WIRED TOGETHER: THE ONLINE CLASSROOM IN K-12

VOLUME 1: PERSPECTIVES AND INSTRUCTIONAL DESIGN

edited by

Zane L. Berge
University of Maryland-Baltimore County

Mauri P. Collins
Northern Arizona University

HAMPTON PRESS, INC.
CRESSKILL, NEW JERSEY

Printed in the United States of America

Library of Congress Cataloging-in-Publication Data

Wired together : the online classroom in K-12 / edited by Zane L. Berge, Mauri P. Collins

p. cm.

Includes bibliographical references and indexes.

Contents: v. 1. Perspectives and instructional design -- v. 2. Case studies -- v. 3. Teacher education and professional development -- v. 4. Writing reading and language acquisition.

ISBN 1-57273-086-2 (v. 1 : cloth). -- ISBN 1-57273-087-0 (v. 1 : pbk.).

1. Educational technology--United States--Case studies. 2. Computer-assisted instruction--United States--Case studies. 3. Teachers--Training of--United States--Cast studies. 4. Teachers--In-service training--United States--Case studies. 5. Language arts--United States--Case studies. I. Berge , Zane L. II. Collins, Mauri P.

LB1028.3.W56 1997

371.33--dc21 97-22976

CIP

Hampton Press, Inc.
23 Broadway
Cresskill, NJ 07626

CONTENTS

PART II: MODELS FOR IMPLEMENTATION

PART III: PERSPECTIVES

PART IV: INSTRUCTIONAL DESIGN

PREFACE

In July 1992, when we sent out the call for chapters for the three previous volumes in this series, *Computer-mediated Communication and the Online Classroom* (Hampton Press, 1995; which we refer to by their project title: CMCBOOK), we received only a handful of submissions that related to computer-mediated communication (CMC) in primary and secondary schools. These mainly described bulletin board systems and other relatively unsophisticated CMC applications. In those days of text-only Web browsers there was little out there to be browsed and, in the CMCBOOK series, only a single, short paragraph was included about the Web. It is hard to imagine that it was such a short time ago. The popularization of easy-to-use graphical interface browsers for the Web such as Netscape and Mosaic have been the catalyst for explosive, exponential growth in the use of the Internet.

INTENDED AUDIENCE

We offer these books to a broad audience of classroom teachers and teacher educators, administrators, and policymakers. The chapters in these books were written with the K-12 practitioner in mind. There are a number of books currently available that examine computer-mediated communication theory and its application in higher education. This is not intended as a theoretical work, but as a series of practical case studies that could be used as models for classroom use. The common thread that unites these books is the classroom use of computer-mediated communications in all its iterations.

As with our previous books we asked the authors to focus on the pedagogical problems they had discovered and to relate how they had used CMC to solve those problems. This seemed to be the most right-headed course. Although technology changes rapidly, the pedagogical issues remain fairly constant. Additionally, teachers and principals continue to emphasize how difficult it often is to provide justification for large funding requirements in the area of CMC to school boards and other central administrators. They have often found that these decision makers are convinced by the weight of the case studies in printed books, as several users of the CMCBOOK series have since informed us. It can be overwhelming to start online, and a seemingly impossible experience if a teacher waits for the complete infrastructure to be installed before beginning. We suggest a good idea is for you to start somewhere—*anywhere* that makes sense! Choose a project that excites you and that will help create the learning environment of which you have a vision. Figure out a way to do it!

THE PROCESS USE FOR THE K12BOOK

When we attended the Association for Curriculum and Development (ACSD) conference in San Francisco in March 1995, we noticed a tremendous interest among these primary and secondary school teachers and administrators in computer-mediated communication in all its forms and the Web in particular. The volumes in the CMCBOOK series were received well in higher education, and there now appeared to be a definite call for a similar set of books to meet the needs of K12 educators and teacher educators. This became *Wired Together: The Online Classroom in K-12* (the project title is simply "K12BOOK").

On May 1, 1995, Zane distributed a call for chapters to selected online discussion groups with a Kindergarten through Grade 12 (K-12) focus. We also distributed, via e-mail, a number of personal invitations for submissions. The closing date for proposals was June 30, 1995, and we received nearly 100 proposals. These were reviewed by an editorial panel of elementary, secondary and higher education faculty, and in July 1995, we issued acceptances to the authors of 73 chapters. At the time, it appeared the content would sort into 3 books. Rather than each of the editors reading all the chapters in all the books (which we found to be a very time-consuming process with the CMCBOOK), we assumed primary responsibility for one book each and invited Patricia Dieter Reidell, a middle school English teacher, to work with us on the third. Of course, as with all such efforts, for a variety of reasons throughout the months following acceptance, several chapters were subsequently withdrawn from the editorial process.

The entire editorial process of the CMCBOOK project up to page proofs had been conducted online, and we found that to be both a time-efficient and effective process, well accepted by our CMCBOOK authors. We decided to use the same process for the K12BOOK, with the addition of a series of Web pages. The first step was to set up a closed discussion group (we used Listserv) so that we could quickly communicate with all the authors, and they with us and each other. The author guidelines from CMCBOOK were revised in light of our prior experience and distributed over the list. We also distributed drafts of two chapters: Santoro's defining of CMC and Collins's explaining of the common terms and terminology of the Internet. We limited authors to approximately 3,000 words and directed the authors to refer to the Santoro or Collins chapters rather than redefine terms and concepts.

Mauri had learned to annotate documents with HTML and felt that a series of Web pages would considerably ease electronic document management. A K12BOOK home page was created, and the Author Guidelines and Santoro and Collins chapters were linked to it. We sent the URL to the authors, via the mailing list, with text versions of everything on the Web pages for those who did not have Web access. An index page with authors and chapter titles was created for each of three books, and as first drafts came in, they were linking to the appropriate entry. Each book was initially divided into two sections, and the authors were invited to read the chapters in their section and to adjust their own content in light of what others had written. First drafts were received electronically during the fall of 1995. Editorial comments were e-mailed back to the authors, and final drafts were received via e-mail through January 1996. The glossary from the CMCBOOK was sent to the authors, and suggestions for additions and annotations were received back. When all the final drafts were received we consulted with the publisher, and the chapters were rearranged into the present four volumes.

The online working process was new to most of the authors, some of whom had not published book chapters before. Even for those authors who had previous publications, they were used to working only with an editor and were often not aware of the other authors nor the contents of other chapters. We had found with the CMCBOOK that authors appreciated a more collaborative mode of working that also kept them updated on the status of their chapters and the general progress of the books.

Using electronic mail, the Listserv group, and the Web pages, we were able to go from the call for chapters to their final delivery to the publisher in 10 months, an impossible feat were we required to do it using conventional mail. Although most of our authors were from the United States, we also have authors from Canada, Australia, the United Kingdom, Israel, Germany, Russia, Singapore, and India. It became obvious to us as we read their chapters that using CMC in the classroom raises the same kinds of issues and is applied to similar pedagogical problems, regardless of the physical location of teachers and students.

WHAT THE AUTHORS THOUGHT OF THE PROCESS

We asked the authors to comment on the editorial process used in the K12BOOK, especially how it compared to other authoring processes in which they had been involved. Several remarked about this being "somehow new." They could not articulate well what that "new" was. The words used to give a sense of how this editorial process was significantly new were "access," "freedom," and "connectivity." Several authors, although seasoned computer-mediated communicators, noted that at first even they felt a little "clumsy." Hardly any of the authors felt they had taken the time or made the effort to interact with other authors to the extent this process would have allowed. There were expressions of regret at this in most cases.

K12BOOK authors expressed concern with the same kinds of limitations as had the CMCBOOK authors. They cited things such as wishing they had more time to take advantage of the flexibility and possibilities of this process, technical problems with sites going down, and lack of convenient access to e-mail or Web sites. Overwhelmingly, though, authors found this process useful because of the ease and convenience in communication between themselves and the editors especially, as well as among other authors. Authors commented that the regular updates from us were important in giving them a sense of "ownership" or "community" in this effort compared with other edited works to which they had contributed.

The Web site, for those having convenient and low-cost access, allowed authors to judge such things as what terminology they need not duplicate, the style being used, and the scope of this work. Several commented that, if nothing else, the review of others' work was reassuring—they were using the appropriate style for the intended audience, and they were not using too much jargon—and that this access served to provide models of writing useful in producing their own contribution to K12BOOK.

The process has proven itself now with seven volumes, and we will continue to refine and elaborate it as we strive to implement the model of collaborative and interactive work, unbound by time and space, that computer-mediated communication fosters so well. We feel this writing and publishing process can be applied within classrooms, schools, or businesses using internal, private Web servers, or openly, across the world, as we have used it.

ACKNOWLEDGMENTS

We raise our keyboards in salute to the late Gerald M. Phillips in recognition of his encouragement and his inspiration that put the words "Berge," "Collins," "book," and "edit" all together in one sentence for the first time on the scholarly discussion group, IPCT-L. (Incidentally, it was on IPCT-L that we met!) Academically and professionally, we hope that all we do carries with it a small spark of his genius. We thank our authors for making their deadlines, regardless of full lives and personal trauma. We acknowledge, with sincere thanks, the help given in the selection and editing processes of the K12BOOK by Nancy Biggs Berge (Fairfax County Virginia Schools) and Patricia Dieter Reidell (The Pennsylvania State University).

DEDICATION

These books are dedicated to the most important people in our lives: our families. It is with special note we dedicate the K12BOOK to Zane's father, Mark R. Berge, who passed away soon after the CMCBOOK was first published.

We also note Nancy Biggs Berge, who again bore the brunt of dealing with two harried editors underfoot for days at a time with patience, tolerance, and hospitality; our parents, who read our books and voice pride in our accomplishments; and to all our children: Jenna Berge; Mark Berge; Doug Collins; Kim and Mike Snyder and their boys, Derek and Sean; Sarah Waghorn; Paul Simon Waghorn; Krys and Scotty Hosmer; Jay Strebel; Benjammin Strebel; Nori Strebel; and Josh Strebel.

Z.L.B.
M.P.C.

Baltimore, MD
1997

ABOUT THE EDITORS AND CONTRIBUTORS

Zane Berge is Director of Training Systems, ISD Graduate Programs, University of Maryland Baltimore County. His scholarship and consulting work is in computer-mediated communication, especially in computer-conferencing. berge@umbc2.umbc.edu

Mauri Collins is a Doctoral Candidate in Adult Education with majors in both Distance Education and Instructional Design at the Pennsylvania State University. She is an experienced online discussion list moderator and facilitator. mauri@cac.psu.edu

* * * * *

Terence C. Ahern is an Assistant Professor in the College of Education who specializes in design and development issues for computer based conferencing. He has designed the IdeaWeb® that allows him to investigate interface and communication issues in using CMC in the classroom. DWTCA@ttacs.ttu.edu

Michael Allen is the technology coordinator for CHOICE 2000 Online School in Perris, CA. mallen@aol.com

Sheryl Burgstahler is Assistant Director of Information Systems, Computing & Communications, at the University of Washington. She directs the DO-IT (Disabilities, Opportunities, Internetworking and Technology) project which was recognized with the 1995 National Infrastructure Award in Education for creative use of the Internet in delivering instruction. sherylb@cac.washington.edu

Kay Day is a media specialist at Norcross High School near Atlanta, GA and completed her Ed.S degree in Instructional Technology at the University of Georgia in 1995. day@hightechnet.gatech.edu

Sara Dexter, a Technology Integration Specialist, focuses on creating and teaching staff development classes that make technology an integral and powerful tool for teaching and learning. The influence of school context on this process is the focus of her doctoral dissertation work. sdexter@informns.k12.mn.us

Daniel V. Eastmond is Coordinator of Academic Services for SUNY Empire State College's Center for Distance Learning. He is involved with instructional design for distance delivery of undergraduate courses using various computer network technologies. DEASTMON@sescva.esc.edu

Kevin Gerrior is the technology coordinator and doctoral student in the College of Education at Virginia Tech University. He is working in a research capacity for CHOICE 2000 Online School. kgerrior@vt.edu or kgerrior@aol.com

Susan Grandgeorge is the Magnet Program Liaison at Bailey's Elementary School for the Arts and Sciences, Fairfax County Public Schools in Fairfax County, VA. Sgrandgeor@AOL.COM

Steven Hackbarth is a computer specialist teacher at P.S. 6 (Manhattan), and a consultant to UNICEF. His passion is in the optimal utilization of diverse media, ranging from print to people, to enhance the quality of interhuman existence. hackbarths@aol.com

Gary Hartley is Coordinator of Alternative Funding at the Shasta County Office of Education and a doctoral candidate at Northern Illinois University. ghartley@shastalink.k12.ca.us

Sally Laughon is a doctoral student in Instructional Technology at Virginia Tech, Blacksburg, VA. She has taught and used telecommunication projects in the K-12 classroom for the last 8 years. laughon@vt.edu

Shabbi Luthra coordinates the elementary school computer program at the American Embassy School, New Delhi, India. She is also a doctoral student in Educational Media and Technology at Boston University and is researching teacher thinking on the use of computers in education. aesindia@attmail.com (Subject line: "For Shabbi Luthra")

Rory McGreal is Executive Director of TeleEducation NB, a province-wide distributed distance learning network. rmcgreal@unb.ca

Karen Norum is a doctoral student in Educational Leadership and Innovation at the University of Colorado at Denver (USA). She researches systemic change in organizations, particularly education settings. kenorum@ouray.cudenver.edu

Gerry Santoro is a Senior Systems Analyst at the Center for Academic Computing at The Pennsylvania State University and adjunct faculty in the Department of Speech Communication. gms@psu.edu

Lynne Schrum is an Assistant Professor in the Department of Instructional Technology, The University of Georgia. She teaches and researches in the areas of distance learning, educational telecommunications, and ethical electronic uses. Lschrum@coe.uga.edu

Amy Shapiro is a professor of psychology at the University of Massachusetts at Dartmouth researching human learning and memory. ashapiro@umassd.edu

Michael Szabo is Professor of Educational Psychology and Technology at the University of Alberta. He has been involved in Computer Based Instruction since 1970 and is currently using a systematic model for change in Alternative Delivery Systems through professional development. mike.szabo@ualberta.ca

Esther Tiessen, an Assistant Professor in the School of Communication at Simon Fraser University, is involved in research and design of discourse and collaboration software environments, particularly for the K-12 context. etiessen@sfu.ca

Doug Ward is an Assistant Professor in the School of Communication at Simon Fraser University where is is pursuing research in the design of interactive discourse environments and information retrieval for knowledge building. dward@sfu.ca

Van Wilkinson is Director of Development and Technology at the Shasta County Office of Education where he oversees instructional connectivity. vwilkinson@shastalink.k12.ca.us

1

TECHNOLOGY AND CHANGING ROLES IN EDUCATION

Zane L. Berge

Economic and technological changes are occurring at an accelerating rate in our information and communication-based society, making life-long learning for everyone a necessity. There is, however, a relative imbalance between the demanding pace of change for students and teachers compared to that in the curriculum and our schools. This chapter suggests that technology needs to become as interwoven in educational delivery as it is in society—in order to become an integral part of teaching and learning throughout the student's life-long learning environment.

CHANGING SOCIETY

In this turbulent transition period from industrial production to a knowledge- and communication-based society, rapid economic and technological changes are also occurring. The confluence of technology, demographics, and work/family requirements make life-long learning for most adults a necessity, and those foundations need to be laid during primary and secondary grades. High school graduates must now be proficient in accessing, evaluating, and communication information, and solving complex problems (Dwyer, 1994). Students are bombarded on every side with information and they need to develop effective filters while building a sense of themselves as members of a global society. This, added to new knowledge about teaching and learning, demands concomitant changes in the roles of students, faculty, the curriculum and our schools.

CHANGING TECHNOLOGY

Not only is the ubiquitous use of technology causing societal and cultural change, the use of computers, telecommunications, and other emerging technologies allow educators to "fulfill age old dreams. We can individualize instruction. We can create simulations through which students can discover important relationships and construct new knowledge. We can even put the reins into the hands of students and watch as these tools take them to destinations they envision" (Peck & Dorricott, 1994, p. 14).

We need to change the way we think about technology in our schools. Even though technology alone is not enough (Reinhardt, 1995), it can be used to create learning environments that boost student achievement, improve student attitudes and self-concept, and enhance the quality of student-teacher relationships We have had such technology available for many years but have not significantly changed the way we do education. Ehrmann (1995) concludes that:

> Ordinarily what matters most is: not the technology per se but how it is used, not so much what happens in the moments when the student is using the technology, but more how those uses promote larger improvements in the fabric of the student's education.

Training of students and teachers is needed, as are new curriculum materials and activities, and, most importantly, changes in the models and strategies we use in teaching and learning. Unless we appropriately use various technologies we cannot meet the access needs, nor improve the quality of, education for tomorrow's students (Twigg, 1994). The following are some ideas about the changes taking place within the technological environment in our schools.

CHANGING STUDENTS

As the learning environment becomes more technology rich, teachers can encourage and guide students in using information resources and in appropriate, collaborative work with other students (Twigg, 1994). Given this, tomorrow's students may learn in ways more like today's researchers and develop qualities of increased independence and self-reliance. Twigg (1994) considers one of the explicit goals of the design of a technology rich learning environment to be that students will learn more independently, using materials that meet their own individual learning needs, abilities, preferences, and interests, and spend more time in small discussion groups or working on collaborative projects with their peers. When working with telecommunications technology in well-facilitated learning environments students become excited about what they are learning and aware they are members of a global community.

CHANGING FACULTY

Teachers often seem to take the attitude of "prove that technology will work for me, in my classroom, and I may give it a try (if I have time)." Although those persons whose mission it is to promote computer technology in the classroom try their best to demonstrate its capabilities to teachers, success takes, as we discuss below, support and direction from the highest levels of administration. Integrating computer technology into classrooms involves shifts to unfamiliar materials, creation of new types of assignments, and inventing new ways to assess student learning often using new techniques and devices (Ehrmann, 1995). Because it is a Herculean task for individual teachers to find the time and resources to implement the changes needed, as members of a community-bases institution, teachers must involve administrators and parents in redefining the school culture to open it up to accommodate changes in their roles and teaching styles.

Yet, as the role of teachers change from expert and controller to facilitator and coach, the teaching/learning process sometimes moves out of the direct control of the teachers. This transition is an often painful and disconcerting change, so much so that veteran teachers might resist the use of computer technologies that can accomplish important goals for students (Jette, 1994).

Computer technology can help teachers extend their most valuable resource—their time. Technology and computer-mediated communication permit learning and instruction to take place even when the teacher and student are not in the same place, nor necessarily communicating at the same time (Klaphaak, 1994). The computer and modem can become a transparent bridge between students and teachers at different locations, without time and energy being wasted in travel by either student or teacher. In the classroom, students can be set to gathering and analyzing information individually or in small groups using the computer while human teachers devote their time to what teachers do best—teaching little human learners (Dexter, personal communication, February 23, 1996).

Many teachers are concerned about changing their delivery methods as, in most cases, a teacher alone can no longer develop all the learning materials and activities possible in a technology rich learning environment. It takes a team of people, sometimes with the serving as subject-matter expert. This is frightening in some ways because it opens a teacher's knowledge base and teaching style to the scrutiny of others.

CHANGING CURRICULUM

Changes to curricula can be facilitated by a technologically rich learning environment. For example, Ehrmann (1995) points out that teachers are more inclined to ask students to "do it over again." When computer technology lessens the mechanical effort of writing and revision, students are more willing to draft, edit, revise, and try again—that is, to take a more authentic approach to problem solving than before (Day & Batson, 1995). The problems posed can become "messy" and require more realistic demands for calculations.

Word processors, databases, spreadsheets, communication, and presentation packages are tools enabling students to plan and revise complex projects, conduct team discussions, and gather resources from around the world. When using project and problem-based learning, teachers can employ these computer technologies to situate problems and help students working in stages to plan, draft, discuss, redraft, and submit their work. Each of these stages offers a chance for students to rethink, expand, rearticulate and generally improve on their problem-solving efforts. In this way computer technology may enable important changes in the curriculum and program even without changing the content. It is when a technology rich environment exists across all problem solving and project areas, available to be used in a seamless way throughout a student's education, that the power of technology to change the curriculum will be realized. When students see their teachers describe, demonstrate, and model expert methods of inquiry, hypothesis generation, and data collection and analysis and begin to practice what experts in each discipline do each day, the true nature of curriculum change due to technology will be seen.

CHANGING INSTITUTIONAL ROLES

In far too many cases, administrators have not examined the role that computers plays in institutional change—at least not in the strategic planning for applying technology to the problems of changing learning and teaching (Ehrmann, 1995; Twigg, 1994). Using technology for place-based and distance teaching is generally brought about by the efforts of individual teachers or school media center personnel for individual assignments or individual classes. It will take a systemic change effort on the part of administrators at the highest levels to have schools reflect ongoing technological and sociocultural changes.

CONCLUSIONS

In essence, computer technology needs to become as interwoven in district strategic planning and educational delivery as it is in society in order to become an integral part of teaching and learning throughout the student's life-long learning environment. This change cannot be forced from the grassroots level by the students or individual teachers or even a department or college. This use of technology as a strategy for learning needs to be part of the strategic plans within and among our schools. To do otherwise is to let the technology support the status quo. Is that what we want?

To work toward changing models of teaching and learning is important. It takes courage to move away from the idea of classroom lectures of stable content, delivered by expert teachers to students who are homogeneous, passive recipients and who work alone as they learn. Computer technology can ease the transition by providing networked access to worldwide information, collaboration with other people, multimedia, and powerful computer simulations while engendering learning environments where students are encouraged to explore and learn in teams, where there is sensitivity to the diversity of students, and which places teachers and other experts as mentors, guides, and collaborators in learning new and ever-changing content.

Certainly there are barriers to technologically rich learning environments: teacher reward structures, "parents" attitudes, high front-end equipment and wiring costs, training, equal access, student support, administrative and technical issues, copyright issues, and teachers' resistance to name a few. But these barriers to the use of technology also involve the culture of our institutions and the people within them. The type of structural changes required for facilitating changing roles are those most resistant to change but most *are* constructed and socially negotiated so they can be reconstructed and socially renegotiated. That will require schools and communities to work hand in hand to ensure a broad base of support for activities that can redefine their individual and collective roles. Communities need to be reassured that the schools will not depart from their traditional role of socializing and teaching students and preparing them for membership in the workforce but doing it in ways better suited to a technologically sophisticated, knowledge-based economy.

How will computer technology affect the changing roles of students, teachers, the curriculum, and schools? Although we cannot predict all these changes, we must surely have an influence upon them.

SUMMARY OF CHAPTERS IN VOLUME 1 OF *WIRED TOGETHER*

Berge opens the first section of this book with a discussion of the use of technology in education followed by Santoro's explanation of what an "online" classroom is. McGreal looks at the effects of technology and computer-mediated communication on school restructuring, and Dexter follows with a description of the process and suggestions for developing district-wide technology plans. Norum examines the principal's vital role as a change agent and acknowledges that little can be done to bring effective technology use into the classroom without the enthusiastic support of the school administration. Acceptable Use Policies, as Schrum and Day explain, need to be in place before students venture onto the information highway.

Introduction

For perhaps as long as there has been a formal educational system there have been attempts to reform education. Reform efforts usually represent the inception of a different model to be used for instruction, often reflecting new educational insights. Berge wonders if using computers and emerging technologies in education should be called *reform*. It may, however, be useful to think how these tools could *transform* various aspects of the educational environment to include more of what we are learning about good practice in teaching and learning. Berge takes the perspective in his chapter that the search for the answers to important questions about education and the implementation of educational goals and objectives should be the forces driving the use of computer technology.

Santoro defines CMC and what is meant by "the online classroom." He categorizes CMC in three ways: computer-based conferencing, informatics, and computer-assisted instruction. Each is described in terms of the level of human-computer use, interaction, and communication. Although the chapter functions similar to the one he wrote to open the earlier, higher education series, *Computer-Mediated Communication and the Online Classroom: Volume I,* (Santoro, 1995) this chapter expands and augments that effort. Among other topics, Santoro includes sections on client/server systems, electronic mail, group-conferencing systems, interactive messaging, campus-wide information systems, online databases, computer-assisted instruction, and the special case of the World Wide Web.

The developing knowledge economy, based on the convergence of computers, telecommunications, and service delivery industries, is also propelling the convergence of learning with the workplace. As McGreal writes, learning and training will become part of everyone's job. With all elements of society adjusting to these new realities, our educational structures are becoming strained. McGreal focuses on strategies for promoting needed restructuring of our educational systems. His concerns are not only in "keeping up" with rapid changes but also taking advantage of the opportunities presented by the new technologies. Some of the topics needed for successful education in the future include changing attitudes, reeducating and training teachers and staff, supporting increased research and development, seeding information technology applications, extending distance education models, and giving attention to systemic change in education to parallel that in other sectors of society.

"Technology, Then Uses" or "Uses, Then Technology"—one or the other of these describes most school districts' technology planning and implementation approaches. They represent two different ways of gathering, sorting, and processing knowledge about technology, then organizing the information for implementation. When a large suburban school district of a major metropolitan area took the "Uses, Then Technology" approach to planning for and implementing technology, Sara Dexter became part of a technology integration staff development framework based on the National Council for Accreditation of Teacher Education (NCATE)/International Society for Technology in Education (ISTE) technology goals. Arranged into a continuum, these goals start with personal productivity and stretch to the use of technology for reforming instruction. This continuum acknowledges that learners must first connect what they are learning to what they already know, after which they can extend meaning making to new areas.

Much attention has been given to the role of the teacher and how it needs to change as innovations such as online classrooms are implemented. However, Norum points out that local school administrators (assistant principals and principals) are a critical connection in creating and sustaining innovations such as online classrooms. Principals play a very influential role in shaping the school culture, and that culture shows up in the classroom. They need to be ready to function as change agents and strategic leaders. Norum describes the assortment of tools change agent administrators will need to sharpen their own understandings of the elements that create organizational change. Norum also discusses new paradigms that need to be created and nurtured for such change to take place.

Many school personnel dream of the day when they will be fully connected to the Internet for professional and curricular activities. However, every classroom teacher and media specialist (who are vitally concerned) knows that open access to unrestricted materials may cause concerns from parents and members of the educational community. Schrum and Day first review of literature, which reveals a great deal of information about the promises of the Internet, but far less is found that addresses how schools are formulating policies concerning appropriate use of the Internet by students. To alleviate these concerns schools need to establish a procedural policy for the use of computers when accessing information, known as "acceptable use policies" (AUPs). Schrum and Day examine the current trends in developing and implementing these AUPs and have compiled both the most recent thoughts from the literature and present school-based Internet users regarding the development of AUPs. Results should guide others as they write their school's AUPs. The chapter concludes with recommendations for school districts as they begin the process of creating an AUP.

Different Implementations of Computer Mediated Communication

Three different implementations of the use of computer-mediated communication is the subject of the next three chapters. Grandgeorge describes an elementary school where CMC is fully integrated into all facets of the curriculum. Gerrior and Allen describe a charter school where all instruction is conducted online. Wilkinson and Hartley describe summer institute where students had the opportunity to meet their faculty mentors face-to-face, then used laptop computers from their homes to continue their individualized studies.

Grandgeorge describes Bailey's Elementary School for the Arts and Sciences in Fairfax, VA. Their Center for Research and Technology offers an environment in which student learning is achieved through interactive and cooperative research on topics that integrate subject areas and are relevant to each other and the real world. Knowledge is generated, sometimes through traditional modes, sometimes via technology. It is assessed, accessed, adjusted, and shared in a variety of technologically appropriate ways. The outcome is the existence of a community of self-motivated, life-long learners who are technologically literate and can confidently travel the information highway making connections, adjustments, assessments, crossovers and/or transfers.

The emphasis at Bailey's is on critical thinking and problem solving as opposed to rote learning, and technology is one tool that is used to motivate, enhance, and stretch student thinking. Technology is critical in another area important to Bailey's "magnet" concept in that it offers a variety of ways for students to show what they have learned beyond a paper-and-pencil test. The uniqueness of this program lies in its ability to promote active student research into concepts relevant to the child's life and interests, to utilize technology, and to teach that which is required by the Fairfax County Public Schools program of studies.

Imagine a school where everything is designed to ensure that all students can realize their full potential—a place where teachers, administrators, parents, and the community are working together as a team with a shared vision. What would it look like? What would it entail? The Charter School Act of 1993 encourages parents and educators to design and create schools that meet all California certification requirements in ways that uniquely suit diverse segments of the state's student population. Gerrior and Allen describe CHOICE 2000, a state-of-the-art, totally online school in Perris, Riverside County, CA. CHOICE 2000 puts a complete, fully certified, Grade 7-12+ adult program within the reach of every student in the state who needs something beyond traditional day school approaches. The school serves students who want to complete their diploma at home via modem from their personal computers. Gerrior and Allen write about how students complete comprehensive courses of study provided to them over a sophisticated computer network accessed from their home computers. This school provides an alternative by innovatively harnessing telecommunications, educational software, and dedicated teachers. This is done by making lessons, designing texts and auxiliary materials, and offering professional guidance and feedback to secondary and adult students via the Internet.

The Shasta County Office of Education received a grant from the California Department of Migrant Education to conduct a summer telecommunications training academy with eight teachers and eight migrant students. Wilkinson and Hartley describe how each participant was given extensive training in the use of e-mail and Internet navigation, as well as a dial-in account and a modem-ready laptop computer. These Southeast Asian students communicated electronically with teachers, school administrators, and each other, and utilized their training to complete "benchmark" activities as well as regular school assignments. Because of the its success, further funding has extended the program into the normal school year.

Perspectives

Hackbarth continues by examining the value that commercial online services can add to CMC for teachers and students. Luthra discovers that CMC is not as easy as it appears when trying to link a school for American students in India with an American service provider. Szabo is concerned that teachers' mental models must be rethought before effective use can be made of CMC in their classrooms. Tiessen and Ward discuss the potential changes in classroom discourse that result from the introduction of CMC technologies and explore one example of how classroom activities can take educational advantage of many-to-many communication. Shapiro reviews the research on learning using hypermedia technology, and this section closes with Burgstahler examining the uses of information technology with students with disabilities.

There is quite a large gap generally between teachers' knowledge of computer-mediated communication and our students' unbridled enthusiasm for all things Internet. Hackbarth illustrates ways in which commercial online services can help bridge this gap. Over the past decade especially, commercial online services have developed well-organized storehouses of information, first-rate tools for easing searches and transactions, and wholesome virtual communities of dues-paying members. Now these services provide friendly gateways to the relatively raw and chaotic Internet. Hackbarth describes how within schooling contexts commercial online services contribute to productive communications, information retrieval, and information sharing. He conclude that they are responsive to teachers' highly regarded criterion of *efficiency* in the achievement of both the mundane and highest of educational aims. Thus, they serve well to bridge the gap between teachers' knowledge of the emerging information superhighway and students' ever-growing fascination with it.

Luthra describes the difficulties she encountered with a project designed to link classrooms around the world via telecommunications. The project's organizers, a commercial company, provided the participants with both the direction and support necessary to creatively integrate communications technology into the classroom. For overseas American schools the idea of bringing telecommunications into the classroom is attractive. An increased awareness of the potential frustrations can make the experience of communicating with other schools educationally beneficial. Luthra explores both the excitement and the technical and logistical problems that turn the information highway into a rather rocky road.

Next Szabo reflect on what he has come to understand as a significant, inhibitory issue in the use of CMC and other innovations for educational purposes. On the surface, the complexity of learning how to use the technology effectively and access to it are certainly inhibitors. But a deeper problem exists with respect to how educators view teaching and learning with CMC. Over the years, Szabo believes we have built up belief systems and ways of knowing about this and other aspects of our real world. He refers to these as *mental models.* Szabo believes many of our mental models are stagnant and need to be reevaluated. He discusses the concepts of mental models from the point of view of constructivism and why they should be reviewed. At the end of the chapter, he selects several topics that relate to mental models possessed by educators based on his years of work with CMC.

The processes and patterns of classroom communication can be significantly altered from their traditional forms through the use of computer-based communication technologies. The use of CMC to shift away from one-to-one or one-to-many toward many-to-many communication patterns offers new possibilities for classroom discourse. Tiessen and Ward describe some specific ways in which CMC technologies can afford nontraditional communication patterns and directly support educationally valuable activities which would be difficult through traditional media. During a 3-week history unit, students used a Computer Supported Intentional Learning Environment (CSILE), a communal hypermedia database system, as a medium for many-to-many communication. Students' distributed and collective efforts resulted in a single knowledge web that explained the relationships among 78 short texts. From this communally created artifact, students were able to construct their own deep understanding of the topic. This unit demonstrates that with CMC software, many-to-many communication can be manageable and productive and can shift the onus for control and content of communication to the students, making them more responsible, active learners.

In the first part of her chapter, Shapiro presents an historical perspective on the debate over the utility of hypermedia (e.g., World Wide Web on the Internet and hypermedia systems) in the classroom. She ends this section by concluding that the shortage of controlled research on the subject precludes any definitive resolution to the conflict. In an attempt to address this need Shapiro next discusses studies aimed at analyzing the effectiveness of Web technologies on learning. This research provides evidence that such systems do offer some advantage over linear presentations of material (as in books). However, it also provides evidence that aspects of learning in this medium are shallow. Shapiro concludes that user training is in need of improvement and draws on the evidence presented in earlier chapters to suggest such improvements.

Burgstahler summarizes the specific benefits of technology to students with disabilities. The approaches to overcoming the barriers to standard computer input, output, and documentation for people with a variety of disabilities are delineated. The chapter concludes with a description of project DO-IT (Disabilities, Opportunities, Internetworking, and Technology), which promotes the education and employment of people with disabilities through extensive use of computes, adaptive technology, and the Internet network.

Instructional Design

The final section of the book is concerned with the use of instructional design of computer-mediated communication. Eastmond examines the topic in general, Ahern focuses on designing learning groups for optimal interaction, and Laughon looks at the design of effective CMC projects.

Given the expansion of Internet resources and possibilities for CMC exchanges, educators can be guided by an instructional design model to develop effective online learning experiences. Through presentation of one such model, Eastmond outlines the steps in analysis, planning, design, development, implementation, and evaluation to which educators should attend in preparing instruction. Also, the production processes for other educational media that possess similar attributes can inform the design of CMC instruction. Eastmond recommends building CMC materials and activities based on one's own educational philosophy and through identification and adaptation of the effective CMC activities of other educators on the Internet.

In general, Ahern argues that in order to achieve optimal participation in online systems a better understanding of the basic nature of the classroom is necessary. The traditional classroom is better understood as a large group. Essential components of the group are discussed briefly as well as the impact CMC has on group dynamics. Finally, a selection model is provided that helps teachers use CMC technology based on planning for different types of goals, structure, and social factors. To improve interaction online, Ahern contends it requires a better understanding of relationship, task, and group dynamics.

Laughon examines projects to determine the features making them attractive to other educators and meet successful completion. The projects discussed here use the Internet for connecting people and classes. The World Wide Web is a source of information for projects but also a conduit for communication between educators as it becomes more interactive. Laughon points to the Web component of courses as providing complementary activities for communication among educators and feels it will become a powerful force in the future. The chapter's focus is on how to develop a project using the Internet as a conduit for connection, not just as a source for information.

This book concludes, as do the other three in this series, with a glossary of commonly used Internet and CMC terms.

REFERENCES

Day, M., & Batson, T. (1995). The network-based writing classroom: The ENFI idea. In Z.L. Berge & M.P. Collins (Eds.), *Computer mediated communication and the online classroom: Vol. II* (pp. 25-46). Cresskill, NJ: Hampton Press.

Dwyer, D. (1994). Apple classrooms of tomorrow: What we've learned. *Educational Leadership, 51*(7), 4-10.

Ehrmann, S. C. (1995). Ehrmann on eval. (Parts 1-3). Asking the right question: What does research tell us about technology and higher learning? [Online] Post to AAHESGIT on January 13. (Archived at listproc@list.cren.net).

Jette, R. (1994). Adopting Educational technology. [Online]. Post to AAHESGIT on August 17. (Archived at listproc@list.cren.net).

Klaphaak, K. (1994). Why invest in info tech? [Online]. Post to AAHESGIT on December 5. (Archived at listproc@list.cren.net).

Peck, K., & Dorricott, D. (1994). Why use technology? *Educational Leadership, 51*(7), 11-14.

Reinhardt, A. (1995, March). New ways to learn. *Byte*, pp. 50-71.

Twigg, C. A. (1994). The need for a national learning infrastructure. *Educom Review, 29*(5), 17-20.

I

INTRODUCTION

2

THE INSTRUCTIONAL TECHNOLOGY TRAIN: WHY USE TECHNOLOGY IN EDUCATION

Zane L. Berge

> Collaborative learning, constructive learning, and apprenticeships—are not new concepts in learning. But they've never been sustainable. Teachers who try them usually burn out. Why? Because they didn't have an infrastructure that supported them. Technology can help establish a supportive infrastructure that makes it possible to use those powerful models without burning out.
>
> —Chris Dede (O'Neil, 1995)

Educational Reform

For perhaps as long as there has been a formal educational system there have been attempts to reform education. Reform efforts usually represent the inception of a different model to be used for instruction, often reflecting new educational insights. I do not know if using computers and emerging technologies in education should be called *reform*. It may, however, be useful to think how these tools could *transform* various aspects of the educational environment to include more of what we are learning about good practice in teaching and learning. The perspective taken in this chapter is that the search for the answers to important questions about education and the implementation of educational goals and objectives should be the forces driving the use of instructional technology.

Are We Left Standing There as the Train Leaves the Station?

The pace of technological change often seems overwhelming. Teachers who deal with emerging technologies everyday sometimes have the feeling that they are left standing on the platform as the train they needed to be on is pulling away. And teachers will continue to feel that way for as long as "technology" is the engine pulling their instructional train. Sophisticated and innovative technologies are constantly being developed in response to market forces well beyond the boundaries and control of education. Although teachers sometimes need to be made aware of technological capabilities they do not know exist, it is the solutions to educational problems that must pull that train, not the technological tools used in the service of creating effective education. Additionally, administrative desires for cost savings and to serve more students with fewer resources should not be allowed to dictate inappropriate technological solutions.

Why Should We Use Computers and Other (High) Technologies in Education?

I am often asked, "Why should I use technology in my classroom?" My response is, "First, tell me what you think teaching and learning should look like, then I will respond to your question." Depending on what the individual tells me, I may suggest he or she should *not* use high technology in his or her teaching. *But* if the person thinks teaching and learning should include such things as real-life, authentic problem-solving; distance and/or distributed learning; a sensitivity to learning styles, an increased collaboration in the learning environments, or more motivated learners, my advice is to consider how technology can help create a learning environment conducive to their educational philosophy and needs. Teachers need to be concerned with what will add *value* to students learning, that is what adds *benefits* to or *reduces the costs of* education.

It is important to remember that benefits derived from the use of technologies are relative to the mission of the educational agency or institution in the community of which they are a part. So, the challenge is to align technology-based changes in the educational delivery system to the goals and mission of the institution. Sometimes the push to incorporate technology in the classroom comes from administrators anxious to reach increasingly large and diverse student bodies while steadily decreasing the cost of educational delivery. But technologically mediated educational delivery is costly in terms of building and maintaining the infrastructure, designing and developing courses, and training and supporting teachers and students. The true value of technology-mediated educational delivery can best be stated in terms of student access to learning and experiences that can be provided *with* technology that may otherwise be difficult or impossible.

QUALITY, ACCESS, AND PRODUCTIVITY

The perennial problems and opportunities faced by teachers can be categorized into three areas: quality, access, and productivity. Quality of instruction (i.e., effectiveness) is mainly determined by the *instructional design* of the educational interventions, not the technology or delivery system (see Eastmond, this volume). The design sets the parameters for quality and *limits* quality—as the effectiveness of the design decreases so does the upper limit of quality in instruction.

Access to educational opportunities for both teacher and learner can be greatly increased through the use of emerging technologies. Various technologies, whether in a classroom or at a distance, can improve or enhance learners' access to courses, other people, and to information in presentation forms to suit most learning styles.

Personal productivity has been increased over the past two decades through the use of technology, and collaborative or collective productivity could surge as we move into the 21st century. Through the merging of computers and telecommunication networks people are linked for conversation, dialog, or collaborative work. We have also seen, especially in business, increases in productivity through automation. Technology can increase productivity—more material that is both more technical and more complicated can be covered in a course of study. The caution is that we need to have the *best* instructional methods and strategies, and the *best* materials, *before* we automate them! Technology needs to be innovated and reengineered *before* automation (O'Neil, 1995). (If General Motors was making automobiles that no one would buy, should they put on another line and make more?)

Overall, we now have the technological tools to improve the quality of education in ways never before possible. As many institutions of higher education develop mission statements like "guiding students toward life-long learning", technology *can* act as a catalyst for meeting this goal. Similarly, as K-12 schools are reshaped to better meet the needs of students, technology can play a significant role. But administrators and teachers need to realize that changes in the agency's mission often means changing roles for teachers and learners. Technology seems to power a move from a teacher-centered environment to a more learner-centered environment which demands significant changes in how we teach and learn.

What Should Education Look Like?

In short, we must turn our attention to situating learning within an environment that recognizes changes in society and persons' lifestyles as important factors in learning. Much of what follows in this chapter rests on the following assumptions about what teaching and learning should look like if technology is to have any significant impact on education: How we use technology to improve quality, access, and productivity will create a learning environment that is oriented toward *life-long learning*, recognizes that *knowledge is socially constructed*, and stresses *authentic* learning that places the learner in an *apprenticeship role*.

Life-long Learning

When the teacher-centered model of education first evolved, teachers could teach all there was to know in a field or discipline. To instill the idea into students, teachers must model life-long learning. Checkley (1995) states: "Rather than helping students develop an ability to memorize facts in a textbook, teachers should teach students metacognitive and self-evaluative skills" (p. 5). Quoting Mary Ellen Verona, she gives the reason for this, so that students "can assess what they need to learn in order to solve a problem or complete a project. What's hoped for is that students will become aware when they need certain skills and they'll go off and learn those skills on their own" (p. 5). The habits of information seeking and study can be acquired by students in the primary grades and strengthened as they progress through their formal schooling.

Critical Awareness

Without a certain level of critical awareness and analysis, students will not think in terms of life-long learning. Even though technology changes quickly and constantly, students equipped with a critical attitude can continue to discover, evaluate, and apply new technology as it evolves and emerges (Johnson & Yahner, 1993). Given the assumptions presented here, our goal is to develop students with an increased interest in various subjects or in learning generally, with higher self-confidence, and a better self-evaluation of their abilities.

Learner-Centered Learning

Over the past century or more, the model used in formal education has generally been teacher-centered: a subject matter expert within a field of study lectures about the content within his or her field, and to a lesser degree demonstrates the skills and processes useful for exploration. (This has been especially true in secondary and postsecondary schooling.)

Students usually take on a passive role of trying to copy the notes from the lecturer's notepad to their own—later, the students attempt to restate those notes for the test. More recently, instructors and designers of instruction have taken on the challenge of developing learning activities that require a more active and interactive engagement by the students. The role of the instructor is shifting from the "sage on the stage" to that of "guide on the side." As we learn more about how learning occurs, and as the shift in teacher and student roles continues, the trend is clearly toward a more learner-centered attitude and approach to learning

Motivation: How do We Engage Students in Learning Activities?

When content is meaningless in terms of the students' needs, when they are taught as if they were passive recipients of knowledge, or when they have little engagement in the instructional tasks, students have no incentive to construct their own knowledge and little motivation to retain information or skills or to transfer them to novel situations. When students perceive instructional activities as relevant to their own interests, important to learning the concepts in their coursework, or practical in learning skills and gaining experience, they are more apt to become engaged in those learning activities. Engagement in learning activities is one way to significantly increase learning effectiveness. Using instructional technology, we can design learning activities that engage and hold students' attention.

Socially Constructed Knowledge

Collaborative learning and increased interactivity are examples of *how* teachers can improve instruction. *Why* these methods are important has to do with improved retention or understanding versus rote memorization. One of the major goals in education is to improve the communication inside (and in some cases outside) the classroom between teachers and students and among students, thereby creating a sense of *community.* It is often within a community of learners that individuals make sense of what they are learning.

Technology is being developed that can help provide these new environments for education, allowing teachers to utilize such methods as cooperative learning, recognize such concepts as interdisciplinary needs in education, and provide an environment in which collaborative efforts are rewarded. These methods foster a view of knowledge in which expertise is distributed and created among the different participants (Collins, 1991), and in which there is a multiple perspective on ideas and knowledge.

Collaborative Learning

School may be one of the few places where people are required, for the most part, to perform individually. In fact, we often call anything else cheating! Yet, teachers are discovering that learning is often best conducted as a social activity. That is to say, although learners construct their own knowledge, many times they do so more thoroughly in interaction with peers and significant others. Technology use provides many learning opportunities that involve increased communication, interaction among students and teachers, and collaborative projects, as shown by dramatic examples in writing classrooms. Through e-mail, real-time conferencing, groupware, and textsharing, a effective supplement to face-to-face tutoring can be designed. Technology can often promote an environment where collaborative projects can be worked on that includes input from experts, other students, instructors, and members of the larger community.

Interactive Learning

Over the past several decades, teachers have moved away from viewing learners as passive, "empty vessels," who are filled by the wisdom and facts poured in by the teacher, to viewing learners as taking an active part in the construction of their own knowledge. Through field investigation, group discussion, and laboratory activities, students can interact with scientific processes, concepts, principles, each other, and the instructor. These kinds of interaction can structure the design of the practice teachers give students through the use of technological tools.

Authentic Learning

One of the overarching principles of effective instructional design is to match student practice and assessment as closely as possible to problem solving and other activities in real-world settings. Technology can often be used to give students the opportunity to experiment in ways that might otherwise be too expensive, time consuming, or dangerous. The more teachers can use technological solutions to simulate real-world conditions and give practice in solving real-world problems, the higher the likelihood that improved attitudes and confidence will result. With greater access through global telecommunication systems, instruction in such areas as language learning becomes very authentic, and cultural awareness is a natural consequence of participation in various activities involving native language speakers. Groups of students are brought together, sometimes virtually online, to learn and to form discourse communities. Technology is often a catalyst for teachers to scrutinize what they teach and to experiment with new ideas. Working with a course development *team* often forces a more conscientious development effort as the group investigates how to design authentic goals, methods, student practice, and evaluation for a particular group of students.

Project-Oriented Approach

The move toward a more project-oriented approach has a powerful effect on teaching and learning. There are problems to be worked out involving evaluation and portfolio assessment of students' projects, especially when considering their admission to college. Still, a project-oriented approach seems right-headed, given the increased potential for a more collaborative and interdisciplinary environment that offers learners greater opportunities for authentic practice in problem solving.

One of the advantages of a project-oriented approach is that it permits students to take an indepth look at phenomena they often could not otherwise explore. For instance, rather than the teacher giving a cursory exploration of many concepts with quick demonstrations, technology allows them to provide access to this information outside of the classroom the school (e.g., home, libraries), and students can easily and quickly retrieve this information for further exploration. Technology-based learning programs provide an alternative method to lectures or reading assignments that students can use to view the same information. Interactive programs promote students' participation and increased attention to the activities being presented. Case studies, simulations, and other problem-based approaches can utilize the rich databases and resources that technology can make readily available. Through the infusion of technology throughout the curriculum, productivity can be increased, often dramatically, as students investigate, analyze, and synthesize issues through project-based approaches.

Interdisciplinary Approach

Schooling often presents a static view of a field of study. Students are given the impression that there is an immutable body of knowledge that must be memorized to know a subject, be it biology, U.S. history, or literature. Scientists, scholars, and professionals know that their fields of study are dynamic in nature—that today's facts may very often be disproved tomorrow. Further, not only are their fields dynamic and ever changing, but they are linked with many other disciplines.

To design courses that show these dynamic links is a difficult challenge. Even so, we are seeing a demand for the integration of school subjects: a conceptual convergence of the natural sciences, mathematics, and technology with the social sciences, behavioral sciences, and the humanities into a coherent whole. In classrooms teachers can use technology such as video footage to view social or natural phenomena using a project-oriented approach that is much richer, authentic, and interdisciplinary. Technologies, such as hypertext and hypermedia, allow advanced students to analyze and investigate links to multidisciplinary information in a way that was impossible a few years ago. This can often lead to stronger interest and motivates the students to further exploration and synthesis (Hartoonian, 1992; Smith & Westhoff, 1992).

Learning Styles

Much research has been conducted into the different ways people learn. Students often have little choice in what to learn, how to learn it, or when to learn it. Gardner (1983) concludes that there are at least seven types of intelligence: linguistic, logical-mathematical, spatial, musical, bodily-kinesthetic, interpersonal, and intrapersonal. Historically, schooling has concentrated almost exclusively on teaching to the intelligences of linguistic, logical-mathematical, and intrapersonal learners. Using technology, we can design instruction to teach to the multiple intelligences of which Gardner speaks. One possibility is to present the course content using different methods and formats for instruction (e.g., small group discussion, graphics, lecture, hands-on labs, writing/reflection, sound, CMC and conferencing), provided that instructional goals and design justify their use. Given that we know students learn in different ways, courses can be designed so important concepts, principles, and skills are presented in different ways.

Apprenticeship Role

During formal schooling, aspiring professionals can only begin to absorb some of the information they will ultimately need during their career lifetimes. The knowledge base in some fields may have appeared static for decades but is now increasing exponentially. Therefore, we must help students to become motivated, skillful, life-long learners by helping them locate the resources to continue learning. Students can be doing that which scientists and scholars do. Dede (quoted in O'Neil, 1995) points out:

> So what people are mastering in work is the ability to make decisions given incomplete information, inconsistent objectives, and uncertain consequences. And that's what we need to be teaching in education—not so much what we know and how we know it, but what to do when you don't know something, and how to act when you don't know exactly how to get to where you want to be. (p. 9)

Locating, accessing, and manipulating resources and data is, to a large extent, the most valuable use for technology within a learning environment. Using computers to help students learn fundamentals and to remove tedium from complex computations, free teachers to work with students on more interesting aspects of their projects (DeSieno, 1995). Apprenticed to scientists or scholars, students can learn their craft; the goal is not so much to teach biology to students but to make biologists out of students. Skills are mastered not from secondary analysis but from practice that relies on primary sources of data collection and analyses. This is occurring in both elementary and secondary classrooms.

BARRIERS TO EFFECTIVE INSTRUCTIONAL TECHNOLOGY

Many of the significant barriers to the effective use of instructional technology involve the infrastructure, failure to align technological projects with the curriculum, and the difficulties inherent in cultural change. Once the *infrastructure* is in place, technology is a catalyst for whatever changes teachers want to make. It is the infrastructure that permits technology to be used for any educational changes one chooses to make, but there are inequities. For instance, as more time shifting and access to resources occur, those persons without access to technology will become more disadvantaged.

Leadership from top administrators will be necessary to align the reporting and reward structures of teachers with the school's strategic plans for technology (see Norum's chapter, this volume). Until this recognition is forthcoming, instructional technology will take a back seat to other priorities that *are* recognized. Until administrators exert this leadership, the use of instructional technology will emphasize only technical requirements and not become an integral part of teaching and learning.

The role of the instructor will continue to evolve as our knowledge of the learning process progresses. Student involvement within interdisciplinary, collaborative environments that utilize technology for students' investigation, analysis, and the synthesis of more authentic problems may evolve many new formats and require changing methods of instruction. It may well be that we will model the use of these technological tools and techniques in the pursuit of our own construction of knowledge. We may be guiding students as we learn alongside them—and that may be more rewarding than much of what we are doing today. However, this type of organizational "cultural change" is very difficult. As Sheingold (1991) pointed out, these ambitious new goals for student learning, along with the radical changes in students' roles those goals bring about, must be met with radical, ambitious changes in the educational process. Indeed, information technology offers options for reorganizing and refining education. Cultural change of such significance is always challenging as new visions of learning drive decisions about the use of technology.

CONCLUSIONS

As we learn more about how learning occurs, it becomes increasingly clear that the educational process takes place in a complex internal and external environment. One of the teacher's roles is to become the creator of an effective learning environment that stimulates students' creation of knowledge, mastery of skills, and fostering of appropriate attitudes toward learning. How do teachers and developers of instruction create environments that are conducive to and enhance student learning?

As can be seen from the broad scope of functions and services described earlier, technology can play an important role in meeting present and future educational needs. I would like to mention two particular trends that may be especially useful when thinking about how technology can help the educational process.

First, the merging of telecommunications and computer technologies can have a significant impact on learning and teaching. Computer-mediated communication (CMC) promotes a type of *interpersonal interaction* that is often lacking in the traditional teacher-based classroom. It allows learners the freedom to explore alternative pathways—to find and develop their own style of learning—in a more learner-centered approach. What if content could be delivered in the form of graphics, text, and/or full-motion video, whenever and wherever in the world it is requested? Tomorrow's telecommunication system fosters *interaction with content* in unprecedented ways. How do teachers responsibly participate in and make use of the inevitable technological changes at hand?

Additionally, one of the greatest benefits of much of the emerging technology is its ability to liberate instruction from the constraints of time and location. The availability of resources from around the world is becoming more and more a reality. A keypal project between countries at an elementary school, a collaborative data collection among dozens of science classes at the middle level, or electronic publishing in a high school journalism class are examples of the many uses of technology occurring today. It is no longer science fiction to imagine teachers and students using full text access to journal articles and other documents, with links to other references from within those articles and documents. The shift toward electronic publishing, archiving, and delivery of multiple-media instructional materials is and will become more commonplace. Teachers and trainers have been searching for the "Holy Grail" of instruction for a long time—to create an environment in which students can learn anything, at anytime, from anywhere (Berge & Collins, 1995). In giving students this type of flexibility, however, comes new challenges. Even with defined instructional goals, students with real choice do not always take the expected path.

Many people involved with technology perceive themselves as standing still as their train leaves the station. Yet it is really up to teachers to drive the instructional technology train. As I have stated before (Berge, 1993), there currently seems to be no shortage of technology, only a shortage of the educational vision necessary to use that technology for creating an educational environment that motivates and engages all of us in learning.

REFERENCES

Berge, Z. L. (1993). Beyond computers as tools: Reengineering education. *Computers in the Schools, 9*(2/3), 167-178.

Berge, Z. L., & Collins, M. P. (Eds.). (1995). *Computer-mediated communications and the online classroom: Overview and perspective: Volume I.* Cresskill, NJ: Hampton Press.

Checkley, K. (1995). Student-directed learning: Balancing student choice and curriculum goals. *ASCD Education Update, 37*(9), 1, 4-5, 8.

Collins, A. (1991, September). The role of computer technology in restructuring schools. *Phi Delta Kappan*, 28-36.

DeSieno, R. (1995). The faculty and digital technology. *Educom Review, 30*(4), 46-48.

Gardner, H. (1983). *Frames of mind: The theory of multiple intelligences.* New York: Basic Books.

Hartoonian, H. M. (1992). The social studies and project 2061: An opportunity for harmony. *Social Studies, 83*(4), 160-63.

Johnson, T. P., & Yahner, T. G. (1993). Computer-based design studios in landscape architecture. In J.V. Boettcher (Ed.), *101 success stories of information technology in higher education: The Joe Wyatt challenge* (pp. 287-293). New York: McGraw-Hill.

O'Neil, J. (1995, October). On technology schools: A conversation with Chris Dede. *Educational Leadership, 53*(2), 6-12.

Sheingold, K. (1991, September). Restructuring for learning with technology: The potential for synergy. *Phi Delta Kappan*, 17-27.

Smith, E. E., & G. M. Westhoff. (1992). The Taliesin project: Multidisciplinary education and multimedia. *Educational Technology, 32*(1), 15-23.

3

WHAT IS THE ONLINE CLASSROOM?

Gerald M. Santoro

In the early 1980s the birth of microcomputing and the declassification of Arpanet into the Internet brought the promise of the "Information Age" to the public mind. During the late 1980s and the early 1990s the complexities of network systems and the need for greater processing speed and network bandwidth made many fear that this promise would pass the way of other unfulfilled techno-predictions such as the "paperless office."

However, by the mid-1990s it has become clear that something is indeed happening to revolutionize the way that people work, shop, interact, and learn. Nowhere is this revolution more apparent then in our elementary and secondary schools, where teachers, students, and administrators are embracing the Internet as a set of tools with great educational promise.

THE INTERNET EXPLAINED

What is the Internet? This is a question that has many answers depending on the reason for the question. Technically the Internet is the set of all interconnected computer networks running the TCP/IP protocol. However, although technically correct, this answer is often unsatisfactory. More useful is a functional definition of the Internet, explained through two analogies.

The Telephone Analogy

Everyone knows what a telephone is. It is a masterpiece of consumer electronics because of its incredible functional simplicity. Even a young child knows that they can, potentially, type a number into a telephone and talk to Grandma.

But most of us really do not know exactly how a telephone operates. What we do know is two important features of telephones that make them useful. The first is that all telephones in the world are somehow connected. This connection may be through wires, through satellites, or (in some cases) through cellular radio.

The second useful feature of the telephone is that we know every telephone has a unique identification number—its "telephone number." When we enter a correct telephone number into an active telephone we can expect to make a connection with that remote telephone. Unless we are paying for the call, we do not even need to know where that remote telephone is located.

The Internet is exactly like the telephone network except that computers are used instead of telephones. Every computer on the Internet is physically connected to every other computer on the Internet. In fact, the Internet uses many of the same physical connections as the telephone network. Also, every computer on the Internet has a unique identification number—its Internet Protocol or "IP" number.

So, when one runs a program on an Internet-connected computer to access information from some remote server, his or her computer is making the Internet equivalent of a telephone call to access that remote computer. Just as people commonly keep booklets recording important telephone numbers, some people keep booklets recording important IP numbers, fully-qualified domain names, or uniform resource locators (explained more fully later in this chapter).

The Highway Analogy

The Internet is also like a highway. The media commonly refer to the Internet as the "Information Superhighway." The intent of this reference is to provide a visual analogy for how the Internet operates. If one looks down on a metropolitan highway system they will see large expressways connected to smaller roads, which in turn connect to smaller roads, and so on. Every road has one or more buildings on it and vehicles travel between these buildings, using the road system. The buildings are like the Internet-connected computers, the vehicles are like data packets, and the roads are the component networks of the Internet.

But more importantly, the Internet acts like a highway system. It is subject to high and low traffic times. There are a number of "rush hours" during which individual data packets compete for available bandwidth. There are occasionally "construction delays" when parts of the Internet, or certain services, may be unavailable. There are sometimes "weather delays" when one is accessing a part of the world that is suffering a hurricane or earthquake.

To use the Internet most effectively, it is necessary to become aware of its highway-like behavior and plan around it in the same way that one would plan for local vehicular traffic patterns when driving somewhere at a critical time.

Client/Server Systems

The basis for Internet function is an approach known as client/server. In this approach, services such as electronic mail, WWW pages, and conferences are provided by computer programs called servers. These servers are addressable through the Internet by IP number and port, Uniform Resource Locator (URL), or some other method.

To access any given service the human user runs another program called a client. The client provides the user with an interface to one or more services, by managing the Internet connection to the server. Client programs are typically developed for different kinds of computers and ideally take advantage of the operating environment of the host computer. So a Macintosh client will utilize the unique features of the Macintosh OS, whereas a Windows 95 client will utilize the unique features of Windows 95, but both clients may access the same service from the same server.

The implication of this for human users is pretty straightforward. In order to access a given service on the Internet one needs to get the proper client program for that service and for the kind of computer system he or she will be using. They then may need to configure the client program to find the correct server. (For some services this configuration information will come from the service provider for the user's Internet connection.)

The Nature of Technology

When using the Internet it is also important to have a good perspective on the nature of technology. Technology is an artifact created and managed by people. Technology is developed for many reasons, although the chief underlying reason typically has to do with economic growth and development.

One of the principle features of technology, and a feature most people find extremely annoying, is that it will sometimes fail. George

Murphy, a designer of aircraft control systems, recognized this when he jokingly referred to what has become known as Murphy's Law—"Anything that can fail will fail, and at the worst possible time."

When I introduce students or other faculty to the Internet I advise them to keep Murphy's Law in mind and to respect it as the "First Law of Technology" to which all technology must ultimately adhere. I remind them that we accept technical failure (albeit grudgingly) in our automobiles, household appliances, and other gadgets on which we have become dependent. When we emerge from our homes on a chilly morning to find that our car battery is dead we may curse and kick the tire, but we get it serviced and continue to drive.

In approaching the Internet, we should expect to be initially confused and amazed. We should rejoice when it works and be wisely accepting when it does not. Above all we should remember that we are the masters and the Internet, for all of its wizardry, is ultimately just a collection of machines. It will come as no surprise that the younger generation (raised on Star Wars and video games) is far more accepting of this than many of us old-timers.

The Special Case of the World Wide Web

Although technically just another Internet service, the World Wide Web is currently recognized as the "killer application" that is helping to bring the potential of the Internet to the average person. Before development of the Web, one had to master a half dozen client programs in order to effectively access information. This changed with the Web (and to a lesser degree its predecessor, gopher) as Web clients incorporate the ability to connect to a variety of Internet services. Further connections to Netscape, Mosaic, and other Web clients promise to continue this trend to such a degree that some will view the Web as the Internet.

Furthermore, the ease of creating Web-based resources has led to an era of electronic publishing without precedent. At the time of this writing over 10 million Web pages, covering everything from ABBA to Zydeco and in between, have been developed. According to one trade journal (*Internet World*) the size of the web is currently doubling every four months.

In recognition of the fact that most of the best documentation and information about the Internet is to be found on the Web, this chapter (like others in the series) contains many references to Web resources.

These references will be in the form of Uniform Resources Locators (URLs) (for example, http://cac.psu.edu/~santoro/) that one can use to access the resource through a Web browser. Later in this chapter URLs, and how to apply them, are explained in detail.

COMPUTER-MEDIATED COMMUNICATION

Computer-mediated communication (CMC) is the name given to a large set of functions in which computers are used to support human communication. CMC can be defined narrowly or broadly, depending on how one defines human communication. At its narrowest, CMC refers to computer applications for direct human-to-human communication. This includes electronic mail, group conferencing systems, and interactive "chat" systems. At its broadest, CMC can encompass virtually all computer uses.

The broad interpretation derives from the recognition that computer systems were developed to receive data from humans (or from the environment in a way that mimics or extends human senses) and eventually return some form of that data to humans for some human purpose. Seen this way, such diverse applications as statistical analysis programs, remote-sensing systems, and financial modeling programs all fit within the concept of human communication.

The meaning of CMC for the purpose of this book is a compromise between these two extremes. The focus is on the use of computer systems and networks for the transfer, storage and retrieval of information between humans. In this definition, the computer/network system is a primarily a mediator rather than a processor of the information.

A special focus of this book will be on the use of CMC as a tool for instructional support in primary and secondary school. The support can range from simply providing students with electronic mail in an otherwise traditional class to actually delivering instruction and supporting student-student and student-teacher interaction at a distance.

The importance of information technology to education and the U.S. economy is reflected in the theme of the Net '91 conference in Washington, DC, "Towards a National Information Infrastructure." This conference drew over 400 representatives from higher education, industry, and government concerned with the future of national educational and research networking (MERIT, 1991). Also, in 1991, Senator Al Gore (then D-Tenn.) introduced Senate Bill 272, which authorizes the National Education and Research Network. This bill demonstrates recognition that a national telecommunication infrastructure is as important to the U.S. economy as the interstate highway system.

Three Categories of CMC

Following the middle-road definition of CMC provided earlier, one can discern three broad categories of CMC function. These categories are distinguished by the nature of the human-computer interaction and the role taken by the computer in mediating the human communication process.

Although these categories are described and explained separately, it is most important to note that they are not mutually exclusive. In fact it is both likely and desirable that functions from each of these categories be combined in a way that meets the specific needs of human computer users—as well as the capabilities of computer-network resources available to these users.

I describe these three categories briefly, with more in-depth descriptions later. The first category of CMC involves direct human-human communication, with the computer acting simply as a transaction router, or providing simple storage and retrieval functions. I refer to this category as *computer-based conferencing*, or simply as *conferencing*. This category includes such functions as electronic mail, interactive messaging, and group conference support systems such as Listserv, Usenet NETNEWS, bulletin-board systems, and so on.

The second category of CMC is one in which the computer has a more active role as the repository or maintainer of organized information that originates with human contributors and is utilized by human retrievers. I refer to this category as *informatics*. Part of the current explosion of interest in the Internet is a result of the rapid growth of Internet-accessible informatics resources including online public-access library catalogs (OPACs), interactive remote databases, and program-data archive sites.

In the third category of CMC the computer structures and manages both the presentation of information and the possible choices available to the human user. In this category the computer is programmed to take a more active role toward the human user in this category as opposed to the other two categories, in which the computer more passively carries out commands. This is the realm of computers as teachers or guides. I use the fairly generic term *computer-assisted instruction* (CAI) to refer to this category.

The differences in the type of human interaction with the computer and in the different roles played by the computer in each of these three categories is quite significant. With conferencing, it might appear that the computer is doing nothing more than playing telephone or postal delivery person. In fact, the messages, destinations, and purpose of communication are entirely provided by the human users. However, the computer, while operating primarily in the background, does have a major influence on the nature and effectiveness of the communication process—particularly in ongoing group communication.

Because of this influence, it is important that design considerations for conferencing systems take into account what is known (or, more importantly, not known) about the nature of human communication interpersonally, in groups and in organizations.

The roles of human and computer in informatics are more involved than in conferencing. Here a true interaction takes place between the human, who is seeking information, and one or more networked computer systems, which potentially have the information being sought. Again, the design of the computer system is paramount to the successful location of needed information.

Two approaches to the design of informatics resources are generally used. The first is to adopt standards (often rooted in technical evolution) that are then documented at great length to make them understandable. This is not an unreasonable approach, because the effort is being placed on training the human users in utilization of the resources. The second approach is to attempt to make the resources more "intuitive" or "user-friendly" by design. At first glance this would appear to be an obviously better approach; however it suffers from two major hangups. First, "intuition" is a very fuzzy concept that varies considerably with cultural background and degree of prior computer experience. Second, the human user can never be sure whether the requested information was really not available, or the inquiry was properly formulated.

With computer-assisted instruction the roles of human and computer are the most complex. The human is cast as student or apprentice and the computer is the teacher or guide. Although the information programmed into the computer originated with some other human, and quite possibly with a team of humans, it is the job of the computer to manage the instructional process within the limitations of its programming.

Each of these three categories of CMC is evolving rapidly. The next three sections describe them in greater detail.

COMPUTER-BASED CONFERENCING

Computer-based conferencing takes three primary forms. The first is electronic mail, the second is group conferencing systems, and the third is interactive messaging systems. Each of these is designed for the support of direct human-human communication.

Numerous studies and analyses of human communication via CMC have shown that this method of communication incorporates aspects of written (literal) as well as spoken (oral) communication. An examination of "smilies" (Lewis, 1986) and the use of CHAT systems such as the Internet Relay Chat (IRC) shows a communication form that is uniquely shaped by the medium, yet unquestionably human in nature.

Electronic Mail

Electronic mail (or e-mail) is unquestionably one of the most commonly used forms of CMC. In its most basic form it involves a human user composing and sending an online "letter" to another computer user. The recipient of this online "letter" may then elect to read it, discard it, save it for later use, print it, reply to it, or send it to another computer user. This form of communication can be thought of as a "one-to-one" communication (Quarterman, 1990), although most e-mail programs permit mail to be sent to multiple recipients.

Electronic mail has been used on mainframe computers for at least two decades. The current explosion in e-mail's popularity derives from two factors. The first is the interconnection of hundreds of thousands of computers, ranging in size from giant supercomputers to inexpensive microcomputers, by electronic data-transfer networks such as the Internet, BITnet, uucp, and so on. The second is the adoption of electronic mail standards that permit the transfer of electronic mail from one kind of computer system (and software) to another without loss of information.

The usefulness of electronic mail as a human communication medium stems partly from its ease of use. A person can send an electronic mail letter to another computer user simply by knowing his or her electronic mail "address." This address encodes the actual physical location of the recipients computer as well as the particular electronic "mailbox" on that computer. In function, this address operates much like a telephone number in the international telephone network.

Another reason for the growing use of electronic mail is that it provides fast "asynchronous" human communication. This is communication in which the participants need not be online simultaneously. Human A composes and sends an electronic letter to human B. It sits in B's electronic mailbox until B (who is doing something else) gets to it. When convenient, B responds to the letter by sending a reply back to A. It waits in A's electronic mailbox until A is ready to deal with it, and so on.

This procedure is really no different than that of sending hardcopy letters through the postal system. However, there are a number of important additional features to electronic mail that make it advantageous for users. One of these is that electronic mail delivery may take mere seconds, even when the recipient's computer is located on the other side of the planet. This significantly reduces overall transaction time when people are working together via electronic mail over a long period of time.

Another useful feature is that local mailer programs often incorporate useful e-mail-management features such as automatic return addressing for e-mail replies, ability to define group nicknames, ability to store and selectively retrieve received e-mail, and automatic redirection of incoming electronic mail to another computer account.

A third useful feature of electronic mail is that it is an extremely convenient tool for managing communications when the user does a lot of other work on the computer as well. Many students, workers, and individuals have convenient access to personal computers. Why not use these systems to manage and support correspondence as well? It can be far easier to take a writing-in-progress from a word processor and transfer it to a colleague (for critical analysis, of course) via electronic mail rather than printing it, addressing an envelope, and waiting for days to make sure it reached its destination. Furthermore, the information transferred via electronic mail is not limited to text. Pictures, sounds, and virtually any type of data that can be encoded into a computer file is fair game for electronic mail transfer. (Although in fairness it must be added that with the current state of technology some pre- and post-transfer processing of the data file may be necessary.)

An interesting side note to electronic mail is the extent to which it is being used for social communication. Some early critics of electronic mail hinged their objection on what they perceived to be a "mechanical" approach. They felt it would be dehumanizing and limited strictly to task-oriented discussion. In fact, the opposite is actually true, and the range of orientation of electronic mail is truly as diverse as the range of human communication. Rice and Love (1987) observed that CMC systems can facilitate exchange of socioemotional content. From this I take faith that technology does not necessarily dehumanize; rather we can humanize technology to meet our needs.

An excellent source for further information on electronic mail is the e-mail chapter from the Electronic Frontier Foundation's "Extended Guide to the Internet" located on the EFF Webserver at

http://www.eff.org/papers/eegtti/eeg_48.html#SEC49

Group Conferencing Systems

Group conferencing systems are essentially an extension of electronic mail. With electronic mail one can send an electronic "letter" to a group of persons as easily as to one person—provided that each of their electronic mail addresses are known. Group conferencing systems were developed to help manage special problems of group-oriented conferencing, including managing large and changing group membership lists, providing efficient distribution of e-mail among group members, and providing retrieval of prior and perhaps related transactions.

There are a variety of group conferencing systems. I mention three popular approaches here. The first is an electronic mailing list system such as the Listserv software program that originated on BITnet-connected IBM mainframes and is now available for most mainframe platforms (unix, VAX, etc.).

E-mail list software handles two primary functions of group electronic mail. First, it manages the group subscription list. This allows (if the nature of the group warrants) computer users to join or leave the group at will, so the list owner does not have to keep track of the current status of all group members. This is a good thing, because some mail list groups have memberships in the thousands. Second, the mail list software takes any single group member's contribution to the conference and copies it to all other group members. Group members participate in the group by sending their contributions to the list address, which makes sure that copies go to all other current group members. This enduring distribution method results in "one-to-many" communication (Quarterman, 1990). The mailing list software typically also keeps an archive of all previous conference transactions. This allows a new group member to examine previous transactions to gain an understanding of the current context in which discussion is taking place.

A second popular approach to group conferencing systems is the "bulletin board system" or BBS. This approach simulates the bulletin board at a shopping center or the lunchroom of a company. Messages are usually written on 3x5 cards and thumb-tacked to physical bulletin boards for all to see. If there are enough entries (and enough space) the board may have separate areas for announcements, items for sale, help wanted, and so on.

A computer bulletin board typically has a number of subject areas into which a user may post messages. Other users may read these messages and elect to respond to the group or to the individual who originated the posting. One example of BBS-type group conferencing is Usenet NEWS. This collection of newsgroups originated on the UUCP network. Individual conference "postings" are transferred through the Internet through a protocol named "nntp." Users access Usenet NEWS through a local client newsreader, such as the NETNEWS program for VM/CMS operating systems or Peter Tatum's "Trumpet" for DOS-based machines.

Usenet NEWS originated with a fairly small group of unix-based computers connected via the UUCP network. It has since developed into a far more powerful system, transferring messages over the Internet and BITnet in addition to UUCP. Hundreds of original topic groups (newsgroups) have exploded to the point where (when I last looked a few minutes ago) over 2,000 newsgroups are represented. These span the breadth of human experience from telecommunication protocols to alternative backrubs.

A third approach to group conferencing is what I call *conference management systems* or *groupware*. These are systems that support conference participants by imposing a structured approach on the conference. The structured approach allows certain features of database management systems to come into play. One example of this is thread management. In a conference, a thread is a particular line of discussion. It can often be difficult to follow threads properly when a conference has hundreds, or even thousands, of members. Sometimes there are multiple discussion threads happening at the same time. Thread management allows a given user to isolate only the thread of interest and track the evolution of that thread through various contributions.

Because of the structured approach, conference management systems can be fairly easy to learn and use. Examples of mainframe conference management systems are DEC VAXNotes, CoSy, Caucus, Confer, and EIES. Examples of web-based conference management programs are Web Forum, Web Caucus, and COW. The thread management capability, combined with other functions in support of group communications, result in a form of "many-to-many" communication.

One of the growing uses of group conferencing systems is to support instructional communication. A number of universities utilize conference management systems such as VAXNotes or LotusNotes for this purpose. At Penn State over 90 courses are taught incorporating private NETNEWS groups for course announcements, discourse, and other purposes.

It is tempting to think of instructional group conferencing as an obvious application of technology to instruction; however, various realities delayed its widespread use until the mid-1980s. Among the problems encountered were lack of convenient access to microcomputers/terminals, lack of centralized support for instructors/students, reluctance of many faculty to explore new instructional approaches, and reluctance of academic departments to give adequate recognition to those faculty who did successfully explore new instructional approaches.

These problems are being overcome in a number of ways. First, technology is increasing in power and decreasing in price. Although this trend may not be following the predictions of Moore's Law (Patterson, Kiser, & Smith, 1989)[1] it has nevertheless resulted in a situation in which $1,000 can purchase a quite usable personal workstation and modem for both local work and telecommunication. Second, large organizations are recognizing the need for both centralized and decentralized provision of training and support. In the 1960s and 1970s the university computer center was a place where mainframe computer access was meted out to users. In the 1990s the computer center is

---

[1]In 1965 engineer Gordon Moore made the prediction that, beginning in 1965, for 20 years the power of a silicon chip of the same price would double annually.

primarily a provider of training and expert support for distributed computing resources. Third, a growing body of literature has reported on various approaches, strategies, and outcomes for instructional conferencing. Finally, there is a growing recognition by academic administrators of the value of technical innovation in instruction. This is partly because of hopes for greater efficiency and partly in recognition of the need to prepare students for an increasingly technical world.

One pioneer in the application of conferencing to instruction has noted that communication within a learning group often increases as a result of computer use (Hiltz, 1986). My own experience over nine years of using conferencing to support Liberal Arts courses shows that students embrace the technology and quickly adapt it to their own purposes (Santoro, 1989).

Further information on Listserv may be found at

http://cac.psu.edu/~santoro/cac/inex/listserv.html

and further information on Usenet NEWS may be found at

http://cac.psu.edu/~santoro/cac/inex/netnews.html

Interactive Messaging

In addition to the asynchronous forms of computer conferencing discussed earlier, many computer systems have the capability for computer users to communicate in synchronous mode. Synchronous communication requires that all participants be online at the same time. As a result, the communication flows much like a telephone conversation. Because of the interaction that results, this form of conferencing is known as *interactive messaging*.

Early interactive messaging took place between people logged into the same computer system, even though they were physically located far apart. As computer networks were developed, some included the capability for interactive messaging between different computer hosts and others omitted this capability. For example, the UUCP network does not support interactive messaging of any kind. The BITnet network supports unsolicited interactive messaging. This means that one computer user on BITnet can interrupt another computer user with a message. (Many systems do include commands for filtering or turning off such messages entirely.) The Internet supports interactive messaging but not unsolicited messages.

If a person on Internet wants to communicate interactively with another Internet user (assuming both have software permitting this), the initiator's software would send a request to the other person. That person would have to acknowledge that he or she is willing to communicate. If he or she does so the software will then establish an interactive messaging session. Simple examples of interactive messaging include the unix "talk" command and the VAX "phone" command. Both establish simple one-to-one messaging that can be useful for brief discussion.

A more robust example of interactive messaging is represented by the Internet Relay Chat (IRC) system. IRC follows the paradigm of a citizen's band radio in providing an environment for interactive messaging. A user first runs a local IRC client program, which then connects to one of a network of IRC servers on the Internet. The client program can be located on the user's PC or on a mainframe computer for which the user has an account. However, the PC or mainframe must have an Internet connection. The IRC servers manage traffic flow between IRC clients to ensure efficient network utilization.

The user selects a "nickname" and a "channel" for communication. If the channel already exists, the user will be joined to it and will be able to communicate interactively with all other persons on that channel. If the channel does not exist, IRC will create it, and the user will be the owner (and initially the only resident) of that channel.

Once on an IRC channel, whatever a person types will be seen by all other channel members and vice-versa. The nicknames will be appended to each message, so each person knows who is saying what. IRC also provides other capabilities for managing interactive sessions, including: maintaining a transcript on a computer file, private messaging, private/public channels, designation of channel topics, listing of available public channels and preset option preferences.
A reference to some Web resources about IRC is located at

http://cac.psu.edu/~santoro/cac/inex/synch.html

INFORMATICS

The second major category of CMC is that in which the computer takes a more active role in storing and retrieving information for the human user. This form of CMC is often referred to as informatics.

With informatics, the computer is programmed to act like an interactive library or database. People access the desired computer system through a variety of methods and issue a series of commands to locate and retrieve the needed information.

For informatics to work the user must first establish a connection with the computer on which the desired information resides. In some cases this interaction is managed asynchronously by sending interactive or e-mail messages to the remote computer, with the body of the message containing the command to be executed.

Users connected to the Internet have the more convenient option of using the telnet protocol to establish a real-time interactive link with the remote computer. Technically, telnet is the Internet protocol for remote terminal access. This allows any Internet-connected user to log onto any Internet-connected host computer as if they had a local terminal connection to that computer, provided they have a login and password for the remote system.

The growth in the number of Internet-connected users has fueled a growth in the number and diversity of informatics applications. I describe a few of these below.

The World Wide Web

The most successful informatics application by far is the World Wide Web. Developed originally as an experiment in Internet-based hypertext, the Web has developed into a global system for electronic publishing and information retrieval.

As an electronic publishing system, the Web's simplicity has allowed schools, corporations, governments, organizations and even individual students to establish an electronic presence on the Internet. According to *Internet World* magazine, the Web contained over 10 million pages as of Fall 1996, and it is doubling in size every 4 months.

For information retrieval, Web clients have been developed that incorporate many Internet service protocols beyond that of hypertext pages, thereby allowing easy access to telnet, ftp, gopher, WAIS, and other services. In this way the Web provides a consistent interface to most of the functionality of the Internet.

Access to the Web comes through a Web client, also known as a Web "browser." The most popular browser as of Fall 1996 was Netscape, a program made freely available for educational and noncommercial use by Netscape Communications, Inc. A link to information about Netscape is

http://home.netscape.com/

The key to the power of the Web is the Uniform Resource Locator, more conveniently known as a URL. This is an address that uniquely identifies any computer file on the Internet. The URL contains information that may identify a specific computer, subdirectory, file, location within that file, and transfer type.

For example, the URL http:/cac.psu.edu/~santoro/cac /internexus.html identifies the transfer type as a hypertext transfer protocol (http://). It identifies the specific computer by its fully qualified Internet domain name (cac.psu.edu). It identifies the subdirectory (/~santoro/cac/), and it identifies the file (internexus.html).

When a Web browser executes a URL, it establishes a connection to the specified computer (which must be running a server consistent with the specified transfer type) and downloads a copy of the specified file. It then interprets the file, in some cases by launching an external application known as a viewer or helper application, to display the contents of the file to the user.

URLs are executed in three ways. One way is when the user selects a link from a hypertext page currently in browser memory. The link contains the URL, and the browser acts on the link by executing the URL. The user sees this as a jump to another hypertext page or to a data object. The second way URLs are executed is when the user types the URL of a desired resource directly into the browser. All browsers contain ways for users to enter a new URL. This allows the user to take a URL from another media type (magazines, books, television commercials, this chapter, etc.) and access the resource directly. The third way URLs are executed is by the user making a selection from her or his bookmarks list. All current browsers allow the user to develop lists of URLs (called *bookmarks*) and call on any of them directly. In this way, when the user finds a particularly interesting item through the Web he or she can save its URL for convenient later access.

Useful resources for learning more about the World Wide Web may be found in the following pages

http://cac.psu.edu/~santoro/cac/inex/www.guide.html and
http://cac.psu.edu/~santoro/283/www.html

Campus-Wide Information Systems

Expanding college/university networks and the ever-improving availability of network-accessible microcomputers/terminals has led to the development of campus-wide information systems (CWIS). These are information servers that combine online database capabilities with menu-driven front-ends to other telnet-accessible information servers.

Typically, the online database function provides users with campus information formerly available through publications or campus newspapers. This information may include the schedule of classes, faculty/staff/student telephone directory, policies/procedures manual, and other "official" information. It may also include a listing of campus events, the semester calendar, and announcements from various clubs and student organizations. In general, the idea behind the database component of a CWIS is to provide the most current information possible without the delays and costs associated with printed versions.

Two popular approaches to campus-wide information systems are MIT's TECHINFO and the University of Minnesota's gopher. Both systems provide users with a hierarchy of menus. The user navigates through this set of menus searching for the desired information. In some cases, the selection of a menu item will result in the display of information. In other cases, the selection of a menu item will result in a telnet session to some remote information server.

Both TECHINFO and gopher are based on a client-server model. The user runs a client program on his or her local PC or a connected mainframe, which provides the user interface and processes menu selections for the server. The server is typically located on another computer and accessed by the client program using telnet. Client programs for both TECHINFO and gopher are available for the Apple Macintosh, IBM-PS/2, various workstations, and various mainframe operating systems.

A slightly different approach to the problem of current information dissemination is found in the Wide-Area Information System (WAIS) developed by Thinking Machines Corporation. WAIS is also based on a client-server model, but in this case the user runs a local client to develop a number of query profiles that resemble problems. Each query profile contains two pieces of information. The first is a set of data that qualifies the kind of information being sought. For example, someone seeking information on computer-mediated communication might use the string "CMC." The second piece of information is the set of WAIS servers to be searched. These are in the form of Internet domain addresses, such as info-mac@sumex.aim.edu. (WAIS FAQ 1993).

The WAIS approach is interesting in that a given user may develop a set of query profiles and issue them periodically to see if any new information has emerged. Such an approach can be extremely useful to persons who are interested in certain topics from online group conferences, but who are too busy to actively screen all conference transactions. If a WAIS server exists for the conference it may be possible to create a query profile to elicit only relevant transactions from the complete set of conference transactions.

On the other hand, WAIS suffers from the same major problem as other online databases. Namely, if a person does not find the desired information it may be because the information does not exist or because he or she has not asked for it using the correct query profile.

Online Databases

With an online database, the user establishes a connection to the remote host computer, issues any appropriate logon sequences, and then issues the proper commands to locate and retrieve the desired information. Hundreds of online databases are currently available through the Internet, with at least a few of these also supporting some kind of asynchronous query mechanism.

Some examples of online databases include online library catalog systems (OPACs), online medical/legal information servers, and weather information servers. Some specialized online databases include interactive game systems, NASA and FDA information servers, and a

Ham Radio Callsign database. Popular guides to online databases include "Accessing Online Bibliographic Databases" by Billy Barron, and "Special Internet Connections" by Scott Yanoff. (Both of these files may be found through the web pages listed in the References.)

Online file archives are network-accessible computers that store libraries of computer files for retrieval by users. The method of retrieval may vary depending on the exact setup of the archive. One of the most popular retrieval methods is the Internet "file transfer protocol" (FTP). Other retrieval methods include electronic mail and interactive messaging requests. With FTP retrieval the file is immediately and interactively retrieved. With electronic mail and interactive messaging retrieval the request is queued to a file server, which sends the file to the requester via electronic mail. (The Listserv program supports queued file retrieval.)

The kinds of information that may be stored in online computer file archives are as varied as the nature of computer files themselves. Files may include programs (both in source and compiled form), data sets (raw and processed), pictures, sounds, text, and even animation and movies. There are only two requirements for the successful use of online file archives. The first is that the user may have to possess a file decryptor or extractor program to process the file after transferring it. This is often necessary with binary programs because they are processed into encrypted or compressed form to ensure successful transfer. The second is that the user possess whatever program necessary to utilize the computer file once it is retrieved. In many cases the necessary decryptor or extractor will be available from the same site as the binary programs. For example, if a user retrieves a weather satellite image from the archive vmd.cso.uiuc.edu (which are stored in GIF format), then the user must have the necessary software for displaying and manipulating the image.

Useful resources for learning more about online databases (accessible through the Web or through telnet protocols) may be found in

http://cac.psu.edu/~santoro/cac/inex/telnet.html

and information regarding file archives and file transfer protocol (FTP) may be found in

http://cac.psu.edu/~santoro/cac/inex/ftp.html and
http://www.matisse.net/files/formats.html

COMPUTER-ASSISTED INSTRUCTION

Computer-Assisted Instruction (CAI) refers to a broad category of computer use whose purpose is provision of instruction to some human user. According to Burke (1982), the terms *computer-based instruction* (CBI) and *computer-managed instruction* (CMI) are also used to describe this category, although CMI also includes the notion of computerized testing, diagnosis, and record-keeping.

The main idea behind CAI is that most instruction can be systematized into an algorithmic process. Once this has been done, it is possible to write a computer program to interactively deliver the instruction. In addition, the program will periodically test the student to ensure that the desired material is being learned. Such a CAI program is commonly referred to as *courseware*.

Two major advantages to CAI courseware are: (a) the ability of a student to learn at his or her own pace, and (b) the effective and consistent distribution of the instructional process to the student, reducing the load on a human teacher. In many cases the role of the human teacher is not eliminated; rather, it is changed into that of a guide and mentor.

In recent years, the principles and approaches of CAI are being combined with the functional capabilities of conferencing and informatics to form the emerging discipline of "distance education" (DE). One pioneer of distance education, Morton Flate Paulsen (of the European SUPERNET project on Distance Learning), sums up the expected potential of this application of CMC: "My proposition is that it is possible to create a virtual school around a computer-based information system and that virtual schools will dominate the future of distance education" (1987, p. 75).

The development and evolution of the World Wide Web is giving new direction to CAI in both application and audience. As a result, Web-based courses are emerging that integrate the interactivity of the web, the interpersonal discourse of conferencing/e-mail, and the structured curriculum of CAI.

Further information regarding CAI (and related instructional technologies) may be found on the Yahoo pages for Instructional Technology and Training

> http://www.yahoo.com/Education/Instructional_Technology_and _Training/ and for Online Teaching and Learning

SUMMARY

The three major areas of CMC described in this overview chapter are different in their purpose and use, yet they are similar in that all three are essentially methods for information transfer between and among human computer users. This leads back to the original premise that computer systems—our grand symbol manipulators— are essentially tools for human communication. Just as communication activities permeate human existence, so will computer systems permeate human endeavor, whether in business, education, socialization, or leisure activities.

It is important to keep in mind that we are both the creator and the object of the creation of CMC. In the final analysis, the potential for benefit or harm stemming from CMC will be up to the humans who design, implement, and use it. On the plus side, CMC technology can permit the worldwide sharing of information in ways that seemed inconceivable only a few decades ago. On the negative side, the potential exists for massive invasion of privacy and the creation of a two-tiered society comprised of those with network access and those without network access.

As one participant in the development of CMC I conclude this overview of CMC technology with the fervent hope that our technical achievements can be paralleled by a dedication to appropriate use and social responsibility.

FURTHER READING

Those wishing to learn more about the Internet and its services have a wealth of material available. Neighborhood book stores now carry many Internet overviews, some including client software and access provider information. High schools and local colleges/universities may provide seminars or continuing education classes about Internet services.

There are also many beneficial articles, catalogs, tutorials, and documents freely available on the Web. A good starting point is a support page maintained by the author at

http://cac.psu.edu/~santoro/cac/internexus.html

This page contains a subject-oriented guide to resources about the Internet and its services.

Examples of class-related pages, wherein the web page becomes a form of interactive syllabus for the student are available at

http://cac.psu.edu/~santoro/283/new283.html and
http://cac.psu.edu/~santoro/283/483.html

To find out more on teaching online and moderating discussion lists, explore the Moderator's home page:

http://star.ucc.nau.edu/~mauri/moderators.html

REFERENCES

Barron, B. "Accessing Online Bibliographic Databases." Accessible at ftp://ftp.udallas.edu/pub/staff/billy/libguide/.

Burke, Robert L. (1982). *CAI sourcebook.* Englewood Cliffs, NJ; Prentice-Hall.

Hiltz, S.R. (1986). The virtual classroom: Using computer-mediated communication for university teaching. *Journal of Communication, 36*(2) 95-104.

Lewis, P.H. (1986, July 8). The summer break. *New York Times,* p. C5.

MERIT. (1991). LINK Letter—Electronic Newsletter of the MERIT/NSFNET Backbone Project. March, 1991. http://www.merit.edu

Patterson, D.A., Kiser, D.S., & Smith, D. N. (1989). *Computing unbound: Using computers in the arts and sciences.* New York: Norton.

Paulsen, M.F. (1987, December/January). In search of a virtual school. *T.H.E. Journal,* pp. 71-76

Quarterman, J.R. (1990). *The matrix: Computer networks and conferencing systems worldwide.* Bedford, MA: Digital Press.

Rice, R.E., & Love, G. (1987). Electronic emotion: Socioemotional content in a computer-mediated communication network. *Communication Research, 14*(1), 85-108

Santoro, G.M. (1989). *Support of group problem-solving instruction through computer-mediated communication.* Unpublished doctoral dissertation, The Pennsylvania State University, State College, PA.

Yanoff, S. "Special Internet Connections". Available at http://www.uwm.edu/Mirror/inet.services.html.

WAIS FAQ. (1993). Available from http://www.cis.ohio-state.edu/hypertext/faq/usenet/wais-faq/top.html.

4

RESTRUCTURING EDUCATION AND THE INFORMATION HIGHWAY*

Rory McGreal

> Today, loving change, tumult, even chaos is a prerequisite for survival, let alone success.
>
> —Peters, 1987, p. 45

The developing knowledge economy, based on the convergence of computers, telecommunications, and service/content delivery industries is also propelling the convergence of learning with the workplace. Learning and training is becoming part of everyone's occupation. As entire industries and economic sectors adjust to the new realities, our educational structures are becoming strained. They are having difficulty not only in meeting the diverse demands being placed on them, but also in transforming from an industrial to a knowledge based model. Strategies for promoting restructuring are needed if our educational institutions are to not only keep up with the rapid changes, but also take full advantage of the opportunities presented by the new technologies.

---

*This chapter is based on a report presented by the author to the Working Group on Learning and Training of the Information Highway Advisory Committee set up by Industry Canada.

Educational systems are being criticized for their inability to compete with those of other advanced nations. The reality is that educational institutions are doing a better job than ever before. The figures used for high school drop-out rates are misleading. Both U.S. and Canadian figures show that the rate has in fact been steadily decreasing to less than 18% today and is continuing to descend. The graduation rate has been rising steadily in all regions of North America since the second world war.

Statistical comparisons of achievement levels with other advanced countries seem unfavorable on the surface because both Canada and the United States test a wide range of students and compare them with elite students in other countries. Top students in the United States and Canada compare very favorably with top students in other countries (Canada, 1991, Trial by false fire, 1994). Koretz (1994) contests the popular negative perception of U.S. test scores and says that scores in fact have not been declining. He advises readers to avoid simplistic interpretations of data, unsupported evaluations of schooling, and a reductionist view, insisting that what works for one may not work for others.

Blaming our schools for supporting an economic system that no longer exists is not the issue. Hodas (1993) contends that schools are not failing, "they are doing exactly the jobs they were set up and refined over generations to perform. It is the world around them that has changed" (p. 26). He further states that the changes in society must have an effect on schools and notes that "they can never be independent of the values of society at large" (p. 27). Schools must accommodate their clients in adjusting to the new knowledge economy.

Current methods of schooling, when based on the industrial model, will not be competent to meet the needs of students and society in the future. A recent Ontario government report noted that "students, through no fault or inadequacy of their own, aren't able to gain from schools what they are entitled to . . . a better chance at a job" (Ontario Report, 1995, p. 3). A radical restructuring is required in all countries.

The directions needed for this transition can be better discerned from an understanding of the principal features of the two economies and the education systems needed to support them. Reigeluth (1994) outlined some of the key differences between industrial age education and information age learning including the need for outcomes-based learning strategies using information technology. They are outlined below:

INDUSTRIAL AGE EDUCATION	INFORMATION AGE LEARNING
Grade levels	Continuous progress
Covering the content	Outcomes-based learning
Norm-referenced testing	Individualized testing
Non-authentic assessment	Performance-based assessment
Group-based content delivery	Personal learning plans
Adversarial learning	Cooperative learning
Classrooms	Learning centers
Teacher-dispenser of knowledge	Teacher-coach-facilitator
Memorization of facts	Thinking, problem-solving
Isolated reading, writing skills	Communication skills
Books as tools	Advanced technology as tools

(Reigeluth, 1994, p. 26)

Our schools need to restructure, and Reigeluth provides us with a concise summary of the directions in which we should be aiming.

How to Promote Restructuring

We must recognize the need for a rapid transition in learning and training to meet the demands of the new knowledge economy. The costs of changing must be weighed against the costs of not changing. Peterson (1990) noted that society is paying now when graduates cannot meet the minimum job requirements and cannot handle the new technology.

The following initiatives are recommended:

1. Invest in technology;
2. Undermine bureaucracy;
3. Change attitudes;
4. Reeducate and train teachers, trainers, and librarians;
5. Support research and development;
6. Support accountability;
7. Seed high technology applications and content development;
8. Extend distance learning;
9. Reform accreditation regulations.

Invest in Technology

"An important technology first creates a problem, and then solves it" (A. Kay, cited in Hammer & Champy, 1993, p. 87). Universal accessibility, as pointed out by Pearlman (1994), is only the first step toward universal participation. He refers to the "critical mass" problem: without widespread local infrastructures, service providers cannot afford to invest, but without these services, schools will not invest in infrastructure. Therefore, both have to be developed simultaneously. He recommends concurrent development of:

1. The InfoHighway backbone, including a public right of way;
2. New educational service industries;
3. Reorganization of schooling; and
4. Local school telecommunications infrastructure.

Few teachers have external phone lines and very few know anything about the online universe. Thornburg (1992) asks whether or not it makes sense to have classrooms without telephones, modems, and televisions. He recommends that institutions should stop investing in the technologies of the past and put their resources into the new multimedia, extending the network in schools to every desktop.

The level of capital investment in information technology (IT) by schools has been scandalously low. In the United States, this amounts to less than $100 per student or $1000 per employee in comparison to the industry standard of $50,000 per employee. In high technology industries the average is closer to $300,000 per employee. Even labor-intensive industries invest between $7,000 and $20,000 per employee. Education has by far the lowest level of investment in technology of any major sector of the economy (Salisbury, 1992).

A major investment through the reallocation of funds must be made. As in industry, the capital investment can be recuperated through restructuring and reducing labor costs, particularly in middle management. The present labor-intensive model of education is incapable of meeting the learning needs of the 21st century at reasonable cost (Twigg, 1994).

Undermine Bureaucracy.

"[c]osts walk, and they usually wear a suit" (Keen, 1991, p. 97). Information technology can be used to undermine the educational hierarchy and to support empowerment at the school level. One third of the employees of many city boards such as the Calgary school board do not teach. Many school boards such as the one in Toronto, now spend 43 cents on support staff for every dollar spent in the classroom (Nikiforuk, 1993). A recent California study (Krop, Carroll, & Ross, 1995) shows that only 46% of state expenditures are spent on classroom personnel and materials. Publicizing the actual ratios of bureaucrats and support staff to teaching staff in different school boards and overall in provinces and states could help parents and other taxpayers better decide on the efficiency of their local system.

The strength of bureaucracies lies in their stability. The existing school organizations have existed in more or less the same form for many years. Present policies tend to reinforce this educational bureaucracy. In a slowly changing environment, this stability is an asset, but in times of change it can hinder progress.

Decentralizing and shifting power from the hierarchy will not be easy. Although bureaucracy readily accepts technology that increases its control (e.g., central marking systems, employee records, intercoms), it can mount effective resistance to any change that takes it away. S. Hodas (1993) wrote, "Organizations seek nothing so much as their own perpetuity." They "experience change as a disruption, an intrusion, as a failure of organismic defenses" (p. 3). "Any practice . . . that threatens to disrupt this existing structure will meet tremendous resistance at both adoption and implementation stages" (p. 4).

Change Attitudes toward Technology

"People don't resist change; they resist being changed" (Senge, 1990, p. 155). The idea of the school environment as a positive place for human socialization as opposed to computer use as dehumanizing is held by some educators. Much of this is based on an idealization of the classroom as a humane, interactive environment. Although this is sometimes true, quite often the ideal is not attained. Likewise, the negative view of computers remains as a legacy of the older computer systems that required arcane knowledge and special operating skills. The new personal computers are very user-friendly and can be used to promote high levels of continuous and humane interactivity.

Jonassen (1995) reminds us that the technology is more than hardware. Attitudes toward it can and will change as pedagogical design is applied to support learning. "Technology is a tool, a partner and a context" (p. 62). Twigg (1995) notes, "Much of our discussion of these issues is clouded by confusion: we confuse the need for student support or structure with the need for interaction" (p. 26).

For all students (whether they use technology on or off site), most studying is done alone. Right now, successful students interact more with textbooks than with teachers. Unsuccessful students rely too heavily on the teacher and the classroom setting. We have to promote more student independence.

Old attitudes nevertheless persist. Few educational institutions or bureaucracies promote personnel on the basis of either a professional's ability to educate or his or her facility with new information technology. On the contrary, a principal's career can be limited if he or she is viewed as a "techie" by his or her superiors. In a study done by Isherwood and Shallwani in Montreal (1992), superiors on a school board thought that "techie principals" were not performing their job very well; they thought the principalship was primarily a "people" role and were suspicious of the principals who used technology. Superiors did not seem to understand how information technology helped principals. Isherwood and Shallwani concluded: "Information Technology, with few exceptions, is not seen as an integral part of Principalship today" (p. 34).

These attitudes can best be overcome by providing the necessary training and introducing teachers to the remarkable potential of computer software for promoting learning, as a creative tool and as a machine that itself learns. This training cannot be imposed on teachers. It must be introduced in collaboration with them.

Unfortunately, all too often it is introduced by fiat. McKenzie (1994) notes, "Equipment is virtually 'dropped' on classrooms and teachers with almost no investment in human resource development. It is an arranged marriage. There is no love and no real consent" (p. 21). Switzer (1992) cautions us to start with those who are ready, noting that imposed changes do not last. The ambivalence and caution that education professionals are expressing is normal. We must provide them with the tools and procedures they need to achieve the goals that are set. When small successes occur, they should be celebrated. Institutions must give strong support to administrators and teachers who are enthusiastic about the new technologies. Appropriate reward and promotion processes can be developed to encourage teachers to retrain and make effective use of the new media.

Reeducate and Train Teachers, Trainers, and Librarians

"Those who implement must make the plans" (Peters & Waterman, 1982, p. 31). Teachers and their organizations should be involved in information technology implementation processes from the beginning. There is an enormous need for reeducation of teachers so they can actively participate as professionals in the introduction of computer applications into their institutions. Thornburg (1992) supports intensive teacher training in information technology. For this, provinces and states have a role in supporting proficiency in information technology for the credentialing of teachers and in insisting on preservice training in information technology at teachers' colleges.

Information technology should be used for the delivery of these new training opportunities for teachers. Through modern telecommunications, using the Internet and the World Wide Web, distance learning, and computer-based training, large numbers of teachers can be trained in the new technologies. By using the technology for their own instruction, teachers can gain a deeper understanding of the potential, and problems involved in implementing the technology in the schools. Combined with programs for encouraging teachers to use computers at home, IT training programs could be an excellent means for delivering the training that is required.

Teachers are not against technology. Carey (1991) noted that much of the resistance of teachers is based on good judgment. Much of the courseware is poorly designed; teachers are given inadequate training and are often not consulted in the planning process. Technology must be presented as a tool to empower teachers, not replace them. The technology should relieve teachers from routine tasks and administration and allow them more time to develop good instructional materials. For this, training in the technology is essential.

User-friendly interfaces are needed to create a more supportive environment for both teachers and students. These must be backed up with simplified documentation and access procedures.

Support Research and Development.

"Reality has outgrown existing theories" (Drucker, 1989, P. 156). Research and development investment in education is extremely low. In the United States, investment averages less than $50 per employee or less than $5 per student, whereas the norm in industry is approximately $5,000 per employee and over $50,000 in high technology industries. Canadian figures are assumed to be similar, and probably worse. The U.S. Army is the largest investor in learning and training R&D. Five percent of their $600 million training budget is reserved for R&D (Perelman, 1992).

Private studies on computer-based training in various educational and training environments support results that show that CBT results in 26% to 37% higher performance in 26% less time with 15% higher retention than traditional teaching. All these results have been achieved at substantially reduced costs (Foshay, 1993). Emphasis on R&D funding should be placed squarely on the development side. There is far too much research in education that has not been acted on. There is also ample research, particularly quantitative research, that is not particularly useful. Funding bodies should not be closed shops for academics. Business, labor, and community groups should have substantial influence on directing the expenditure of R&D funding.

Support Increased Accountability

"TACO BELL: If something was simple, we made it complex" (Hammer & Champy, 1993, p. 172). Change cannot come easily to large organizations in which there is little accountability. Businesses that have adopted new technology have done so because there were negative consequences for not doing so. In educational hierarchies there are few mechanisms available for rewarding good management using technology, nor are there mechanisms for penalizing those that do not make effective use of the media available. Too many educational institutions treat inputs (money, staff, time, real estate) as positive rather than as costs to be reduced. The administrators and teachers are not themselves accountable for the bottom line.

Pearlman (1993) argued for a devolution of control to the schools. Large schools must be broken down into separate self-managing clusters. As the student evaluations move toward accountability and competency-based assessment, so too must the administration and teaching staffs. Smaller units must be allowed more freedom and autonomy in choosing different learning models using various organizing principles, learning philosophies, and technological media.

We must explore ways to ensure that local accountability does not come at the expense of equality in our public schools. All children must be guaranteed equal opportunities for learning. The challenge is to find different ways of promoting local autonomy while ensuring equity and fairness in the overall system.

Seed IT Applications and Content Development

"The primary threat to jobs is not too fast a pace of technological change, but a pace that is too slow in comparison with the competition" (Adler, 1992, p. 4). Learning institutions could prepare effectively for the knowledge economy by first terminating many of the curriculum development projects that are based on the old paradigms. "What is the value of a textbook that results from a 4 year adoption process in a world where half the information in that book might be obsolete the day it is opened by a student for the first time?" (Davis, 1987, p. 74). Existing resources should be directed toward the development of new quality IT content materials. They are urgently needed to encourage teachers and students to make effective use of the new technology.

The flexibility that comes with a wide range of content materials is essential for building the new learning environments. Resource allocation should focus on multimedia projects that have direct application in the local classrooms and significant export potential. Costs are too high to be taken on at the local level without some possibility of sale or collaboration with other institutions. Preference should be given to projects that are based on partnerships among institutions in order to implicate a wide range of learning professionals. These projects can be used to train teachers and other professionals in the new technology. While providing quality content to students, we can be training teachers and developing the information technology courseware and applications industry.

The development of a strong learning and training service sector should alter the ways in which institutions operate. Public institutions that are strong in the content areas make natural partners for new courseware producers. Distance education can be used to help drive the development of the IT courseware and applications industries. Distance education funding should be not just for equipment and staffing but also used to help seed the development of IT expertise.

Extend Distance Learning

"In any given system, there are very few 'high leverage points' where one can intervene to produce significant lasting changes in the overall behavior of the system" (Buttner, cited in Briggs & Peat, 1989, p. 177). The need for restructuring grows more urgent as access to distance learning opportunities becomes more widespread. Celis (1991) wrote, "local control takes on new meaning when school districts can choose among many televised offerings . . . local leaders cannot then dictate the course contents." When bureaucracies lose their monopolies, change becomes high on the agenda.

Distance learning is nonelitist and tends to bypass bureaucratic control. Students no longer have to travel to a specific site for their education. As more and more institutions offer a wider selection of courses and programs, effective power and control is transferred to the students who become free to choose among courses, programs, and institutions. New institutions are opening up, delivering educational services to small communities and directly to the home. Perelman (1993) wrote: "There is no way distance learning can be adopted without violating and ultimately reconstructing the fundamental bureaucratic structures that tie established institutions together . . . bureaucracies are powerless to exercise an effective veto over the spread of telelearning" (p. 311).

The development of a ubiquitous, affordable, high-bandwidth telecommunications infrastructure is essential for the spread of distance learning. However, this is not enough. Resources must also be reallocated to ensure that distance learning services based on quality content materials are equally affordable and ubiquitous. An electronic telelearning network must be built at the same time as the physical infrastructure.

Accreditation

"Every profession is a conspiracy against the lay person" (George Bernard Shaw). Accreditation is a means of maintaining control. As students gain a wider choice of learning options through distance education, problems of accreditation among multiple institutions will become more common. A global market for credits is already developing. By adopting a universal system for recognizing credits, we effectively give more control to students at the expense of traditional educational bureaucracies.

Institutions must adjust their accreditation policies to be more flexible in accepting credits from other institutions. Articulated credits that permit students to take courses for credit at multiple institutions (but especially among secondary schools, community colleges, and universities) should be encouraged. In the past, many students have had to redo courses that they previously completed in order to satisfy stringent accreditation requirements. As more opportunities become available, students will be able to bypass institutions that are inflexible. Institutions should be encouraged to collaborate and work together, possibly creating consortiums to avoid duplication and standardizing programs for flexible accreditation. In addition, partnerships should be encouraged to promote the establishment of more independent, bona fide, officially recognized accrediting agencies that will allow students to bypass institutions if necessary.

CONCLUSION

The challenges we see ahead are formidable. Educational departments and organizations worldwide are facing the same difficulties . All are trying to adjust to the new knowledge economy. Learning institutions that can develop partnerships built on a clear understanding of where they are going and how they are going to get there, along with the resolve to carry it through, will certainly be the new leaders in the 21st century.

The need for systemic change in our educational institutions is no less urgent than the need for changes in other sectors of society. The rapid pace of change brought about through the global development of microcomputers and telecommunications is forcing this on us. The information economy is already being transformed into a knowledge economy in which learning and training will play a crucial role. The need for change has become critical. Reverend Coady, a leader in the Antigonish movement on Cape Breton Island more than 50 years ago, suggested how people can best regenerate society: "They must have the brains, the techniques, and above all, the *will to do it*" (Coady, 1943; emphasis in original).

REFERENCES

Adler, P. (1992). *Technology and the future of work*. New York: Oxford University Press.

Briggs, J., & Peat, F.D. (1989). *The turbulent mirror: An illustrated guide to chaos theory and the science of wholeness*. New York: Harper & Row.

Canada. (1991). Learning well . . . living well. [Consultation Paper of the Prosperity Secretariat]. Ottawa: Ministry of Supply and Services.

Carey, J. (1991, March). Plato at the keyboard: Telecommunications technology and education policy. *ANNALS, AAPSS, 514*, 11-21.

Celis W., III. (1991, April 7) Inventive curriculums. *The New York Times, Special Report on Education.*

Coady, Rev. M. M. (1943). *The Antigonish way: A series of broadcasts over CBC.* Antigonish, N.S., Canada: St. Francis Xavier University.

Davis, S. (1987). *Future perfect.* New York: Addison-Wesley.

Drucker, P.F. (1989). *The new realities: In government and politics / in economics and business / in society and world view.* New York: Harper & Row.

Foshay, R. (1993). *Effectiveness of computer-based training: An annotated bibliography of reviews, 1980-1993.* Edina, MN: TRO Learning.

Hammer, M., & Champy, J. (1993). *Reengineering the corporation: A manifesto for business revolution.* New York: Harper Business.

Hodas, S. (1993). Technology refusal and the organizational culture of schools 2.0. *Education Policy Analysis Archives, 1*(10), 1-33.

Isherwood, G.B., & Shallwani, M. (1992). Principals beliefs about information technology, school administration and leadership. *ECOO Output, 13*(1), 31-34.

Jonassen, D.H. (1995). Supporting communities of learners with technology: A vision for integrating technology with learning in schools. *Educational Technology, XXXV*(4), 60-63.

Keen, P.G.W. (1991). *Shaping the future: Business design through information technology.* Cambridge, MA: Harvard Business School Press.

Koretz, D.M. (1994). *What happened to test scores and why.* Santa Monica, CA: Rand. (Originally in Educational Measurement: Issues and Practices, Winter 1992)

Krop, C.S., Carroll, S.J., & Ross, R.L. (1995). *Tracking K-12 education spending in California.* Santa Monica, CA: RAND Institute on Education and Training.

McKenzie, J. (1994). *From technology refusal to technology acceptance: A reprise.* Unpublished manuscript.

Nikiforuk, A. (1993). *School's out: The catastrophe in public education and what we can do about it.* Toronto: McFarlane, Walter & Ross.

Ontario Report. (1995. *For the love of learning.* Toronto: Queen's Printer for Ontario.

Pearlman, R. (1994, May 25). Can K-12 education drive on the information superhighway. *Education Week*, pp. 48-38.

Pearlman, R. (1993). Designing the new American schools. *Communications of the ACM, 36*(5), 46-49.

Perelman, L.J. (1992). *School's out: Hyperlearning the new technology and the end of education.* New York: Avon Books.

Peters, T. (1987). *Thriving on chaos.* New York: Knopf.

Peters T., & Waterman Jr., R.H. (1982). *In search of excellence*. New York: Harper & Row.

Peterson, G.A. (1990). *Schools and national telecommunications policy*. Washington, DC: National Geographic Society.

Reigeluth, C. M. (1994). The imperative for systemic change. In C.M. Reigeluth & R. J. Garfinkle (Eds.), *Systemic change in education* (pp. 3-11). Englewood Cliffs, NJ: Educational Technology Publications.

Salisbury, D.F. (1992, July). Toward a new generation of schools: The Florida schoolyear 2000 initiative. *EdTech*, 7-12.

Senge, P.M. (1990). *The fifth discipline: The art and practice of the learning organization*. New York: Doubleday/Currency.

Switzer, T.J. (1992). Empowering for technological change. In M. Wagonner (Ed.), *Empowering networks: Computer conferencing in education* (pp. 215-229). Englewood Cliffs, NJ: Educational Technology Publications.

Thornburg, D. (1992). *Edutrends 2010: Restructuring, technology, and the future of education*. Toronto: Starsong Publications.

Trial by false fire: Education's role in U.S. economic decline. (1994). RAND Institute on Education and Training. [Abstract].

Twigg, C.A. (1994). The need for a national learning infrastructure. *Educom Review, 29*(5), 23-26.

Twigg, C.A. (1995). The value of independent study. *Educom Review, 30*(4), 24-27.

5

DISTRICT TECHNOLOGY PLANS; "TECHNOLOGY, THEN USES" OR "USES, THEN TECHNOLOGY"

Sara Dexter

"Technology, then Uses" or "Uses, then Technology"; one or the other of these two approaches describes most school districts' technology planning and implementation approaches. They are two different ways of gathering, sorting, and processing knowledge about technology, then organizing the information for implementation. The approach planning and implementation efforts resemble is very influential because it determines what information becomes an organizing principle and what information is discarded. Based on the values, assumptions, and logic of the involved planners, the approach chosen determines what will serve as the technology plan's foundation.

A "Technology, then Uses" planning approach focuses on hardware and software first and results in equipment, network, and communication-line purchases for schools. Then, after the technology arrives, the thinking starts on what to do with it all and who to train in its use. On the other hand, a "Uses, then Technology" planning approach focuses on integrating technology and leads first to the identification of the "peopleware," that is, instructional goals, staff-development needs, and the necessary personnel for training and technical support. The peopleware then clarifies and directs subsequent hardware and software purchases.

The "Uses, then Technology" approach undergirds my district's technology plan. The planners focused first on relevant curricular and instructional uses for technology and then on the technology appropriate for those uses. This emphasis on the educational applications of voice, data, and video technologies resulted in a technology-integration plan the stresses curriculum and instruction and peopleware. This chapter describes the technology-integration staff-development framework that resulted when this large suburban school district of a major metropolitan area took this tack to planning for and implementing technology.

Technology-Integration Plan

Because this school district's 26 buildings follow a standard curriculum and the integration of technology into teaching and learning was the premise for the technology planning, the Superintendent created a district-wide Technology Coordination committee to write and then implement a comprehensive technology plan. This committee was made up of representative membership from administration, support personnel, and K-12 instruction. Its charge was to develop a district-wide, long-range plan to provide for effective and efficient implementation of current technology in the areas of teaching, learning, and information management.

The Technology Coordination committee's co-chairs were the Coordinators of Instructional Media and Technology and Information Systems. Together, they strongly emphasized and kept the Technology Coordination committee focused on the classroom uses of technology. As a result, the committee created a technology-integration plan with a bold vision statement: "To empower learners through technology by providing all students and staff with access to information through voice, video, and data technologies for the purpose of processing and communicating information and ideas, and constructing knowledge." The technology plan, of course, mentioned hardware, software, and technical support, but tacked onto nearly each and every statement of the plan were the words "for curriculum and instruction" or "for teaching and learning." Teaching and learning was to be at the front of all technology decisions.

Furthermore, the Technology-Integration plan went beyond implying that an educational rationale had to be present behind all purchases to suggest that technology do the necessary work to help schools manage the reforms that educational leadership organizations and journals have been writing about over the last five years, such as granting credit only *after* proficiency is demonstrated, or continuous progress multiage classrooms.

Sprinkled throughout the pages of the plan are reform-oriented quotes such as: "Our students must be prepared for life in the next century—a time of unprecedented change" and "We must first identify the solid curricular and pedagogical ideas that we believe in, and then equip our classrooms with the best technologies currently available to do this job." Additionally, the plan is congruent with and supports the school district's mission and the state's proposed high school graduation standards. In this case, the technology planning is about what to do with the technology, then what equipment is needed to do the job.

Foundational Pieces

The Technology Coordination committee that wrote the plan recognized the direct link between desired instructional outcomes and teacher technology education and support. The planning committee acknowledged that not only do teachers need to be provided with hardware and software, they need peopleware as well. As a result, the plan specified personnel for district-level staff-development and technical support as the foundational pieces of the plan. Learning opportunities specifically emphasizing the application of technology to teaching and technical support for these implementation efforts are critical for sustaining the staff's efforts to learn about technology.

Three staff positions, Technology-Integration Specialist, Technical Support Specialist, and Network Manager were created to provide district-wide support. Additionally, technology teaching and troubleshooting responsibilities were added to each building's Information Technology Specialist's (formerly called a Media Generalist) job description. This created the necessary structure of personnel with required job duties to implement and support a reliable "train-the-trainer" model.

I hold the role of Technology Integration Specialist in this school district of 22,000 students. Working out of District Media and Technology Services, my responsibilities focus around designing and teaching the staff-development classes necessary for staff to integrate technology into their teaching and the curriculum. Prior to starting this position, I was teaching science at both the senior high and junior high levels over an 8-year period. I had always used technology as much as it was available to me, and I was also very involved in my buildings' efforts at restructuring. When the Technology Integration Specialist position was created, I jumped at the opportunity to get in on the ground floor of implementing a plan that emphasized technology use to help restructure how learning and teaching occurs.

Staff-Development Standards For Technology-Integration

The organizing framework for technology staff-development in my district is the National Council for Accreditation of Teacher Education (NCATE) technology standards. These standards were developed by the

International Society for Technology in Education (ISTE) which recommends that every teacher acquire these foundational skills and concepts related to technology, regardless of the teacher's area of specialization. These standards are congruent with the district's dual commitment: to integrate technology into teaching and learning and to make students processors, communicators, and constructors of knowledge.

The NCATE standards were introduced into the technology planning process by the Coordinator of Instructional Media and Technology and myself. We arranged the NCATE standards so they created a continuum that started with using technology for personal productivity and stretched to using technology for reforming instruction. The continuum acknowledges that learners must first connect what they are learning to what they already know; afterwards they can extend meaning-making to new areas. Mastery of the steps in the NCATE standards would indicate mastery of technology use as an instructional tool in a teacher's subject area.

A team of principals and district administrators further refined the continuum by creating four divisions and adding the labels Entry, Progressive, Proficient, and Exemplary. (See Figure 4.1 for the four levels of standards.) The directors of elementary and secondary education printed and distributed these standards with the statement: "It is a goal [of the district] that all teachers will reach the proficient level and strive for the exemplary level of these technology-integration staff-development standards." As the teacher appraisal process is revised over the next year, these standards will be made a part of that appraisal process.

The standards serve two purposes. First, they describe the technology proficiencies staff are to strive for and second, they serve as an organizing framework for staff-development. Having a clear picture of the desired end result and a shared framework for getting there among our district's 1,200 teachers assists with teacher placement in technology staff-development classes and creates common vocabulary and shared goals. It also allows trainers in all of the buildings to coordinate and share resources for offering classes.

Technology-Integration Staff-Development Standards

Entry level. The first level of the standards, Entry, is the starting point for beginning computer users. In entry level classes the emphasis is mainly on teachers learning basic capabilities of the standard software and how to operate the hardware. Entry level classes create an awareness of what computer technology-based materials are capable of and their proper uses. Participants learn how to utilize the operating system of a computer, access information on computers, and produce materials for

Entry level

- Operate a computer system to use software successfully
- Explore, evaluate, and use computer technology-based materials
- Demonstrate knowledge of equity, ethical, legal, and human issues of computing and technology
- Use computer-based technologies to access information to enhance personal and professional productivity (for example, reference CD-ROMs, database, telecommunications)
- Demonstrate skill in using productivity tools for professional and personal use (for example, word processing, presentation software, multimedia authoring, spreadsheet, graphic utilities)

Progressive level

- Evaluate and use computers and related technologies to support the instructional process
- Apply current instructional principles, research, and appropriate assessment practices to the use of computers and related technologies
- Evaluate, select, and integrate computer technology-based instruction in the curriculum of one's subject area(s) and/or grade level(s)

Proficient level

- Demonstrate knowledge of uses of computers for problem solving, data collection, information management, communications, presentations, and decision making
- Design and develop student learning activities that integrate computing and technology for a variety of student grouping strategies and for diverse student populations
- Demonstrate knowledge of multimedia, hypermedia, and telecommunications activities to support instruction

Exemplary level

- Apply computer and related technologies to facilitate the emerging roles of the learner and the educator
- Identify resources for staying current in applications of computing and related technologies in education

Figure 4.1. Technology-integration staff-development standards

classroom use. The focus for classes at the entry level is to allow teachers to find out, "How do I use the software's capabilities for my own work?"

An example of this might be a teacher using the district's standard word processing software to create a worksheet or a test. Teachers at the entry skill level might also utilize technology to present electronic lectures, or to create a spreadsheet that tracks their department's or grade level's budget. The uses of technology associated with entry level classes are oriented toward personal productivity—technology as a new way to deal with teacher's traditional work. Staff-development classes at the entry level would be typical "Introduction to <Software package>" and "Additional Features of <Software Package>" classes.

The acquisition of these entry level skills is essential for progressing to the next level where the emphasis is on moving technology use from the teacher's desk to the student's desk. However, if a teacher's skills stay directed at their own personal productivity—no matter how well they can use a program—they are still at the entry level in our district's technology-integration staff-development framework. Although entry level skills are legitimate starting points for staff, they are not an end goal.

Progressive level. The second level of the technology-integration staff-development framework is a starting point for teaching staff familiar with using computers for their personal productivity. The progressive level is characterized by the use of computer-based technology in the classroom by students. Teachers at this level adapt instructional practices as they start to realize how technology can assist them with the instruction and assessment of their curriculum. It is solid entry-level skills that allow users to spend less time managing power cords and commands and, as described in the progressive level outcomes, more time on the classroom uses of computer-based technology.

Classes at the progressive level focus on helping teachers to find out, "How do I teach my students to use the software's capabilities so they can accomplish classroom work?" This shift in teacher's thinking and planning from how they can use technology for their own work to how their students can use technology is a natural one as teachers become more familiar with the technology. An example of technology-integration at the progressive skill level might be using the district's standard word processing software program to have students complete a writing assignment, or using the standard multimedia authoring program to have students create a presentation or tutorial that they can share with their classmates. This level is extremely important as it represents the point at which students, through their teacher's lesson planning, gain access to computer technologies.

At this relatively early point in our implementation, progressive level classes are created by drawing on our district's Curriculum

Specialists and my responsibilities as Technology-Integration Specialist. Together we have identified subject area outcomes that would benefit from the introduction of computer-based technologies. We also work with teachers on curriculum advisory teams to identify curricular areas, units, or outcomes most well-suited for integration with technology. "Student Products with PowerPoint," "Creating Graphs with Microsoft Word and Excel," and "Students Reports with HyperStudio" are examples of classes we are offering. They not only teach additional features of the programs, but more importantly, how to use the program in the classroom. A Curriculum Specialist and myself prepare training materials and illustrate the technology-integration by team teaching these classes. Progressive-level classes also provide materials to help teachers teach the operation of the hardware and software to their students.

At the progressive level of skills, there is also a movement toward selecting technology-based curriculum materials. These materials provide students with technology subject matter information sources in addition to their traditional classroom resources. This selection process is combined with the ongoing Teacher Advisory Teams who meet throughout the year and advise Curriculum Specialists on subject area decisions. Also, throughout the district's regular program improvement process, as teachers and administrators focus on a curriculum area the Curriculum Specialist and myself organize previews of appropriate software to consider during the selection of core instructional materials.

Proficient level. The third level of the technology-integration staff-development framework is characterized both by technology being altered for instruction and instruction being altered by technology. The proficient technology users create learning environments with increased emphasis on thinking strategies such as problem solving, information management, and decision making through the integration of technology into their classroom. This requires teachers to draw on and combine strong technological and curricular backgrounds in order to achieve curricular goals. Like the entry and progressive-level skills, this level is also a goal for all teaching staff.

This level is unique in the technology-integration staff-development framework because it encourages using a software's capabilities, in perhaps new or innovative ways, to create the type of curriculum outcomes and learning environments that the educational reform literature has been calling for over the last five years; for example, curriculum outcomes in formats such as problem solving, data collection, information management, or decision making, and learning environments such as cooperative learning, student-centered, project-based teams, or individually paced instruction. A simple way to describe classes at the proficient level is they help teachers to find out, "How do I leverage the technology's capabilities to obtain [perhaps] new classroom goals?"

In proficient-level classes, teachers explore the philosophy of and theory behind these classroom goals along with exploration of the hardware and software. Teachers focusing on learning and motivation theory at the same time as technology and curriculum expands their conceptualization of their classroom and subject area and increases the consciousness of the environment they operate within. Encouraging teachers to think creatively with technology and theory increases the solutions they can imagine for the teaching concerns they have. Examples of uses of technology in classrooms of teachers at the proficient level of technology-integration might include students collaborating over a network on a shared research process or students creating a multimedia presentation to report the results of their problem solving.

Proficient-level classes create an expanded awareness of computing possibilities such as telecommunications and multimedia, are tightly integrated with curriculum material, and are specialized to a subject area. In some cases, they make creative and unconventional use of aspects of the technology to better suit the instructional goals. An example of a staff-development class for the proficient level of technology-integration is "Supporting Inquiry with Technology: The District Research Process." In this class teachers learn how the local area network resources and the district's standard software can be used to facilitate students learning the research process. "Dealing with Data: Database Use for Grades 5-12 Social Studies and Science Teachers" illustrates how the database's field creation, sorting, and filtering capabilities can be capitalized to teach inferring and hypothesizing skills. I team up with our district's Curriculum Specialists to create and team teach progressive-level classes.

Exemplary level. The fourth level of the technology-integration staff-development framework is exemplary. This would be a starting point for teachers with prior experience creating transformed learning environments through technology-integration. The exemplary level of technology-integration is characterized by new technologies being researched and new technology uses being developed. Teachers at the exemplary level of technology-integration ask, "What can we see now that was not possible without technology?"

A classroom example of exemplary technology-integration might be students directing their own investigation, then publishing their findings on World Wide Web pages where they collect input from others who are researching the same topic. Technology teacher education at this level is directed toward supporting teachers' experimental uses of technology. This level represents a research and development approach to integrating technology into teaching and learning. Staff-development at this level would not be represented by classes but rather by investigations.

CONCLUSION

The values, assumptions, and the logical basis of the district's "Uses, then Technology" technology planning and implementation approach are clearly oriented toward integrating technology into curricular and instructional goals. This ensures that the resulting technology staff-development is relevant, appropriate, and welcomed. Adopting the NCATE standards as a staff-development framework while allowing curriculum specialists and teachers to specify the most appropriate classroom uses of the software and hardware ensures that a solid, yet flexible, teacher education structure is in place. This allows teachers to direct their energy and dreams for technology uses toward integrating technology into classroom teaching and their students' learning.

6

THE ADMINISTRATOR AS THE CRITICAL CONNECTION IN LEARNING ENVIRONMENTS

Karen Norum

Computer-mediated communication (CMC) opens the door for changes in the delivery of education, and this potentially changes the role of the teacher (see Santoro's chapter, this volume). Teachers are now expected to be competent users of technology. Indeed, "the challenge for teachers in their classrooms is how to engage effectively with the images and technologies of the postmodern world without jettisoning the cultural analysis, moral judgment and studied reflection they threaten to supersede" (Hargreaves, 1994, p. 76). CMC also may change the role of the school.

During the years to come, students will barely need to go to the school building to get information. But they will need to get some basic skills, including those of collaborative learning and process judgment: learning how to put together, reflect on, and use knowledge. New employees today are not arriving at the workplace with these crucial survival skills because schools do not provide them effectively. To provide them would mean getting the teacher out of the front of the room and into the role of guide and model, helping students find and manage the information they need or want (Senge, Roberts, Ross, Smith, & Kleiner, 1994, p. 491).

As the role of the teacher and potentially that of the school changes, the role of the administrator (assistant principal and principal) also changes. For some educators, the online classroom is an innovation that represents a paradigm shift; a shift in the nature of education and the roles of educators. The purpose of this chapter is to explore the critical role administrators play in influencing what can happen in the classroom.

Changing Roles

When online classrooms are implemented in a classroom or school, the roles of the student, teacher, and administrator all change. Berliner (1992) states that in the information age, teachers are seen as managers of complex environments (executives), whereas students are treated as knowledge workers. As students are asked to take on increasing responsibility for their own learning, the relationships among staff, administrators, and students shift considerably (Hawkins, 1993). Changing the role of teaching (which is called for in such learning environments) requires changing the role of the administrator (Bailey & Lumley, 1991).

ADMINISTRATORS AS CHANGE AGENTS

Principals and assistant principals are in a prime position to be change agents—people who intervene in the problem-solving efforts of a social group or organization (Havelock, 1995). Change agents can act as catalysts by upsetting the status quo: as solution givers by identifying how a proposed solution satisfies needs and concerns; as process helpers by assisting the system in every aspect of the change process; or as resource linkers by bringing together needs and resources (Havelock, 1995, p. 9, 10).

Administrators who are change agents provide the critical connections that are necessary to create and sustain online classrooms. Because of their position both in the school and the community, they are the ones who can find out who will support the change at the local school level, the district level, and in the community. But to take on the role of change agent, administrators must be aware that leaders who initiate change cause uneasiness, insecurity, and risks not only for themselves but for those around them (Anderson & Lavid, 1986). No one is sure of the outcome or the multiple ramifications a change will bring.

As change agents, administrators need to tolerate this uncertainty and assure and support those affected that the idea or project is worth trying (Anderson & Lavid, 1986). They need to work with parents, students, and teachers to create an atmosphere conducive to change (Fishman & Duffy, 1992).

Being a change agent is not easy. In fact, Hodas (1993), when writing about the introduction of technology to the classroom, painted a dismal picture of the acceptance of change and even despaired of the administrator's ability to take on the role of change agent:

> Given that long-term school workers are well adapted to a particular ecosocial niche, it is understandable that their first response to attempts at innovation would be one of resistance. Calls for change of any kind are seen as impositions or disturbances to be quelled as soon as possible, as unreasonable attempts to change the rules in the middle of the game. (p. 7)

Hodas went on to say that because teachers are not motivated to change anything, "school administrators are relieved of the responsibility for developing the creative management skills that would be required for teachers to develop new classroom skills" (p. 13). In fact, Hodas continued:

> Administrators, for their part, have equally few organizational incentives for inviting this disruption into schools. Not only would they be required to respond to teachers' demands for the time and resources needed to attain proficiency, they themselves would need to attain some minimum level of competence in order to retain authority over teachers. Since there is no way for the system to reward this kind of involved, responsible management, nor any way to penalize its absence, school authorities' most sensible route is to ignore or quell demands for the implementation of such potentially disruptive processes. (p. 15)

Other aspects of the education system also make it difficult for administrators to take on the role of change agent. For example, the quest for school improvement suggests that schools have failed. When support for change is promoted, ironically, one response could be an attitude of why put more into a system that has failed (Hutchins, 1994)?

Acting as a change agent is not easy; however, a culture of change has to be created in a school if online classrooms are to be created and sustained. Administrators are in a prime position to create a culture of change in their school. Providing strategic leadership is an aspect of the change agent administrator's role.

CHANGE AGENT ADMINISTRATORS AS STRATEGIC LEADERS

According to Senge (1990), effective strategic leaders are designers, stewards, and teachers. As designer, the change agent administrator is the architect of the organization. As online classrooms are implemented, educational objectives, curriculum guidelines, textbooks and materials, teachers and their knowledge capital, staff development, student assignment, resources and time allocation, testing, assessment, school organization, technology, and incentives all need to be aligned to support the changes that are taking place in the classroom (Pearlman, 1993; Stasz, McArthur, Lewis, & Ramsey, 1990).

Change agent administrators prepare and create opportunities for their schools while providing stability in change: Scaffolding is designed that allows experimentation with new ideas, risk taking, and dismantling of ineffective aspects of the organization without losing an overall sense of the framework in which everyone is working (Conley, 1993). The role of the designer is to shape and create ways to bring about the desirable future—change by design (Banathy, 1991).

As steward, the change agent administrator ensures that the organization is vision-led (Senge, 1990) and understands that the vision for the school must permeate the organizational space, for it is this vision that will shape the organization (Wheatley, 1992). The vision provides the overall conceptual scheme, that is, the theory that guides the change ("Motivating students," 1993). One way change agent administrators can keep the vision active is through careful hiring practices (see Grandgeorge, this volume). Teachers hired to facilitate learning in a school committed to creating and sustaining online classrooms should match with the philosophy of the school, understand and believe in the vision, be committed to demonstrating both personal growth and flexibility, and understand they may be asked to adapt their skills and roles frequently throughout their teaching careers (Conley, 1993).

As teacher, the change agent administrator helps the staff to achieve more accurate, insightful, and empowering views of reality by helping them to see the big picture: How different parts of the organization interact, how different situations parallel one another because of common underlying structures, how local actions have longer term and broader impacts than local actors often realize, and why certain operating policies are needed for the system as a whole (Senge, 1990). They foster the long view, guided by their sense of mission and strategic direction (Conley, 1993). Fostering a long view may mean explaining to teachers why they need to learn new teaching techniques and strategies, defending the reorganization and alignment of the curriculum so that it supports the online classroom, or changing how traditional teacher evaluations are conducted so the emphasis is on facilitating learning rather than dispensing information.

Change agent administrators need a set of tools that will enable them to sharpen their own understandings of the elements that create organizational energy (staff, time, resources, education, and information, among others; Wheatley, 1992). A description of the assortment of tools that might be found in change agent administrator's toolbox follows.

THE ADMINISTRATOR'S "CHANGE AGENT" TOOLBOX

Creating a Culture of Change

Creating and sustaining online classrooms means creating a culture of change that will enhance motivation, skill, and collegial support for improvement (Bellamy, 1993). The administrator's support (or lack of it) sends a loud and clear message about the importance of the change (Murray, 1992). Administrators create a supportive climate for change by providing clear statements of important goals, serving as examples of consistent action toward those goals, using stories and conflicts to communicate important themes, and creating ceremonies and rituals to mark important school events (Bellamy, 1993).

Being an effective "symbol manager" is an important part of the administrator's toolbox (Carlyle, 1987). Ziegler, Boardman, and Thomas (1985) state that in an organization, people operate within a general administrative environment created by the policies and practices of top management. That climate is established by how leaders and followers relate to each other. Teachers tend to imitate the behaviors and attitudes of their principals (Carlyle, 1987). This means that mismanaging the change process may lead to teacher frustration and skepticism (Murray, 1992). Encouraging the expression of feelings, opinions, pride, and loyalty through team management, sensitivity, humor, and personal example becomes a crucial piece of the administrator's toolbox (Valentine & Bowman, 1991). This also helps to create a safe environment that encourages the disclosing of beliefs (Nolan & Huber, 1989).

Adding Value to Professional Effort

According to Bellamy (1993), the school organization can improve the students' learning environment by adding value to professional effort. Because of the nature of professional effort, it is the administrator who is the critical connection here. Professional effort includes resource development, support for operations, the culture of change, and organizational renewal. Resource development refers to ensuring that resources are available to fulfill and improve the responsibilities of the learning environment. School leaders can influence the quality and amount of these resources through budget requests, district services, and community support. Support for operations refers to enabling activities through the allocation of staff, facilities, time, equipment, and space.

This includes looking at schedules and assignments of professional staff, environmental support, and organizational support. The culture of change has to do with enhancing motivation, skill, and collegial support for improvement, whereas organizational renewal is the process by which schools establish priorities for change, set goals, and implement reforms. This requires the acceptance of ongoing changes as a natural and valued part of everyday life in schools (Bellamy, 1993).

Crafting the students' learning environment so it will support the implementation of online classrooms requires effort from the school's faculty and staff. The change agent administrator is in a position to motivate this effort and enhance its success. A school culture that supports the implementation of online classrooms will be reflected in the classroom itself.

Building Relationships

When implementing online classrooms, change agent administrators need to work not only with the staff within their own school, but with parents, students, the district, the community, and all the elements of the system to create an atmosphere conducive to change (Fishman & Duffy, 1992). They need to provide the kind of leadership that is willing and able to take the risk and criticism that will follow the initiation of change ("Motivating students," 1993). Bellamy (1993) suggests that a leadership team consist of the principal, teachers, and community members and that the principal provide regular, ongoing information to the school and community to facilitate school change and keep all involved informed of school changes. Thus, skill in building relationships becomes a major piece of the administrator's toolbox. Not only must the administrator be able to manage effectively the day-by-day operational procedures for the school, he or she must also nurture the climate of the school through the development of positive interpersonal relationships (Valentine & Bowman, 1991).

Change agent administrators must forge connections and create interdependencies that will connect teachers within and across disciplines and connect people inside and outside of the school community to one another (Conley, 1993). According to Wheatley (1992), relationships are what facilitate processes, and it is the quality of relationships that gives organizational energy its charge (positive or negative). Sergiovanni (1990) calls this "leadership by bonding," a model of shared commitment and vision. Building relationships nurtures critical connections that are necessary for innovations to grow and evolve. The skills of listening, communicating, and facilitating groups cannot be taken for granted and need to be in the administrator's toolbox if online classrooms are to be created and sustained.

A NEW PARADIGM FOR ADMINISTRATORS

A new kind of administrator is called for to effectively use the toolboxes needed to create and sustain online classrooms. For administrators to become the critical connection in creating and sustaining online classrooms, the paradigm of "Administrator as Manager of Administrivia" needs to be shattered and replaced with a paradigm of "Administrator as Creator and Nurturer of Critical Connections." Because of their role both inside and outside of the school, administrators are in a wonderful position to turn their schools into learning organizations: organizations that can continually expand their capacity to create their future (Senge, 1990). Discovering, building, and nurturing critical connections and being critical connections themselves are fundamental roles for change agent administrators.

Transformation needs to occur if online classrooms are to be successfully created and sustained. Tribus (1993) cites the following as elements that are needed for transformation to occur:

> Aim, for without it, there is no sense of direction.
> Philosophy, for without it, there will be no followers.
> Vision, for without it, there will be confusion.
> Strategy, for without it, there will be false starts.
> Skills, for without those, there will be anxiety.
> Resources, for without these, there will be frustration.
> Rewards, for without them, there is bitterness.
> Organization, for without it, there is no coordination.

All of these fall within the role of the administrator. Change agent administrators need to be able and willing to provide all eight elements for online classrooms to be successfully implemented in their schools and communities.

Ultimately, transformation needs to occur throughout the system. Administrators who are willing to create and sustain online classrooms need to be acutely aware of the entire system they are attempting to influence. November (1993) says that for transformation to occur system-wide, wisdom needs to be honored:

> Teachers need to honor the wisdom of teachers: design the faculty to create an organization that shares.
>
> Teachers need to honor the wisdom of students: recognize that humans want to create and be a part of a community.
>
> The school needs to honor the wisdom of the community: the community needs to have a voice in how schools (and learning environments) are designed.
>
> The community needs to honor the wisdom of the school: after all, educators have studied their field and may even know what they're talking about!

Providing the eight elements for transformation as outlined by Tribus and honoring the wisdom of teachers, students, the community, and the school as November (1993) suggests, will create the conditions necessary to create and implement online classrooms. To sustain such learning environments, critical connections need to be nurtured through the building of relationships. Administrators can build relationships with their staff by examining the toolbox their staff has been given to ensure that it is adequate to help them function in a new school and classroom culture (Waters & Andrade, 1993). Administrators can build relationships with those outside of the school by ensuring their own toolbox allows them to function effectively as a change agent and strategic leader.

The literature repeatedly points to the administrator (principal and assistant principal) as having a powerful influence over the culture of the school and that culture effects teachers, students, and even the community. Because of their position in the system, administrators are the critical connection in creating and sustaining online classrooms. Wheatley (1992) provides words to nurture the "Administrator as Creator and Nurturer of Critical Connections" paradigm:

> Leaders are being encouraged to include stakeholders, to evoke followership, to empower others. . . . Leadership is always dependent on the context, but the context is established by the relationships we value. We cannot hope to influence any situation without respect for the complex network of people who contribute to our organizations. (pp. 144, 145)

Because it is indeed a complex network of people who contribute to the system in which online classrooms are to be created and sustained, more research is needed. Administrators and teachers need to shift from being the "learned" to being "learners." How well does the current professional development of teachers and administrators-to-be prepare them for such roles in new comprehensive instructional systems? How easy is it to find an administrator with the creative management skills that are required for teachers to develop new classroom skills (Hodas, 1993)?

Research is needed to explore how current professional and staff development programs could be structured to prepare administrators to discover, build and nurture the critical connections needed for instructional systems such as online classrooms to be implemented in schools.

REFERENCES

Anderson, R. E., & Lavid, J. S. (1986, April). The effective principal: Leader or manager? *NASSP Bulletin*, pp. 82-84.

Bailey, G. D., & Lumley, D. (1991, July). Supervising teachers who use integrated learning systems: New roles for school administrators. *Educational Technology*, pp. 21-24.

Banathy, B.H. (1991). *Systems design of education*. Englewood Cliffs, NJ: Educational Technology Publications.

Bellamy, G. T. (1993, October). *The whole school framework: A guide for systemic school-level reform*. Unpublished manuscript, University of Colorado at Denver, School of Education.

Berliner, D. C. (1992, October). Redesigning classroom activities for the future. *Educational Technology*, pp. 7-13.

Carlyle, T. (1987, April). *Principals as symbol managers: Measures of meaning in schools*. Paper presented at the annual meeting of the American Education Research Association, Washington, D.C.

Conley, D. T. (1993). *Roadmap to restructuring*. Eugene, OR: ERIC Clearinghouse.

Fishman, B. J., & Duffy, T. M. (1992). Classroom restructuring: What do teachers really need? *Educational Technology, Research, and Development, 40*(3), 95-111.

Hargreaves, A. (1994). *Changing teachers, changing times*. New York: Teachers College Press.

Havelock, R. G., with Zlotolow, S. (1995). *The change agent's guide* (2nd ed.). Englewood Cliffs, NJ: Educational Technology Publications.

Hawkins, J. (1993). Technology and the organization of schooling. *Communications of the ACM, 36*(5), 30-35.

Hodas, S. (1993, September) Technology refusal and the organizational culture of schools [Education Policy Analysis Archives]. *Electronic Journal*. Seattle: School of Education, Leadership and Policy Studies, University of Washington.

Hutchins, C.L. (1994). State systems of education and systemic change. In C.M. Reigeluth & R.J. Garfinkle (Eds.), *Systemic change in education* (pp. 15-25). Englewood Cliffs, NJ: Educational Technology Publications.

Motivating students: School leaders can make a difference. (1993, Winter). *Leadership and Learning*, pp. 1-2.

Murray, G. J. (1992, Fall). Cooperative learning: What's the administrator's role? *Schools in the Middle*, pp. 7-10.

Nolan, J. F., & Huber, T. (1989). Nurturing the reflective practitioner through instructional supervision: A review of the literature. *Journal of Curriculum and Supervision, 4*(2), 126-145.

November, A. (1993, June). *From smart toilets to smart schools.* Keynote presentation at the Technology in Education (TIE) Conference, Steamboat Springs, CO.

Pearlman, R. (1993). Designing the new American schools. *Communications of the ACM, 36*(5), 46-49.

Senge, P. M. (1990). *The fifth discipline.* New York: Doubleday/Currency.

Senge, P. M., Roberts, C., Ross, R. B., Smith, B. J., & Kleiner, A. (1994). *The fifth discipline fieldbook.* New York: Doubleday/Currency.

Sergiovanni, T. (1990, May). Adding value to leadership gets extraordinary results. *Educational Leadership,* pp. 23-27.

Stasz, C., McArthur, D., Lewis, M., & Ramsey, K. (1990, December). *Teaching and learning generic skills for the workplace.* Berkeley: National Center for Research in Vocational Education, University of California.

Tribus, M. (1993, November). Keynote presentation at National Quality and Education Conference, Denver, CO.

Valentine, J. W., & Bowman, M. L. (1991, December). Effective principal, effective school: Does research support the assumption? *NASSP Bulletin,* pp. 1-7.

Waters, T., & Andrade, E. (1993, November). *Designing high performance systems: Transforming schools through systemic change.* Workshop presented at the National Quality and Education Conference, Denver, CO.

Wheatley, M. J. (1992). *Leadership and the new science.* San Francisco: Berrett-Koehler.

Ziegler, V., Boardman, G., & Thomas, M. D. (1985, April). Humor, leadership, and school climate. *The Clearing House,* pp. 346-348.

7

THE INTERNET AND ACCEPTABLE USE POLICIES: WHAT SCHOOLS NEED TO KNOW

Lynne Schrum and Kay Day

Stories abound regarding students who are actively engaged in the learning process and educators who are communicating with their colleagues using the electronic superhighway. Many schools dream of the day when they will be fully connected to the Internet for professional and curricular activities. However, every classroom teacher and media specialist knows that open access to unrestricted materials may cause concerns from parents and members of the educational community, for "the freedom of scanning the Internet carries a much greater weight of responsibility than simply checking a book out of the media center" (Sperber, 1995, p. 5).

Some schools have chosen to confront the concerns in a proactive manner, whereas others encountered problems as they implemented Internet access into their curriculum. Regardless of the impetus, most schools will ultimately need to address these concerns by establishing a procedural policy for the use of computers when accessing information, known as an Acceptable Use Policy (AUP). An AUP is "a written agreement signed by students, their parents and their teachers outlining the terms and conditions of Internet use . . . rules of online behavior and access privileges" ("Keeping students," 1995, p. 12). In this chapter, we review the current literature surrounding this important topic, discuss the pressing issues, and summarize the essential components of an Acceptable Use Policy. We also suggest guidelines for implementation and provide resources for model policies.

REVIEW OF THE LITERATURE

A review of the literature can reveal a great deal of information about the promises of the Internet, but little is found that specifically addresses how schools are formulating policies concerning appropriate use of the Internet by students. As more and more schools grant K-12 students access to the Internet to expand their educational experiences, our educational community faces new challenges. Fishman and Pea (1994) attribute these new problems to the fact that "since the Internet was not designed with children in mind, many potentially difficult issues must be discussed by both the education and the Internet community" (p. 1). They continue that it is the school's responsibility to determine "what safety, liability, and above all, educational concerns must be addressed before the schools are ready to tap into the Internet" (p. 2). One of the most serious concerns seems to be protecting children from being exposed to or finding inappropriate material. Another concern is to protect the schools from litigation arising from inappropriate use of the Internet.

Even though the need for schools to establish AUPs is ever increasing, a review of the educational literature reveals a void in formal research on how schools establish policy on computer use. After reviewing online and print articles, however, we have identified the following framework of components necessary for the construction of an AUP.

Definition of the Internet

Educators should not "assume parents know what the Internet is" ("Keeping students," 1995, p. 12). The educational community must bear the burden of informing parents about the Internet and all of its capabilities, both good and bad. Parents and students also need to be conscious of the fact that because "the Internet is a fluid environment, the information which will be available to students is constantly changing, therefore, it is impossible to predict with certainty what information students might locate" (Minnesota Coalition, 1994, p. 1).

Netiquette

Just as people have referred to Emily Post and her rules for etiquette for social situations, there is a need to establish rules for interacting with others via the computer. LaQuey and Ryer (1993) have pointed out that "with all the people and networks and government agencies participating in the Internet, there are bound to be rules, restrictions, and policies for parts of it" (p. 29). In education, we see that "every school has a code of conduct for its students that details appropriate school behavior, outlines rights and sets expectations for students" (Fishman & Pea, 1994, p. 7).

Connolly and Webster (1993) concur by stating, "We as educators need to recognize that although the context for learning may be changing, the underlying values ought not change. We must develop and advocate policies specifically to protect those underlying values" (p. 28). The AUP's netiquette guidelines should be an extension of the school's code of behavior and make clear "that certain forms of behavior are unacceptable" (Johnson, 1994, p. 49). Many of the articles reviewed cite *The Net: User Guidelines and Netiquette* (Rinaldi, 1994). Rinaldi's guide seems to have become a standard application in the area of online behavior.

Ethical Issues

The third major component of an AUP addresses ethical issues and naturally extends from netiquette. In fact, the two are often confused. However, netiquette usually addresses the social behavior, and ethics addresses the principles of right and wrong and legal issues. "Ethics has been defined as the code or set of principles by which people live. Ethics is about what is considered to be right and what is considered to be wrong" (Forester & Morrison, 1994, p. 14). In the K-12 educational setting, Protheroe, Wilson, and Kluge (1994) recommend that as we "encourage students to use this communication tool responsibly, schools should consider integrating issues around technology and ethics into the curriculum" (p. 29).

Some schools are addressing these issues as part of the curriculum for computer classes or by "implementing agreements regulating students' use of the school computers" (Hagans, 1995, p. G1). Many of these agreements list acceptable and unacceptable uses while students are online and consequences for violating the policy. Rinaldi (1994) emphasizes that each student must be made aware of his or her responsibilities while accessing network services. If a school decides to grant students access to the Internet, it "must also teach them responsible and ethical use of on-line resources" (Johnson, 1994, p. 6). Typical ethical behaviors that are addressed by AUPs deal with such issues as copyright, intellectual freedom, viruses, worms, and hackers.

Schools have been guiding their students on the issue of copyright for print materials for many years. There is a continuing debate concerning copyright protection in the realm of electronic transmissions. However, as Webster and Connolly (1993) point out, "by law, a work is protected by copyright as soon as it is committed to a medium, including an electronic one" (p. 35). At this point in time, the recommendation most frequently advocated is that schools continue to follow fair use and software reproduction guidelines until there is a "change in the U.S. Copyright law aimed at providing greater protection for copyrighted information that can be accessed electronically" (Henderson, 1995, p. 56). Put simply, if you are not sure that you have permission and the right to post something, don't do it.

In regard to intellectual freedom, the educational community should regard media specialists and librarians as valuable resources in this area as they have dealt with this issue for many years. As Flanders points out, "Many librarians feel strongly that access to information should be unrestricted and that Internet resources provide valuable information to K-12 students" (1994, p. 35). Johnson (1994) has recommended that a school's AUP become an extension of its selection policy and that "board adopted selection policies must cover on-line resources if they do not do so already" (p. 4).

Students need to be aware that hacking and the placement of worms or viruses on computer networks is an unacceptable and illegal behavior. Indeed, laws exist, such as the Federal Computer Fraud and Abuse Act of 1986, for the purpose of protecting computer networks.

Objectionable Material

Just as print materials may offend certain people, so too will the Internet. "Like other forms of publishing, materials that appear on the network may be judged as pornographic by some users" (Proctor & Allen, 1994, p. 26). The Communications Policy Forum recommended in 1993 "that a warning statement be developed to advise schools of the presence of materials on the Internet that may be deemed inappropriate for minors" (Fishman & Pea, 1994, p. 4).

It is for this reason that "schools develop clear policies regarding Internet use" and when developing these policies, "schools need to exercise reasonable oversight while realizing that it is almost impossible to absolutely guarantee that students will not be exposed to objectionable materials" (Protheroe, et al., 1994, p. 26). Many schools have developed a procedure for dealing with objectionable materials within their media selection policies which could be extended to cover the use of the Internet.

Many schools have also chosen to use this as an educational opportunity, to encourage students to use the resources wisely, and to voluntarily limit their searches to appropriate materials. Some young students may have trouble understanding many abstract principles, such as the Bill of Rights or the school's AUP behavior codes. One teacher sought to bring these concepts into the students' personal world by using a combination of computer graphics, online research, town meetings, and community outreach (Reissman, 1994). She had students draft model legislation, conduct research to find varying types of bills of rights, survey peers and teachers, and write persuasively. This model could serve to make AUPs pertinent and relevant to students' lives.

Privilege, not a Right

Another essential component of an AUP is the inclusion of a clear statement that access to the Internet is a privilege and not a right. "Policy statements of many districts and institutions treat computing as a privilege so as to more easily enforce rules surrounding its use or abuse by the threat of revoking the privilege" (Connolly & Webster, 1993, p. 30). The AUP must make it clear that if a student violates any rule, then specified consequences will follow. Webster and Connolly (1993) suggest consulting the Bill of Rights and Responsibilities for Electronic Learners (1993) as a way of stimulating discussion of issues when formulating a school's policy.

It is also important, however, to identify the rights of network users. For example, students who use online resources have a right to equal access to network resources, to be safe from harassment, to intellectual freedom, and to privacy in electronic communications and work (with the understanding that system administrators may perform spot checks).

Legal Issues

As this area of technology has developed, many legal issues have evolved that have not yet been tested in the courts. Groenewold (1994) indicates that some of the troublesome areas will be property rights, mischief and criminal activity, censorship, security, commercialization, and individual tort liability. "Many of these dilemmas constitute new gray areas for which there are few accepted rules or social conventions, let alone established legal case law" (Forester & Morrison, 1994, p. 10). Stager (1993) noted, "Educational institutions are struggling to word their network use policies so as to accommodate First Amendment Rights while upholding their responsibilities to maintain a non-intimidating environment" (p. 42). He concluded that we must also ask, "Can an institution deprive electronic citizens of access to the network and its resources without due process?" (p. 43).

Schools would be wise to confer with their legal advisors and state or provincial codes when writing an AUP, in order to comply with current laws. Finding the proper balance between preserving individual rights and protecting the schools from litigation should be an objective of any AUP.

Penalties and Repercussions

Students and parents need to be aware of any penalties or repercussions, such as financial restitution, loss of Internet access, warning letters, or legal action, that will be incurred for failing to abide by the guidelines setup in the AUP. States have varying laws, but typically, conviction of certain computer-related crimes can carry financial fines and/or imprisonment. The AUP must be explicit in addressing these issues in order to protect the students' due process and the school from litigation.

Permission Form

A permission form for Internet access has been viewed as essential. It has been recommended that once a student and parent have read the AUP, they should be required to sign a form stating that they have read and understood the items included. Then the school must retain these forms as a legal, binding document ("Keeping students," 1995).

One final suggestion is that the AUP be made user friendly and as unambiguous as possible in order to help students and parents understanding its contents. One way to do this, according to Tannenbaum (1993), is to include an appendix with a glossary of terms used in the AUP.

AUPs are rapidly becoming an integral part of education. As educators continue to delve into the new electronic frontier, a well written AUP will help to make the journey a little smoother by setting forth a strong statement of expected behaviors and consequences.

RECOMMENDATIONS

It is important to note that not all school districts or individuals agree that an AUP is the correct way to proceed. Dr. Clancy Wolf, with the Puget Sound Educational Service District in Washington, has a different perspective. In an interview, he described his reasoning and recommendations (see suggested resources). Still others prefer to use technological solutions, such as filters that limit the access to certain types of material, or those that block certain words. But many feel just as strongly that it is the process of developing an AUP that is the most important aspect because the school board, employees, community members, students, and others are forced to discuss and air the issues and concerns.

In an effort to discover further information on how schools are developing and implementing AUPs, we interviewed educators who have assisted schools in developing an AUP. The participants were volunteers who had AUPs in place for a minimum of six months. Most of the policies discussed were district policies and the remaining were individual school building policies. The reasons varied for developing an AUP, but all of these participants had their policies in place before students accessed the Internet. Respondents described a variety of procedures in designing and developing their AUPs that ranged from one person writing the policy to one designed by committee.

Interviewees were invited to give recommendations that might help schools develop AUPs. Some suggested using other AUPs as a guide and talking to people who have had policies in place to see what has or has not been effective. Advice included engaging the school staff and school board in a discussion about the implications of the AUP, putting the AUP in place before allowing students access, and including language that reflects a concern for students' intellectual freedom. They suggest that the policy use simple terminology, be flexible in cases of misuse, have a positive tone, and take into account each community's values. It was also recommended that schools provide guidance or tutorials in properly using the Internet as a resource.

A school that has access to the Internet may well want to spend time searching for the most current examples of district AUPs and recent information on their design, development, and implementation (see resource section). In addition, it is important to continually remain aware of new interpretations of legal issues and court decisions. Perhaps a yearly review of the district AUP would be beneficial.

It is clear that writing and implementing AUPs is in an early and evolutionary stage of development. Although our interviews did not reveal one universal approach for developing an AUP, several guidelines emerged and were consistent with those in the literature. Although the AUPs reviewed for this study were developed in different manners and managed in various ways, they all had a majority of the eight components that have been discussed. Even though this commonality of the components of the AUPs existed, much diversity existed. It appears that the diversity was a result of particular community values and an individual school's code of conduct.

Based on the results of this study, we suggest keeping the following steps in mind when writing an AUP:

1. The school should appoint an individual to gather information and write a draft of an AUP, using searches on the Internet and an examination of other AUPs.
2. The school should form a committee to review and revise the draft of the AUP. It should have representatives from the

district and school level, and include teachers, media specialists, and computer technologists.
3. A policy should anticipate and address all eight of the previously recommended topics.
4. The tone of the AUP should be as positive as possible.
5. The policy should be reviewed by people outside of the committee. This should include the school board attorney. The local school board may want to formally adopt this collaboratively produced AUP as one of its policies.

CONCLUSION

The importance of this chapter resides in its compilation of current thoughts from the literature and educators regarding the development of AUPs. Results of this chapter should guide others as they write their school's AUPs. We have discussed the concept and creation of an Acceptable Use Policy and offered suggestions for its implementation.

Schools today are challenged to meet the demands of a changing society, including using and teaching with information technologies. It is necessary that schools be prepared to confront the issues involved with introducing students to these technologies, and creating an AUP may make that transition much easier.

REFERENCES

Acceptable Use Policies: Defining what's allowed online, and what's not. (1995/December/January). Classroom Connect, Available online: http://rice.info.rice.edu:80/armadillo

Bill of Rights and Responsibilities for the Electronic Community of Learners. (1993). [Online]. Available: gopher://rice info.rice.edu: 1170/00/More/Acceptable/brrec; WWW: http: //gopher://riceinfo .rice.edu:1170/00/More/Acceptable/brrec.

Connolly, F., & Webster, S. (1993). New policies for an evolving future. *Educom Review, 28*(3), 28-30.

Fishman, B., & Pea, R. (1994). The Internetworked school: A policy for the future [Online]. Available: gopher riceinfo.rice.edu,information by subject area, education, acceptable and unacceptable uses of net resources (K12); http://rice.info.rice.edu:80/armadillo

Flanders, B. (1994). A delicate balance. *School Library Journal, 40*(10), 32-35.

Forester, T., & Morrison, P. (1994). Introduction: Social, ethical and professional issues in computing. In T. Forester & P. Morrison (Eds.), *Computer ethics* (2nd ed., pp. 1-22). Cambridge, MA: MIT Press.

Groenewold, G. (1994). The net meets the law [CD-ROM]. *Unix Review, 79*(4), 12. (Article from: Computer Select: Record #16 300 577)

Hagans, G. (1995, February 26). Tired of mischief, schools tackling computer etiquette. *The Atlanta Journal-Constitution*, p. G1.

Henderson, C. (1995). At stake: Electronic fair use of copyrighted materials. *Educom Review, 30*(1), 56-57.

Johnson, D. (1994). Crime, abuse, and hacker ethics. *Educom Review, 29*(5), 40-50.

Keeping students in line, online. (1995, December/January). *Classroom Connect*, 12-13.

LaQuey, T., & Ryer, J. (1993). Internet: The lowdown. In T. LaQuey & J. Ryer (Eds.), *The Internet companion: A beginner's guide to global networking* (pp. 21-39). New York: Addison-Wesley.

Library Bill of Rights. (1980). American Library Association [Online]. Available: gopher://riceinfo.rice.edu:1170/0R0-1724-/More/Acceptable/ala.

Minnesota Coalition Against Censorship (1994). Minnesota Public School Internet Policy [Online]. Available: gopher riceinfo.rice.edu,information by subject area, education, acceptable and unacceptable uses of net resources (K12); WWW: http://rice.info.rice.edu:80/armadillo

Proctor, L., & Allen, A. (1994). *K-12 education and the Internet*. East Lansing, MI: National Center for Research on Teacher Learning. (ERIC Document Reproduction Service No. ED 373 798)

Protheroe, N., Wilson, E., & Kluge, L. (1994) *The Internet handbook for school users*. Arlington: Educational Research Service.

Reissman, R. (1994). Rights conflict computer scenarios: Storyboarding and "righting" our responsibilities. *The Computing Teacher, 22*(2), 34-35.

Rinaldi, A. (1994) . The netuser guidelines and netiquette [Online]. Available: FTP:LIB.BERKELEY.EDU Directory: /pub/net.training/FAU.

Sperber, C. (1995, Fall). How to write an acceptable use policy. *Enhance: Bringing Teachers and Technology Together*, 4-8.

Stager, S. (1993). Individual rights versus institutional responsibilities. *Educom Review, 28*(3), 41-44.

Tannenbaum, R. (1993). A code of rights and responsibilities for access to computing resources. *Educom Review, 28*(3), 19-22.

Webster, S., & Connolly, F. (1993). Responsible citizenship in the electronic community. *Educom Review, 28*(3), 32-35

SUGGESTED RESOURCES

ERIC Services:
http://ericir.syr.edu/ (Look in Internet Guides & Directories, Acceptable Use Policies) Rice University/Houston Independent School District http://riceinfo.rice.edu:80/armadillo/acceptable.html
Learning Through Collaborative Visualization (CoVis), templates for Network Use Policy: http://www.covis.nwu.edu/CoVis_AUP.html
Bellingham, WA School District: http: //riceinfo.rice.edu:80/armadillo /About/bellingham.html
Consortium for School Networking: http://cosn.org/

Wolf, C.
I conducted research a few years ago on what districts were trying to address in their Internet Use Policies, and a discussion of my findings has been on a few gopher sites for a couple of years. Lynne found my work while researching this chapter and asked me to jot down a few thoughts on acceptable use policies based on my decade of experience with kids on the Internet, and several years helping individual districts develop their own policies.

My first piece of advice is: Don't create a new policy. I base this on the following two points. First, I have been told by many lawyers (I am not one) that any policy you generate is worth the paper it's printed on. It's often equated to a field trip permission slip. As I understand it, even if a permission slip is signed—supposedly relieving the school of all responsibility—the school is still responsible for whatever happens. The permission slip is a show that might bluff some parents from suing, but it's worthless in court. Check this with your own legal council.

Second, I would argue that most schools and districts already have policies in place that address most issues. For example, if a middle-school boy takes a pornographic magazine into the building and passes it around, most administrators would have some idea on how to handle the situation. Inappropriate materials brought in via computer networks should be handled the same manner—it's just our unfamiliarity with the medium that makes it seem different.

What we really need to do is educate our students and parents as to what this medium is and what it is not. It is not like television in that you are passively served whatever the programmers send out—the user must take some action to retrieve it. Inappropriate material doesn't "just appear" any more than pornographic magazines. And if something does come up as a result of a search, a simple click or keystroke will clear the screen. I would argue that it all boils down to citizenship and how schools teach students to become members of a community.

The Internet is a community—not a service. It's not like the phone company or some of the large information services. It's a community of businesses, schools, universities, governments, nongovernmental organizations (NGOs), and people. If we approach it from that viewpoint, we may be better able to deal with the issues in an appropriate manner.

Consider it a public relations opportunity. Highlight some of the neat things your students can or have done. Educate the parents—or let the kids educate them—and dust off those existing policies and reread them in a new light.

Clancy J. Wolf, Ed.D.
Interactive Curriculum Institute
cwolf@ici.wednet.edu

II

MODELS FOR IMPLEMENTATION

8

INFORMATION HIGHWAYS, BYWAYS, CONNECTORS, AND MIXING BOWLS: THE INTEGRATED USE OF TECHNOLOGY AS AN INSTRUCTIONAL TOOL

Susan Grandgeorge

Bailey's Elementary School for the Arts and Sciences: A Center for Research and Technology, Fairfax County Public Schools first elementary magnet school, offers an environment in which students learn through interactive and cooperative research on topics that integrate subject areas and are relevant to each other and the real world. Knowledge is generated, through traditional modes and via technology. It is accessed, assessed, adjusted, and shared in a variety of technologically appropriate ways. The outcome is the existence of a community of self-motivated, life-long learners who are technologically literate and can confidently travel the information highway making connections, adjustments, assessments, crossovers, and/or transfers.

The program is successful for all language minorities (75% to 80% of Bailey's students speak English as a second or third language), and English-speaking students of varying ability levels. Using the basis of the conceptual unit method of instruction and the Fairfax County Public Schools Program of Studies as a springboard, teachers plan in grade-level teams. Resource areas such as the science discovery laboratory, technology resource center, library media center, performing arts theater, music technology laboratory, and the communications laboratory (TV studio) enhance and extend the classroom curriculum using technology in varying degrees.

The emphasis at Bailey's is on critical thinking and problem solving as opposed to rote learning, and technology is one tool that motivates, enhances, and stretches student thinking. Technology is critical in another area important to Bailey's magnet concept in that it offers a variety of ways for students to show what they have learned beyond a paper-and-pencil test.

The uniqueness of this program lies in its ability to promote active student research into concepts relevant to the child's life and interests, to utilize technology, and to teach that which is required by the Fairfax County Public Schools Program of Studies.

THE HOW AND WHY OF THE MAGNET PROGRAM

Bailey's Elementary School for the Arts and Sciences, located in Bailey's Crossroads, VA, is the most culturally, linguistically, and economically diverse elementary school in Fairfax County. The 850 students come from 45 countries and speak 20 different languages. The economic backgrounds are equally diverse; however, the majority of the student body receives free or reduced price lunches. Although the benefits of diversity were and are celebrated, concerns were raised regarding the imbalance of English to nonnative English-speaking students and the educational impact in the classroom.

Through the lobbying efforts of Bailey's parents to achieve educational equity and quality for their children, the Fairfax County School Board, in March 1991, designated Bailey's to be its first elementary magnet school. A planning committee, comprised of teachers, parents, administrators, education specialists, technology resource specialists, and university and museum representatives, worked throughout the following year to devise a program that would best meet the needs of Bailey's then-90% language minority and simultaneously be attractive enough to draw proficient English speakers to the school from outside the attendance area. Aware of the increased use of technology in the workforce, the necessity for its inclusion in education, and its instructional potential with language minority students, the committee sought to combine use of technology with contemporary learning theories in the program's design. In June 1992, the Fairfax County School Board voted to fund and implement the educational program proposed by the Bailey's Magnet Committee.

PHILOSOPHICAL BASE

Discussed in Renate Caine's (1991) book, *Making Connections: Teaching and the Human Brain*, are the results of recent brain research that verify that learning depends on students making connections between what they know and what they are learning. Actively solving a problem rather than being told the right answer has meaning. In "Restructuring for Learning With Technology," Karen Sheingold (1991) points out that effective learning hinges on the active engagement of students in constructing their own knowledge and understanding. Such learning is not a solitary process; it occurs through interaction with and support from the world of people and objects and through the use of technologies of many kinds. Anna Uhl Chamot (1981), "Applications of Second Language Learning Research to the Bilingual Classroom" stated: "Few children care about language for language sake. They want an immediate and practical purpose to which they can put the language. This means creating situations in which children can use the new language for functional ends. Structured drills that have no communicative function have little value in helping the child acquire the language."

These theories of learning and language acquisition formed the framework for the program design. The Bailey's program addresses the curriculum through a multidisciplinary, inquiry approach. Knowledge is acquired through active student research and communicated or shared in a variety of technologically appropriate ways; for example, videos, computer slide shows, multimedia presentations, dramatic performances, or interactive museum exhibitions. Subjects are interrelated through a "conceptual unit" method of instruction. A broad concept is selected to give organization, consistency, and real-world relevance to components of the curriculum. This helps students see and make connections in meaningful ways, which is an essential ingredient in language acquisition and acculturation.

Technology is an integral component of the Bailey's magnet program, which emphasizes critical thinking and problem solving. The interactive nature of computers provokes decision making and allows learning to become individualized. Working collaboratively with technology, students develop more initiative, leading to more independent and self-motivated learning. The goal of technology use is to enhance and enrich instruction. The instruction of technology use is not to be assessed as a separate entity. Technology is integrated into classroom instruction across all areas of the curriculum.

PROGRAM RESOURCES

Magnet program technology resources include a technology resource center furnished with 24 computer work stations, two black-and-white scanners, one color scanner, one black-and-white laser printer, and two color ink-jet printers. A multimedia station, comprised of a TV monitor, CD-ROM, laser disc player, and VCR utilizes video capturing and graphics audio animation capability to provide multimedia presentation opportunities for students and staff. Also available in the technology center are digital cameras and a poster maker.

The technology resource center is operated by a full-time technology resource teacher. Instruction is provided in technology use as well as lessons devised utilizing the equipment to enhance the conceptual units being studied in the classrooms. The resource teacher also assumes the duties of "technology trouble shooter" for the entire school and is responsible for identifying software or hardware purchases and minor maintenance.

The technology center is adjacent to the library media center, which has an automated circulation system networked to the county library system and online research tools that include several encyclopedias on CD-ROM and a computerized data base of community and parent resource capabilities. With completion of the school's renovation (Fall 1996), complete networking will provide multiple access to telecommunications modems.

The science discovery lab is staffed by a full-time science teacher, trained as a science and technology lead teacher, who supports research projects and demonstrations and provides additional science instruction consistent with the conceptual units of study. The lab is equipped with a microscope that is projected into a monitor, stereo microscopes, 12 computer stations using interactive physics and other exploratory software and CD-ROMs, probe ware, a laser printer, modem, laser disc player, Lego sets with programming software, a ripple tank, a stream table, a growth lab, and more.

The music technology lab, with its full-time music teacher, offers six workstations equipped with digital keyboards and headphones (one with a synthesizer) and computers, all networked with a central lab station for the teacher and with a TV monitor for instruction. Using graphics and music software, students learn names and positions of notes on the treble clef, create simple themes, and orchestrate and arrange them. There is a listening center and a games and information center that allow students to listen to a variety of music styles and play and create musical games. Instruction in the music lab meets music curriculum objectives and is done in collaboration with conceptual units.

In the Bailey's communications lab, students produce a live daily news program, public service announcements, book reports, videos documenting conceptual units, and infomercials. It is staffed by a full-time teacher with a communications background. The studio is equipped with three video cameras on tripods, a TV monitor, a still camera visual presenter, and a teleprompter. The control room houses a video switcher that allows the camera person to switch from one camera to another, a "play" VCR, and a "record" VCR with monitors, a character generator, a CD player and tape deck, and a 16-channel audio mixer. The editing room contains a video editing system with character generator and special effects generator, and four computers for writing the news and doing simple video editing. Students perform the duties of news reader, camera person, video and audio mixer, news writer, and video editor.

The performing arts theater does not play a significant technological role; however, it is integral in enhancing conceptual units and in attracting students to the school. The performing arts strand is directed by a full-time teacher who works with the students and available video capability to produce dramatic presentations that explore and extend the concepts being learned in the classroom. Students choose their roles to include lighting and sound technicians, as well as performers and set and stage crew. These resource areas build on the already established Model Technology Initiative program, which equipped each classroom with four computers and teacher training.

OBJECTIVES

In the Bailey's magnet program, technology is used as a knowledge sharing or dissemination tool as well as an avenue for knowledge acquisition. Laser discs, CD-ROMs, telecommunications, and a computerized community resource bank serve as valuable research sources. Word processing, spreadsheets, interactive science, music composition, graphics, and video software are utilized in the learning process as well as in the sharing or exhibition stage. Students at Bailey's have the capability to do an entire research and presentation project technologically.

The objectives of the educational program are to emphasize skills and knowledge required in an information age, combine teaching and learning strategies with the well-integrated use of technology across the curriculum, utilize community resources, create a model that insures all students will be challenged, and make the programs and opportunities so attractive that out-of-boundary English-proficient students will choose to attend Bailey's. In addition the following instructional goals strive to have students:

- become competent researchers
- develop the ability to question and solve problems
- demonstrate an appreciation and understanding of various cultures
- demonstrate science literacy and independent use of the scientific method
- use technology to gather, organize, and process information and to communicate research outcomes to others
- work effectively with others in a multicultural society.

In order to implement the magnet program, physical building changes as well as staffing changes and staff development were necessary. Renovation, room remodeling, and equipment procurement were required to create the technology resource center, science discovery lab, music technology lab, communications center, and performing arts theater.

PROCESS

This unique program promotes active student research into concepts relevant to the child's life and interests, utilizes technology, and teaches that which is required by the study program. It can be best explained by providing a specific example. The first-grade teaching team devised the conceptual unit "Winter Adaptations" to introduce the scientific method, volume, area, and animal behavior in winter. Student interaction with temperature permeates the unit. Students take the temperature daily and report their findings in daily weather reports on the Bailey's News Program, broadcast from the communications center.

Graphing skills, done by hand and on computer, are taught as they correlate temperature with weather-dependent clothing the students wear each day. The scientific method is utilized as students make predictions regarding the effect different materials have on temperature. In the science discovery lab, they measure the time it takes for snow to melt and for hot chocolate to cool to a drinking temperature in different containers. Using computerized temperature probes, they compare their hand temperatures before and after holding ice until it is melted.

The scientific method and snow are used to introduce the concept of volume, as students predict, then determine, the differences in the volume of snow in its frozen and melted states. They continue to study volume with hands-on exercises such as estimating the number of handmade paper snowballs or snowflakes it would take to cover a giant paper snowman. Counting by twos, a math objective, is included in these exercises.

Science objectives—the study of winter animal behavior, language arts objectives, and beginning research skills—are taught using the winter adaptations concept. Books selected deal with winter and animals, such as *The Mitten* and many others. Students become more involved with the stories and the study of animal behavior in the technology resource center, where using graphic arts programs they design scenes of animals camouflaging themselves in winter's environment. After graphically illustrating and verbally narrating portions of a winter story, they learn sequencing by creating a computerized slide show. Classroom learning is enhanced as students interact with the CD-ROMs about animals.

Students demonstrate results of their research on animals' preparation for winter by scanning pictures of their selected animal and "pasting" them into a "template" indicating the animal's winter preparation behavior, such as it "gathers food," "stores food," or 'hibernates."

In the music lab, students use computerized keyboards and synthesizers to compose "theme" music to accompany a sentence they have written about winter. The performing arts team works with the children to produce dramatic performances of Native Americans' winter adaptation customs. In art, the children design and create from paper maché a life-sized winter scene revealing animals in their winter habitats. Available video technology is used to film these learning activities.

A culminating activity is held at the completion of the unit, in which students share their knowledge through a dramatic performance and student-guided tours of the many "products" created during the unit, for example, graphs, snowmen, paper maché scenes, computer slide shows, animal templates, and experiment results. Also shown is the video portraying the many learning activities in progress that captured the important stage of "process" for review and sharing.

It is apparent from this review of one conceptual unit that with this method of instruction, all curriculum areas—math, art, science, language arts, and music—are integrated. Curriculum objectives are related to each other as well as the real world, and technology plays an important and cooperative role in the learning.

TECHNOLOGY INTEGRATION

Presented in this section are additional examples of technology use in the enhancement of the conceptual unit method of instruction. During the fifth-grade unit instruction on Ancient Civilizations, the science lab component is based on plants along with experimental design. The students devise, through brain storming, experiments to perform with growing plants. One group experiments with the effects of changing variables on growing plants. Using specifically related software, they record all data weekly on spreadsheets. Another group uses Legos and computers to build a temperature-controlled greenhouse. Another group uses graphic arts programs to draw plants from their native countries, whereas some students create cosmetics from herbs.

In the technology resource center, students create computerized slide shows revealing information on pyramids and mummification. They create labels and advertising, as well as document and illustrate the work of all fifth-grade groups in a guide book, for the culminating exhibition, "The Ancient Egyptian Museum." Using communications equipment, one group produces an eye-witness news program in which student-researched life in ancient Egypt is portrayed. Clips of chariot and sail ship races are edited from films and included in the sports segment of the video. Modern-day commercials advertising Egyptian clothing on sale for Egyptian currency are included. News stories feature government officials of ancient Egypt. The study of the Nile River is brought to life in the science lab as students create a delta in the stream table.

During the second-grade unit instruction on Communications, a postal service is set up in school. Computers are used to make street signs, and postage stamps are made from photographs of classroom teachers using a digital camera. A simulated e-mail program networks classrooms for writing letters, and different fonts are used to create secret codes of communication. In the third-grade unit instruction on Patterns, students learn about tessellations by creating them on the computer using math software.

In the unit instruction on Explorations, the fourth grade studies the solar system. In the science lab they design and construct Lego vehicles with capabilities compatible with the environment of the planet to be visited. For example, the vehicle built to visit Mars' rocky terrain is equipped with spiked footed legs rather than wheels. In music, the students compose planet national anthems and devise notation systems for writing the music.

Using the Internet, fourth graders conduct research, discuss, gather, and enter data along with 64 classes worldwide while working on the Global Wonderful Water Project through Virginia PEN. Fourth and fifth grades participate annually in the Jason Project via the World-Wide Web. First graders telecommunicate to all states requesting others send leaves to them to examine and information on winter adaptations. Bailey's Vietnamese students answer a telecommunicated request for information about Vietnam from a student in Colorado planning a visit there. Questions fourth graders have while working on pendulums using an interactive physics program are directed to "Ask the Science Teacher" on a VA PEN network. Several grade levels use Iris and Kids Sphere to exchange information with distant classes using a pen pal format.

IMPLEMENTATION

Members of Bailey's staff and administration served on the magnet committee, which designed the program, implemented in phases over three years. Prior to its implementation, the entire staff received staff development sessions on creating integrated thematic units, using technology to support the curriculum, integrating subject areas, and utilizing experimental research design and the museum approach to learning. The staff met in the summer in grade-level teams with specialists to plan their conceptual units. Ongoing planning and decision making is done in weekly team meetings with input from resource teachers and the principal.

Classroom teachers and many specialists have received computer training as part of the Model Technology Initiative Program, and many have received the Technology Lead Teacher training. Frequent staff development sessions and in-services are offered with substitutes available to allow classroom teachers to participate. Teachers are kept abreast of available school based technology, its operation, and possible uses in regular, after-school mini-Mac training sessions conducted by the technology resource center teacher. They are kept abreast of countywide technology use through frequent and regular meetings with all Model Technology Initiative Program schools. In hiring staff, emphasis is placed on an applicant's technology background. Curriculum is outlined by the Fairfax County Public Schools Program of Studies, but is addressed by the conceptual unit instructional approach. Conceptual units are devised by grade-level teams in collaboration with the resource specialists. Ways to utilize technology are born out of conversational exchange of needs and capabilities.

Programs used and activities done in the labs are continued in the classroom. In fact, in many cases, instruction is provided to the classroom by the students who have acquired the skills in the labs. There is no permanent schedule for resource use; scheduling is done on an as-needed basis. It would be counterproductive for Mrs. Parker's class to be using the technology resource center from 1:00 to 2:00 because it is Tuesday, when Mrs. Noel's class needs the computer time to finish transforming data from their survey on languages spoken in the home into pie charts before Wednesday's presentation. A brief description of the intended project or material being studied is provided so the resource teacher can make suggestions. A continual database of use, including number of students, name of classroom teacher, projects addressed, and programs used, is updated daily. Resource area teachers devise lab schedules and distribute them to the staff on a weekly basis. The technology usage is always related to the ongoing conceptual unit.

Students can be sent individually, in small groups, or as a whole class. There can be students from several classes within any given lab, doing several projects simultaneously.

A complete commitment on the part of the entire Bailey's staff is necessary for its success. Staff members who have not shared this commitment have opted to transfer to other schools, as offered, free of negative consequences. Newly hired staff are made completely aware of the program and its job implications. Staff members exercise their commitment and leadership by conducting numerous in-services and offering presentations all over the country on technology use.

Bailey's hosts multiple visiting teachers, principals, administrators, and public officials from all over the world. Fairfax County Public Schools central administration has demonstrated commitment by providing leadership from the Office of Instructional Services and the Office for Training and Staff Development. A school system technology specialist provides expertise to all schools in the "pyramid" (schools that feed into and including the high school). On site leadership is provided by the Bailey's technology resource and science discovery lab teachers and the many classroom teachers and instructional assistants who have received the Technology Lead Teacher training. The PTA provides volunteers, trained in technology in the resource center, to assist in the classroom, and it has established a Technology Support Committee made up of parents with that expertise. A partnership with Thomas Jefferson High School for Science and Technology, Fairfax County's selective science and technology magnet high school, brings in student tutors on a weekly basis to work with Bailey's students on projects using technology. Collaborative relationships are plentiful through telecommunication networks and Bailey's is currently developing a World-Wide Web home page.

EVALUATION

The Model Technology Initiative Program is monitored and evaluated annually by Fairfax County Department of Instructional Services. The Bailey's magnet program is monitored and evaluated by the Fairfax County Public Schools Office of Planning, Testing, and Evaluation. A progress update was presented in May 1993. The findings were based on a staff survey, parent survey, and classroom observations. The six-person observation team consisted of an administrator with expertise in elementary curriculum and instruction, a computer technology coordinator, an editor of a children's science journal, and university professors with expertise in language arts instruction, English as a Second Language (ESL), and school restructuring.

The progress update, evaluating the first year's implementation of the magnet program, indicates that outcomes serviced the program objectives and goals. It states that implementation of the science lab, technology in the classrooms, hands-on, interactive learning methods, and emphases on problem-solving and critical thinking, cooperative learning, and interdisciplinary units was deemed successful, and parents indicated these components to be important to their children's education. The majority of teachers agreed that the program offers a rich and socially supportive educational environment in which students' academic and cultural needs are met. Teachers stated that students from outside the Bailey's community are good language models and bring with them outside experiences that the teacher can use in classroom discussion.

The expert observation team found the school to be a warm, inviting, respectful, and congenial place for learning. An ethic of equity is exhibited by the staff, a variety of innovative teaching approaches is evident, and students and teachers appear at ease in their transition to using computers to enhance instruction readily, easily, and frequently. Teachers are adept at maintaining high levels of student interest and in building rapport with a wide range of learners. Conceptual units are varied to meet student interests, structured for active student involvement, and designed to lead to meaningful student products. Science and computer resource teachers are proactive in planning jointly with classroom teachers to integrate some classroom projects with laboratory activities. Teachers provide frequent opportunities for student choice and encourage students to reflect on their learning. When explaining their work, many students are articulate and demonstrate a good knowledge of the subject matter. They are able to state clearly the relationship of their computer and/or science laboratory activity to what they are learning in their classrooms.

The program is also monitored and evaluated regularly by the staff. Grade-level teams meet weekly, and specialists meet monthly to discuss student progress and achievement. Technology use is not evaluated in and of itself, but by its effectiveness as a tool in enhancing instruction. In addition, each of the hundreds of visitors to and observers of the program who frequent Bailey's are presented a survey. Responses are documented as an evaluative device.

POTENTIAL FOR REPLICATION

The integrated, hands-on, conceptual unit method of instruction and its complementary use of technology are all replicable to other sites. Although the replication of the extensive technology resources available at Bailey's would be ideal, the same results could be achieved with much less. Staff development programs can be easily duplicated, and successful ideas and technology uses can be shared. The extent of necessary training depends on staff knowledge of computers and other technological equipment. There has been some documentation of specific conceptual units; however, the staff feels strongly that the magic of the units is their flexibility to bend with student interest and desire. The dissemination of rigid unit summaries would be equivalent to a "canned curriculum." Staff are eager to share processes. Strategies and procedures can be relayed, as they have been thus far, through presentations, publications, workshops, and in-services. Although difficult to initiate and maintain, a prevailing sense of creativity and commitment by the staff is essential.

Minimal requirements for replication include one or more computers with printers per classroom, a technology and science lab with multimedia and telecommunications capability as well as several computers, printers, and scanners. A performing arts strand can be implemented with moveable stage pieces, sound and lighting equipment. If video editing equipment is available for use by the school system, the communications strand can be implemented with only one video camera and tripod, a VCR and monitor, a computer, and a small permanent space to be used as a studio. Teaching positions, or instructional assistants in some cases, are required. The music lab can be staffed by the existing music teacher and equipped with computers, keyboards, and a synthesizer.

Program replication capability is evidenced by the implementation in 1995 of a second elementary magnet school program and two focus programs patterned after the Bailey's program. Also initiated in 1995 was the effort to design a model middle school that extends the fine arts and technology strands at Bailey's.

PROGRAM ACCOMPLISHMENTS

Technology use in the Bailey's magnet program is unique and significant in its dedication to enhancing, enriching, and complementing the conceptual units rather than functioning as technology education in and of itself. Students make connections between subject material and real-world uses through technology. The learning process flows continuously into products. Technology is the medium for the research and the dissemination of student-generated knowledge. Experiencing the relevance of what is being learned sparks an excitement and an initiative that hastens and deepens the learning. Curriculum objectives are met and useful computer techniques acquired in an enthusiastic learning endeavor.

A distinct significance of this method of instruction is its ability to address the learning needs of students at all levels of academic and language ability. Those of higher academic ability can progress individually through technology use and serve as instructors and learning role models to other students. Students of lower ability are given more opportunities and avenues to produce and are stimulated to progress through the positive reinforcement of discovery and technology use.

Second-language learners are able to participate in a hands-on, language-independent way, acquiring academic concepts while learning English as a by-product. For example, a fifth-grade ESL student studying geographical concepts creates them in the technology lab using a graphic arts program. Included in his design is a peninsula, mountain range, oasis, river with mouth and delta, and natural harbor. In limited English, he asks questions regarding some of these land forms. The graphics program facilitates rapid and complete explanation while providing him with the freedom to independently acquire the concepts, technology, and self-esteem. Success is evident as he verbally expresses tremendous excitement and satisfaction with "Jose Island" and its "Jose Peninsula," "Jose Oasis" and so on. Students with limited English writing skills create computerized slide shows depicting how caves are formed and the regions of Virginia for a museum exhibition on Virginia.

The project responds to state-of-the-art standards, its relevant utilization of state of the art technology, and contemporary brain-based learning theories. The first-grade Economics conceptual unit is an example of outcomes demonstrating the achievement of program goals and objectives. The curriculum areas to be taught include counting by 5s and 10s, measurement, money, plants, seeds, reading and writing. Each class selects an item to manufacture and to sell at the First-Grade Market Place.

All classes grow bedding plants from seeds, an exercise enhanced in the science lab by interactive experimentation on plant growth using relevant software. One class produces bubbles, researching ingredients, using measurement skills, and working cooperatively through the assembly-line method. Another class may create play dough, using the science lab to discover the effects air exposure has on different objects. They also use measurement and weighing skills and experiment with color combination. A third class bakes brownies for sale, and another creates a coloring book depicting the steps in growing a garden, which first graders tend behind the school. All classes use the technology resource center to create advertisements and packaging materials. A promotional video is created in the communications lab and broadcast on the morning news. Labor schedules and inventories are done on spreadsheets. Some children invest in their businesses. Storefronts are designed and built, products are promoted through advertising, and retail prices are determined, all by the children.

The Market Place opens for several days, selling goods to the entire school. Students work their scheduled shifts, collect money, make change, and document inventory depletion. Supply and demand are evaluated daily, and production is modified accordingly. When the Market Place closes, gross income is used to pay start-up expenses, labor costs, and dividends to investors. Upon completion, all classes document the real-world experience with the writing of class books. Obvious accomplishments are the development of skills and knowledge required in today's world, integrated use of technology across the curriculum, a multidisciplinary approach to subject matter, active student involvement in the learning process, cooperative learning, communication of knowledge in a variety of meaningful ways, student ability to question and solve problems, and use of the scientific method. All of these provide avenues for students of varied academic and language abilities to acquire and communicate knowledge.

Results obtained by the magnet program are immensely important in meeting the educational needs not only of Bailey's unique student population, but of the entire community of learners. This method of instruction teaches children to be independent life-long seekers of relevant knowledge. It provides new options for shared learning beyond pencil and paper. It offers challenging environments to the bright, the learning disabled, "the regular kid," and the minimal English speaker, in which they can all participate, contribute, and communicate. It prepares students to be productive participants in the increasingly technologically dependent world. It gives them the vehicle in which to travel competently and confidently the information highway, gathering information in one location and transporting it to another.

In 1995, after three years of the magnet program, test scores revealed desired accomplishments as well. Bailey's students' Iowa Test of Basic Skills scores increased in science by 34 percentile points, in social studies by 35 points, in math by 32 points, and in language arts by 19 points. Degrees of Reading Power Test scores show an 18% increase in numbers scoring in the highest quartile and a 15% decrease in numbers scoring in the lowest quartile.

In addition to meeting these goals, the innovative nature of the program has been successful in meeting another need for which it was designed: attracting proficient English speakers from other attendance areas. There are approximately 200 students attending Bailey's from 52 schools outside the boundaries. Bailey's receives over 300 applications for some 75 slots that are open each year.

Bailey's staff is willing to extend its current outreach efforts to assist with replication in other sites. Based on these efforts, Hunters Woods Elementary School began a magnet program in 1995, and two other schools began focus programs, all patterned after Bailey's. An initiative to create a model middle school, incorporating Bailey's fine arts and technology strands, is in the design phase. The Bailey's program functions as a showcase, hosting a continuous stream of observers comprised of educators, community members, news media, and public officials from all over the world. Staff continues to do presentations, in-services and workshops, and publications to share aspects of the program with others.

In addition, since the inception of the magnet program, Bailey's has won the following awards recognition:

- Selected by Virginia State Board of Education as one of 10 schools in the state demonstrating "Exemplary Uses of Technology in Education"
- One of 5 schools in the country chosen to receive the *Business Week*/McGraw-Hill Award for "Instructional Innovation: Schools in the Age of Technology"
- Cited in U.S. Department of Education, Public Affairs Release as one of the "Examples of Exemplary Schools" in the nation
- Selected by *Redbook* magazine as one of "America's 142 Best Schools"
- 1994 Principal of the Year; 1993 Teacher of the Year; 1990, 1991, 1992 Teacher of the Year finalists
- 1995 A. Heath Onthank award for outstanding public service.

CONCLUDING COMMENT

The Bailey's Elementary School for the Arts and Sciences staff is an unusually talented and dedicated group. That which motivates their long hours and creative approaches is seen daily in the incomparable excitement for learning exhibited by the children—from the newly arrived immigrant to the GT Center eligible. By being able to develop research skills, work cooperatively with peers, independently utilize technology, and find meaning in what is taught, the students claim personal ownership for their knowledge, which not only enhances learning but makes major strides in developing powerful self-esteem. This is rewardingly visible during the learning process as well as during presentations when children nearly burst with pride and elation as they share what they know and how they have come to know it.

An open invitation is extended to visit Bailey's Elementary School for the Arts and Sciences, to see that which, after first-hand experience, anyone would conclude must be the right way to teach.

REFERENCES

Caine, R. (1991). *Making connections: Teaching and the human brain.* Menlo Park, CA: Addison-Wesley.

Chamot, A.U. (1981, May). *Applications of second language learning research to the bilingual classroom.* Paper presented at the International Bilingual Bicultural Conference of the National Association of Bilingual Education.

Sheingold, K. (1991, September). Restructuring for learning with technology. *Phi Beta Kappan, 73*(1), 17-27.

9

CHOICE 2000: ATTAINING A HIGH SCHOOL DIPLOMA ONLINE

Michael Allen and Kevin Gerrior

Imagine a school where everything is designed to ensure that all students can realize their full potential. A place where teachers, administrators, parents, and the community are working together as a team with a shared vision. What would it look like? What would it entail? How would it be made up?

CHOICE 2000 is a state-of-the-art online school in the beautiful city of Perris, Riverside County, in sunny southern California. CHOICE 2000, California's newest charter public school, puts a complete, fully certified, grade 7-12 plus adult program within the reach of every student in the state who needs more than traditional approaches. The school serves students who want to complete their diploma via modem from their personal computers at home.

A SOPHISTICATED COMPUTER NETWORK

CHOICE 2000 students complete comprehensive courses of study provided to them over a sophisticated computer network that they access from their personal computers. CHOICE 2000 realizes the goal of individualized instruction by taking advantage of the fact that students in California have personal computers in their homes. CHOICE 2000 provides an alternative by innovatively harnessing telecommunications, educational software, and dedicated teachers.

THE CHARTER SCHOOL ACT

The Charter School Act of 1993 encourages parents and educators to design and create schools that meet all California certification requirements in ways that uniquely suit diverse segments of the state's student population. This is done by developing lessons, designing texts and auxiliary materials, and offering professional guidance and feedback to secondary and adult students via the Internet.

LEARNING 24 HOURS A DAY, SEVEN DAYS A WEEK

CHOICE 2000 gives students in any part of California a charter school of their own 24 hours a day, 7 days a week. CHOICE 2000 students are not passive learners. Students participate in cooperative projects through teleconferencing, master software tools by using them in creative tasks, sharpen communication skills through using electronic mail and become independent life long learners. Graduates will know how to analyze problems, define solutions and employ the most advanced technology.

Benefits of this Form of Schooling

Throughout their programs students are guided by the teachers who can evaluate their work through instantaneous communication and feedback. CHOICE 2000 radically reduces the costs of serving special students and those with disabilities. The simple convenience of having a school that comes into the home or office via a computer network removes some of the obstacles to educational opportunity and growth.

In addition, computerized learning is widely regarded as particularly beneficial for students with special needs. Economic growth and security depends entirely on how well people can prepare themselves for careers in the exploding knowledge industries.

The CHOICE 2000 Nuclear Community

The school has developed a unique virtual community. Unlike other distance education programs, the school has developed a tight-knit community of learners. Recent events included the face-to-face Christmas Party held at a community center, the Sweetheart Dance held at the Church Hall, and the 1995 Perris Graduation Ceremonies held at the Perris Public Library. The school has a very active parent council and an extremely excited student body and staff. The school even has a yearbook and individual class pictures.

A Training Resource for Business

CHOICE 2000 does not just simply describe advanced computer technology for its students, it is an integral part of the program. It offers basic data processing, computerized accounting and bookkeeping, office automation, and word processing. Our students, trained according to industry standards, are ready to become the workers of the future.

The CHOICE 2000 Extended Community

The school is based on the conviction that quality education is not based on mandates from distant administrators but by communities. CHOICE 2000 is no exception. It is fortunate to count parents, business people, and educators as members of its school community.

WHY WE FEEL THIS KIND OF EDUCATION IS IMPORTANT

"It has been said that when children born today, by the time they reach their eightieth birthday, 97 percent of all knowledge will have been produced during their lifetime. Compare this to the sixteenth century: the greatest total of knowledge then—all one could acquire in a lifetime—was about what is now contained in one weekday issue of the *New York Times*. Today anyone who has access to a computer, a phone line, and a modem has access, in one evening, to more information than both his or her parents had in an entire lifetime. A new learner fortunate enough to have a satellite dish can access more information in one evening than all his or her forebearers in history and . . . it is impossible to know everything about anything. Your best hope is to learn how to access information and utilize new nontraditional methods for your continuing education. This can be done via satellite, fiber optics, interactive video disks, and computer driven information systems" (Ogden, 1993, p. 15).

A recent statistic from the U.S. Department of Labor stated that by the year 2000, 44% of all jobs will include collecting, analyzing, synthesizing, storing, and retrieving data. In some instances, whole communities and provinces like New Brunswick in Canada) are building multipurpose computer networks. For the past 18 months, a partnership between the town of Blacksburg, VA, Bell Atlantic, and Virginia Tech University has operated a communal network called the Blacksburg Electronic Village. By the end of 1994, the project has hooked up a majority of the town's businesses and 36,000 citizens, including 24,000 students at Virginia Tech, whose campus is situated in town. All these people reach the Internet through a local network that ties Blacksburgians to a town hall, hospital, stores, restaurants, and to one another ("Welcome to cyber space," 1994).

Why has schooling evolved so slowly, while society has made rapid changes? In the last 10 years we have seen fax machines, car phones, and CDs proliferate. We have seen the fall of communism, the emergence of a free trade agreement, and the end of apartheid in South Africa. What will the next 10 years bring? How does the classroom prepare students to deal with all these changes? The Internet—the huge (2.2 million computers), global (135 countries), rapidly growing (10-15% a month) network—has captured America's imagination and provides a virtual world library. Throughout the history of human communication, advances in technology have powered paradigmatic shifts in education and as Yogi Berra (1990) said: "The future ain't what it used to be.

ABOUT CHOICE 2000

CHOICE 2000 Online School started in September 1994 and has already drawn over 250 students from areas of Riverside County California and beyond.

"We have 250 students online and they are rabid about it," said director Michael Allen, a high school chemistry teacher and the mastermind behind the charter school that is under the auspices of the Perris Union High School District. Unlike traditional schools, charter schools are governed by the students, parent, and teachers. They can select their own materials and teaching styles.

There are no boundaries for the computer school: Anyone who wants a high school diploma and has a home computer with Windows and a modem can apply. Students must sign a contract pledging to log on to the school at least two hours a day, five days a week. The computer system automatically tracks how much time they spend working.

Here is a typical day for student Shannon Wheeler: Shannon Wheeler gets up late almost everyday but has not had to bother her father for a ride to school all year. Class starts when she switches on her IBM 486DX computer sitting in the living room of her Sun City home. "I do not like to log on until I am really awake, and that is around noon," said

Shannon, who is enrolled in the school, which is believed to be the first in the nation to offer a diploma via a home computer.

Wheeler logs on and immediately checks for messages and assignments from her teachers. She is taking sophomore-level courses in English, algebra, Spanish, computer science, and art. A sound card in her computer one day will play language assignments through her stereo speakers. She keeps track of her physical education activities such as line dancing and aerobics and sends them in for credit. Following instructions on the computer, she typed and sent in an essay on a hypothetical case in which school officials were deciding to switch from a graded system to pass-fail.

If she had a question she could e-mail a teacher, page the teacher directly online, or talk to the teacher directly in a teleconference, which is an interactive conversation conducted online. Testing is done on the system, with test questions flashed on the screen, and students type in the answers. CHOICE 2000 offers a grade 7-12 program and has proven so popular that the Perris Union School District is capping enrollment until enough telephone lines, computers, and staff are added to adequately serve them all.

The biggest problem for parents is to pry students off the system, especially the ones who would like to work late at night or into the wee hours of the morning. The school is open 24 hours a day, 365 days a year. Students cannot get enough.

"My daughter got busted using the system at 11 p.m.," said Cheryl Carson of Perris. A teacher sent an electronic message saying that it is late and was time for her to go to bed. At eight years old, Shawna Carson is the youngest girl in the school. She is working at a 7th-grade level, but occasionally does a few 10th-grade assignments for fun. She has already passed a preadmittance test for Mt. San Jacinto Community College and the GED test, which could get her a high school diploma.

"But I do not want her on the high school campus," said her mother. "This way she can do work that is challenging and I can have her home to protect her." Shawna said she does not mind being away from other children during the day. She says she has plenty of time in the afternoon to play with her friends, go to Brownies, and socialize with other girls her age. "All my friends live in the same complex, and I play with them after school," she said. Most of the students in the program are teenagers; however, four adults are using the program to get their high school diplomas.

Safety was the big issue for Sherryle Lemessurier, whose thirteen year old daughter is in the eighth grade at the school. Like many of the parents in the program, Sherryle tried home schooling, but the responsibility of being the teacher proved too great. She purchased a computer and enrolled her daughter in CHOICE 2000. She said it was definitely worth it.

Another student, Amy Briggs, said she felt lost in a traditional school, which sometimes has more than 30 students in a class: "I did not like it. One teacher cannot help all those people in one hour. With this school, my mom can help me and my teachers can help me." Another thing she likes about the school is chatting with other students on the network after her lessons are done. Amy thinks this type of a school is an option, which she loves.

Dawn Regalla has two children in the school and she is using the opportunity to get a high school diploma she missed 16 years ago: "My daughter asked why I didn't go back to school, and she would be able to help me."

Jason Regalla has a different kind of problem. He is a child actor and needs a flexible school schedule. The flexibility the school offers him enables him to follow a dream that he has while not neglecting his studies. All this and more is happening at this innovative school.

HOW IT CAME TO BE

Michael Allen asked himself a question. He sat back and freed his mind of conventional thought and started to dream. In this dream he envisioned what education will be like in the 21st century and beyond. Michael had a vision of what education would look like in the future. He, as a classroom teacher, thought there could be more that we could do as educators to prepare the students of today for the 21st century. Other people also shared these common beliefs. Thus, a vision became combined with action, and a small nucleus of people started their voyage.

Other educators with the same belief shared that vision. Myque Jeffers became the administrator, and Dave Peterson took on a major role of teaching and sharing in the development of the newly formed school. Kevin Gerrior came onboard in a research capacity and has moved to Blacksburg, VA, home of the Blacksburg Electronic Village and Virginia Polytechnic University, to take doctoral studies geared toward online education. More importantly, parents and the community came on board.

PURPOSE

The purpose of CHOICE 2000 Online School is to educate students to be the workers of the future. CHOICE 2000 realizes that the students of tomorrow have to be prepared for the Communications and Information Age. It is imperative that educators adapt to this ever-changing world for the benefit of our future, for our children. The proactive stance that we are taking is a philosophy that will not only empower students, but everyone involved in the process. It is to be creative and self-directive in the quest for knowledge in the process of reaching their highest potential. We believe education is a journey, not a destination.

FORCES THAT ALLOWED IT TO BECOME A REALITY

CHOICE 2000 would not have come together without the support of the Perris School District, the state of California, and the creation of charter schools. A charter school in its purest form is an autonomous educational entity operating under a contract negotiated between the organizers who manage the school (teachers, parents, or others from the private sector) and the sponsors—usually local or state education boards—who oversee the provisions of the charter.

Another guiding light was found in the foundational beliefs set forth by Goals 2000, a national standard for educational guidelines. It was shaped during a historic education summit with the nation's governors in 1989. It detailed educational goals for the year 2000 and beyond. The principles of GOALS 2000 are the backbone of the direction that CHOICE 2000 is striving to attain.

THE PROGRAM

The educational program has several areas of emphasis. Self-motivation is very much tied together with self-esteem. For students to function and get involved in the learning process, they need to feel that they are in a safe environment. A safety net needs to be created so that students will feel free to participate without fear of ridicule. This can be accomplished at home and in the community with the effort to include on- and offline social activities that foster inclusion.

CURRICULUM

The cornerstone of the curriculum is based on the California State Frameworks. Emphasis is on developing process skills, computerized information gathering, higher level thinking skills, and utilization of multiple learning strategies. CHOICE 2000, through staff development, will implement a process of outcome based education for creation of future measurable outcomes.

The identified knowledge, skills, and attitudes may include, but are not limited to, portfolios including work and test samples based on reading and writing. Standardized assessments will be administered including required state performance reports. Educational successes will be measured partially by standardized test scores, but success should also be measured by the overall improvement of students' abilities. "Student outcomes" means the extent to which all students of the school demonstrate that they have attained the skills, knowledge, and attitudes specified as goals in the school's educational program.

CHOICE 2000 has identified a set of competency-based outcomes that are used to measure student skills, knowledge, and attitudes as described in the school plan and district curriculum guides. The school, in its continuous cycle of planning, implementing, and evaluating, has recently focused on the need to clarify its mission and vision of educating students who can transfer school learning into meaningful real-life applications.

Teachers are establishing transitional program and attitudinal outcomes, accompanied by the rubrics with which they will be measured. The program and attitude (affective) outcomes provide the linkage to the transformational, real-life exit outcomes. Our exit outcomes are powerful demonstrations of knowledge, skills, and attitudes that could literally transform to the "real world" after graduation.

ACCOUNTABILITY

CHOICE 2000 will continue to use the current accountability system with annual revisions to reflect the school programs. At each level, specific knowledge, skills, and attitudes will be established to determine a student's readiness to proceed to the next level. Ongoing student monitoring and parent communication utilizing progress reports, phone, or e-mail communication, student conferences, and parent/teacher conferences will be used.

These outcomes will be based on the state frameworks and course of study and will be developed jointly by teachers, curriculum directors, and system administrators.

PROGRAM SUCCESS

The program success will also be measured by the impact on the educational system this program will produce and the success of the students. Upon graduating from CHOICE 2000, the students will be on their way to becoming critical thinkers, collaborative workers, concerned citizens, and life-long learners. There is certain to be some negative opinions, but a program that is not controversial is not innovative. However, the real key, as with any endeavor, is teamwork and sustained cooperation of everyone involved, which reminds me of a short story:

> *If we were as smart as a goose.* In the fall as you see geese heading south for the winter, flying along in a "V" formation, you might be interested in knowing what science has discovered about why they fly that way. It has been learned that as each bird flaps its wings, it creates an uplift for the bird immediately following. By flying in a "V" formation, the whole flock added at least 71% greater flying range than if each bird flew on its own.
>
> Whenever a goose falls out of formation, it suddenly feels the drag and resistance of trying to go it alone, and it quickly gets back into formation to take advantage of the lifting power of the bird immediately in front. When the lead goose gets tired, he rotates back in the wing and another goose flies point. The geese honk from behind to encourage those up front to keep up their speed. And like geese, people who share a common direction can get where they are going quicker and easier because they are traveling on the thrust of one another, and cheering each other on. (Anonymous)

This is why we think that it is a key that all parents, teachers, administrators, and the community look at adapting education to the enormous change that society will undergo during the 21st century and beyond. Our children are our nation's most valuable resource and it is our responsibility to educate them to the best of our knowledge.

REFERENCES

Ogden, F. (1993). *The last book you will ever read.* Toronto: MacFarlane, Walter & Ross.

Welcome to cyberspace. (1994, Spring). *Time*, p. 34.

10

MIGRANT SUMMER CONNECTIVITY ACADEMY

Van Wilkinson and Gary D. Hartley

Rural, resource-poor regions like Shasta County in California's extreme north face poor academic performance among a wide base of students who have little access to connectivity for information processing and decision making. Rural and migrant students in California have difficulty accessing world-quality information at a level comparable to other students. Furthermore, students of parents who migrate to seek agrarian-based work defined by migrant education are the least likely to have access to telecommunications for learning because of the cost of purchasing hardware, language problems in learning software and technical language, and geographical mobility. These factors contribute to migrant students being radically underrepresented in leadership roles in their schools, while at the same time becoming disproportionately involved in gangs and other negative activities.

Our means to address these problems was computer-mediated communication (CMC). We trained pairs of teachers and migrant students on the educational uses of the Internet, while simultaneously equipping each of them with laptop computers for dialing into our local Internet point of presence. The model progressed in five stages:

1. We identified and recruited eight migrant-qualified students from middles school and eight teachers to spend three weeks in a summer training academy, operated by the Shasta County Office of Education in Redding, CA.
2. We involved California State University subject-matter specialists in science and language arts to assist in developing instructional units that were congruent with the California Department of Education's curricular frameworks.
3. We conducted a 20-hour preinstitute for the teachers separately, bringing them to an operational level of Internet navigation and hardware usage prior to being paired with the students.
4. Students joined the academy and spent 57 hours with their teacher partners in a computer laboratory setting, co-learning Internet navigation, scientific thinking processes, and language arts skills through structured writing and reporting. During this time, each participant was issued a laptop computer with dial-in capability, configured to operate with a minimum of difficulty.
5. After the end of the academy, the pairs worked together in tutorial relationships online with their laptops, in preparation for the start of the 1995-96 school year. A benchmark-checking reunion was held one month into the first semester to evaluate progress and make appropriate adjustments for the remainder of the first semester.

Preliminary results from pre- and posttesting, anecdotal evaluations, and performance in the school setting strongly indicate that this CMC-based solution appears to be a rapid and effective means for addressing the identified problems. Using laptops for remote dial-in provided access to world-quality information with little dependency on location. Having the students supported online with a teacher tutor provided practical support. Having the teachers and students working together on science projects provided for authentic-framed development of lesson plans to be used with all students; and, having the students using telecommunications at home and at school provided a leadership propulsion system hitherto unavailable to these underrepresented students.

The outcome we hoped for was a reversal in the predictable cycle of rural, migrant student underachievement in school. Traditional intervention programs focused on in-school remedies and, because they were generally viewed as remedial in design, carried with them the stigma of low performance. Few California school systems provided laptop computers to students on anything beyond a limited check-out basis for the already skilled. Taking technologically unskilled students and preparing them, in three intensive weeks, with computer skills, the capacity for Internet navigation, and a set of academic projects aimed at benchmarks beyond their current grade level was an untried model. Additionally, having the students assume at-home and at-school responsibility for a new laptop computer added a dimension of uncertainty.

PROJECT SETTING

An overview of Shasta County helps paint the picture of what some refer to as "Cal-Appalachia," a Delaware-sized county with 30,000 students scattered among 25 small school districts. Redding is the only city large enough (80,000) to have an urban center. Economic problems, due to a major shrinkage in the land-based economy (e.g., timber, mining), are evidenced by 14% unemployment; 11,906 community members who receive food stamps, nearly 10,000 recipients of assistance from the local Aid for Dependent Children program, 467 children in foster care placements, and of over 4,000 Medi-Cal recipients.

The county's school children, like those in most counties in the extreme north of California, are predominately White and in the lower and lower-middle income brackets. It was not until June 1994 that any form of educational connectivity for Internet access reached the Shasta County Office of Education. The nearest four-year state postsecondary institution is 75 miles away. Most of the county's high school graduates who remain enlist in service-related work not requiring extensive postsecondary education. A few (estimated at 2%) attend four-year postsecondary institutions and matriculate through to graduation at the bachelor's level in four years.

The Migrant Population

Into this setting, a new Asian population was introduced in the 1980s. Mostly tribal people from Cambodia and Thailand, these Southeast Asian immigrants were relocated as agreements were reached in the post-Vietnam War era. These Hmong and Mien residents have had a somewhat difficult time succeeding, due to many factors.

They have little or no formal education, they lack exposure to the English language, and their own native spoken languages have no written alphabets. Shasta County offers them limited opportunities for employment, but is the scene of much racial discord. Children growing up as American teenagers often serve as the family's interpreter on important issues.

THE ACADEMY MODEL

Program Participants

The eight students were selected for the summer academy because they were the most at-risk of all populations, and as new seventh graders they occupy a window of teachability. All were eligible for benefits as "migrants," seven were Asian, and none had computer skills before attending the summer academy. Three school districts were represented by the students, with six from a single school and seven of the eight female. It was our hope that the academy would help advance females to leadership roles in school, at home, and in the Southeast Asian subculture.

The eight teachers came from eight different school districts, and all were White. Teachers were selected on the basis of experience with migrant students, computer literacy, and enthusiasm for the program. Each filled out an application and was interviewed by telephone. Some were recruited through e-mail announcements, some through administrator referral, and some by our contacts with them in school and prior to the academy. For the 8 available positions, some 22 applications were submitted, and three teachers consented to being on the alternate list.

Program Structure

The academy was structured in two phases. Phase one was a three-day, teacher-only preinstitute in which teachers acquired or refined computer skills aimed at Internet use and assisted in planning some of the lessons for the students. The 11 days remaining included the students, who were immediately paired in a tutorial learning relationship with the teachers. Pairs rotated throughout this period so that all had contact with each other. In the final days, teacher-student "permanent pairs" were made, and it would be these pairs that worked together between the end of the summer academy and the start of the regular school year.

Lessons in the academy were provided by several teachers and presenters. The lead designer was the director of the Shasta County Office of Education's Technology Resources Center, but much of the science and language arts content was developed by technical networking staff, consultants, and local teachers who were part of the California Telementor program. A presenter from the local museum community (Shasta Natural Science Association) and a California State University at Chico Science Project representative also made contributions. Teachers sat side by side with the students as they first learned in a networked lab equipped with full, direct Internet access, and then later as they learned to operate their laptops and dial in to the Internet server.

The academic content was crafted around six scientific processes (observing, comparing, ordering, communicating, categorizing, and relating), a conceptual set appropriate for middle schoolers but new to these students. The Internet was used as the source for over half the assignments. E-mail was the primary means of communicating, and it immediately became the single most popular tool of the academy, allowing as it did for close communication without the fear often experienced by these students in face-to-face interaction. Students began taking their laptops home with them on a limited basis in the last week so that technical snags could be addressed and relearning could occur before the students were on their own for an extended (6-week) period. One student had technical problems, and when her system came back online she had over 70 e-mail messages waiting.

Woven into the academy was a strong family component, which required responsible adults to be present at designated times to sign various permission forms and Internet use agreements, while simultaneously being shown the benefits of what was being learned. Given that most of the students' parents were non-English speaking and unfamiliar with Internet connectivity, it was an unanticipated positive consequence of the academy that each student's family became involved in the program. On the last day, we held a luncheon celebration in which the students served as tutorial guides for their extended families and a number of local civic dignitaries and businesspersons who were present to inspect the academy's results. That moment was an authentic demonstration in which shy, computer illiterate students became confident presenters with their laptops dialed in, taking family members and community leaders out for "drives on the Information Superhighway."

Performance Benchmarks

In the six weeks between the end of the academy and the first reunion of the 16, there were several monitored benchmarks to be achieved. One was the safe care and use of the laptop as an educational tool that would not sit idle. Students and teachers had to be in regular communication with no more than a 3-day interval between communications. (The Shasta County Office of Education staff involved in the academy was also a part of this communication circuit.)

Another outcome was the completion of a weather-watching science project in which students were given thermometers and an Internet online Netscape form for data submission, so that they were taking local temperature readings and comparing them with both the Internet temperatures for our area from the National Weather Service and with a city of their choosing on another continent. A third outcome was the completion of seven separate lessons that reinforced their Internet access skills and language arts proficiency. Work toward all outcomes was exchanged electronically, even though home phone numbers were exchanged between "permanent partners" on a need-to-know basis in case the laptops malfunctioned and they could not use e-mail.

One of the stipulations for teachers in the academy was to become an advocate with the students' regular classroom teachers when school resumed in the fall. One of the anticipated challenges in this model was making the bridge between the regular classroom teachers' lessons and the new skills these eight students would possess. Most classroom teachers design lessons and evaluate results based on students not having ready dial-in access to the Internet, so a major question in our minds was: "To what extent would the students be able to successfully use their laptops to perform better in regular classes?" We had evaluation data taken at the end of the academy, which strongly suggested the students had grown in several content areas, such as computer literacy, technology and scientific vocabulary, and Internet information management. Anecdotal data suggested growth in communication skills as measured by an ability to present to others, but we had no indication as to growth in language arts, and we could only guess about how the power of portable Internet connectivity would be used for performance growth as measured by nonacademy regular teachers.

OUTCOMES OF THE ACADEMY

A reunion with MSA teachers, students, trainers, and staff was held one month into the school year, and the overall outcomes were pleasingly within expectations. We gathered the 16 participants together for a day of evaluation, skill acquisition in more advanced computer applications, and preparation for the next 10 weeks of laptop use before they had to return the machines to the County Office of Education for use by the next Academy.

After six weeks of use, only one laptop computer had sustained any damage, specifically to a floppy disk drive. Although some students registered less activity with the computer than others, all used them on a regular basis. One student reported some fear in working with the computer centered around his apprehension about doing something to "mess up" the machine. Anecdotal reports from the students indicated their comfort in using the computer, their creativity in solving problems (e.g., getting documents printed), and their willingness to use the units for classroom projects that had been on the rise. Students had written reports on the laptops, used them in GATE programs, and e-mailed school and government officials. Some had trouble remaining in contact with partner-teachers, although some of the problem was culturally based fear of authority figures. School administrators at the participating schools provided positive reports of these students using computers in their homes and the potential for greater use at school.

The teacher participants reported that their own lessons had grown in richness due to Internet-gleaned source material, and that they had been given opportunities to present their newfound knowledge at inservice meetings and in the classroom. Several benchmarks for MSA students in the remaining weeks of the semester were developed by teachers and trainers, and teachers were asked for feedback on the progress of students in the program. This set of student assignments included in-class connectivity exercises, electronic communication links with others online (e.g., principals), and Internet demonstration activities.

CONCLUSIONS

The summer academy was an experiment in telecommunications training and application focused on an unlikely population of students that is often on the outskirts of educational progress. For many in the program, computers were still a mystery, and special attention was an unknown. At the conclusion of the program, eight students were leaders in technology knowledge in their schools and had become resources to their teachers, peers, and families, indicating a solid future for these kinds of projects.

One of the planning elements of the summer academy was the anticipated grant for a three-year expanded program in the same arena. The Program Improvement Project grant awarded in August was designed to further the work with migrant students begun by the MSA, primarily by extending the work of the trained teachers and students into other grade levels during the regular school year. It was necessary to plan for the purchase of additional laptop computers and other equipment to recruit more teacher participants, to arrange for space usage and substitutes in the schools, and to alter training schedules in the County Office of Education to accommodate a much larger group. In addition, the Department of Migrant Education was required to identify students who were eligible for migrant programs in order to insure equity in selecting student participants. In effect, the MSA served as the springboard for a much more extensive effort at moving migrant students to the forefront of school success.

The California Department of Migrant Education had various staff on hand to observe the operation of the MSA and ensure the progress of the program. They also sent representatives to the reunion, and a local television station with network affiliation was on hand to interview students and teachers. Continuation into the 1996-97 regular school year includes 16 new students and 5 new teachers, and funding for the program is nearly $50,000. Evaluation of the program, related to the benchmark activities, will continue into the Spring semester.

Suggestions for Replication

Because of the timing of the program, some limitations on school involvement were encountered. The following observations may help others wishing to replicate this program:

- Taking place during the summer, the program had few links to school sites and administrators.
- The connection with curriculum was weak because the students did not have an active curriculum context during the summer months.
- Students were hesitant to take laptop computers to school for fear of loss, damage, theft, and "sticking out" socially, the latter being somewhat attributable to the Southeast Asian subculture with its emphasis on unassuming, reserved behavior.

Our experience is that the strength of the curriculum and the support network (staff, teachers) during the regular school year is important for the success of the program. Partnering students with teachers is a vital link, and this group of students in particular needs continual encouragement and affirmation from respected adults not just to perform, but to excel.

III

PERSPECTIVES

11

EXPLOITING EDUCATIONAL FEATURES OF COMMERCIAL ONLINE SERVICES

Steve Hackbarth

GAPS BETWEEN TEACHERS' KNOWLEDGE AND STUDENTS' INTERESTS

We hear of teachers and students collaborating internationally on projects via the Internet. This past year I've been installing computers in Manhattan classrooms and trying to persuade the more hesitant teachers that they might be of some use. At both of the elementary schools where I consult, plans are underway to "get wired." This past year I have restored to life scores of classroom computers that had only loose wires (often merely unplugged).

A few years ago I obtained four more commercial online service accounts in addition to the one I had been using primarily for e-mail while studying to satisfy state teaching credential requirements at New York University (NYU). This enabled me to draft a concluding chapter for *The Educational Technology Handbook: A Comprehensive Guide* (Hackbarth, 1996b). After two years of reading, classes, conferences, workshops, and online experiences, it still took me several months to bring that chapter up to date for publication. Internet gophering was out; Web browsing was in. However, few of the teacher credential candidates I met at NYU (1993-95) took advantage of the free e-mail accounts, and none of the courses I completed in 45 units of elementary and special education made any use of computers. I took courses in "computer literacy" and "photorealistic imaging for instruction" as electives, not to fulfill degree requirements.

Strong evidence that my experiences have not been unique is presented by Edwin George ("What Should We Be Teaching Preservice Teachers About the Internet?") in Volume III of this series. At the end of the school term (June 1995), I asked my Public School (P.S. 6) third and fourth graders what they wanted to study the coming fall term. On nearly every team list was the "Internet." The next fall term, as students walked into the P.S. 116 library, where three new Macs had been installed with reference software, their first question was: "Are they connected to America Online?" During a midterm assessment, I asked them what they would like to add to our computer sessions. The Internet and the World Wide Web were mentioned as often as "more games."

As I continued installing computers in fifth-grade classrooms, one teacher said, "I think we can perhaps start some keyboarding practice next month." Another said that the students would have some essays to type next spring. A consensus among resistant teachers was: "We don't have time for that stuff." A justified attitude among many was: "I may not know much about computers, but what I do, I do very well!" On the contrary, many teachers were enthusiastic about the arrival of new computers, although few used their own for anything other than word processing.

Student classroom use generally was not integrated into the curriculum—bits of Oregon Trail (shoot the buffalo), SimCity 2000 (pick a disaster), Kid Pix (blow it up), and Wheel of Fortune (guess). No wonder that when I administered my Computer Literacy Assessment Tool, over 90% of the students selected in response to "How do you feel about computers?" the option "I love them."

Even among the most enthusiastic teachers there has been very low tolerance for printer woes, much less RAM jams and software complexities. Let the custodian unplug the machines over the weekend, and they soon disappear under stacks of books, reams of paper, and piles of dust. In one classroom I found diskettes buried under pencil sharpener shavings. Low levels of integrating computer use into classrooms is documented well in Henryk Marcinkiewicz's "Will Teachers Use Educational Computing Technology?" (in Volume II of this series).

Why is there such a gap between teachers' pedagogical expertise and computer utilization? Between teacher priorities and student interest in electronic media? How might progress be made in bridging these gaps? The primary purpose of this chapter is to suggest some ways in which teachers and students can quickly and confidently get up to speed on the information superhighway, largely by exploiting for valid educational purposes the rich features of easily navigated commercial online services.

EDUCATIONAL AIMS

Use of computer technology in schools must be justified in terms of aims of education. Think for a moment about such aims. Go ahead and write them.

Steeped in the history and philosophy of education as I am, my list ranges from "prepare for productive citizenship" to "develop good character." Perhaps you placed "becoming independent learners" at the top of your list, or "empowerment." There are no wrong answers as long as they satisfy the criterion implied in the word "education," that is, that the aims be "worthwhile" ones.

Educational aims are a bit unwieldy. To facilitate communication and planning we tend to speak in terms of goals and objectives. Thus, we have districtwide, year-long goals for each of the subjects taught in schools, and from these teachers (ideally) collaborate with students in deriving instructional objectives for lesson units. Very broadly speaking, most goals have to do with facility in the acquisition and utilization of knowledge, what we call "information literacy." Included here are development of skills in problem finding and solving, disciplinary and multidisciplinary modes of inquiry, and, of course, communications, both oral and written. Equally important are the development of positive attitudes and sound values.

Placed in the context of curricular goals, it becomes clear how computer technology generally, and online services particularly, can contribute. Those of us who see value in a focus on each student's construction of personally significant meaning within a socially constructed reality can find rich multimedia resources in addition to "quality literature." Those of us who are asking "Who is going to find cures for breast cancer and AIDS, negotiate settlements among warring ethnic factions, and prevent collapse of the biosphere?" find promise in computer-based learning and telecommunications.

EXPLOITING ONLINE FEATURES

Throughout the four-volume series, "Wired Together: The Online Classroom in K-12," and in the references listed at the end of this chapter, are detailed descriptions of features of computer-mediated communications. See especially Gerald Santoro's foundational "What is the Online Classroom?," in this volume and Mauri Collins' instructive "Computer Networks and Networking: A Primer" in Volume III. But do not be overwhelmed by buzzwords like TCP/IP, FTP, WAIS, Gopher, Archie's friends, URLs, HTML, Mosaic, Hot Java, and VRML. Basically, we plug our computers into a telephone jack and thereby gain direct access to thousands of institutional computers and, indirectly, to people similarly connected. Thus, we are able to send and receive messages, obtain information, and share information.

In this section, I describe how these basic capacities are embodied in America Online (AOL), CompuServe, and Prodigy, all of which I have subscribed to for several years. Although I do not describe here features of the relatively new Microsoft Network, published sources assure us that it is equally refined and valuable. Also not covered are those commercial enterprises (e.g., International Discount Communications, which boldly advertised "unlimited sex"; Netcom, an award winning service) that provide direct access to the Internet and its World-Wide Web, rather than being based primarily on intermember communications and in-house resources.

Communications

Language arts surely is at the core of the school curriculum. Advocates of "whole language" watch for and cultivate "emergent literacy" while immersing students in the world of print. Others stress acquisition of basic skills, yet still in the context of acquiring and sharing information, or "constructing meaning," if you prefer. Listening, speaking, reading, and writing rightfully dominate classroom life from prekindergarten through graduate school.

Facility with language enables us to function effectively as social beings and as productive citizens. The quality of thought, per se, the efficacy of decision making, perhaps even the depth of compassion, all may be rooted in language. What opportunities for language use, including social interaction, are afforded by commercial online services?

Research findings by Kallen Tsikalas (1995) about youngsters' use of the Internet should come as no surprise. Kids love to chat and send e-mail, and making friends takes precedence over gathering information. The commercial online services provide niches for unstructured interactions among children that are, I believe, a bit better monitored than those found on the raw Net. AOL has a "Kids Only" area; CompuServe has separate student "forums" for kids, teens, and adults; and Prodigy has its "Kids Zone" and "Teen Turf." Within these carefully constructed and monitored virtual communities, children can express themselves in chat rooms, on bulletin boards, and via e-mail.

Adherence to well-publicized and enforced rules of "Netiquette," with their admonitions to be considerate of others, serves to shape and generally reinforce proper conduct.

Verbal expression without knowledgeable guidance and feedback, however, is of limited academic value. Better are the classroom-based Internet projects that engage keypals across the globe in collaborative writing and research. For example, see the enlightening chapter by Annette Christy, "Key Pals: The Goodwill Ambassadors of the 1990s," in Volume IV. See also Tom Brush's chapter entitled "Using CMC to Bring Real-World Expertise into the Classroom: The Electronic 'PenPal' Project." Wentworth Worldwide Media's periodical, *Classroom Connect: Your Practical Monthly Guide to Using the Internet and Commercial Online Services*, regularly describes collaborative classroom projects and lists requests for student keypals by grade level. Fortunately, the commercial online services all provide easy access to the Internet where these virtual learning communities blossom.

Teachers, too, might like to exchange ideas with colleagues and parents. Prodigy has a "Teachers' Center" area linked to its "Education/K-12" Web page. CompuServe has teacher and parent areas within its "Education" section. AOL has its "Educators' Network" with links to an "American Federation of Teachers" area, an "Association for Supervision & Curriculum Development" area, "The Idea Exchange," the "Forum on Technology in Education & Training," the "National Education Association Public Forum," the "National Principals' Center," and "The Teachers' Forum," to name a few.

Teachers and students alike also can interact (read, post, and chat) with like-minded souls in special interest forums. A sample of AOL's "Clubs & Interest" areas include "Astronomy Club," "Black Voices," "Book Nook," "Deaf Community," "Image Exchange" (including "Art for Kids"), "Religion & Beliefs," "Writers Club," and "Youth Service America" (ServeNet: The Action Network for National and Community Service). Prodigy has its own topical "Bulletin Boards," where members can read and post messages. Within the "Education BB" alone are listed over 20 topics, from "Arts in Education" and "Distance Learning" to "Software/Technology" and "Special Education." CompuServe members can find people sharing their interests under "Home & Leisure." Within this area is a section on "Hobbies," where I discovered the "Photography Forum." Here aspiring amateurs and professionals alike upload samples of their work and receive suggestions for improving it. Such mingling is an example of "scholarly apprenticeship," a wonderful way for students to learn, one that is highly engaging and that ensures transfer to "real life." CompuServe's "Education" area has a "Foreign Language Forum," a "Science and Math Forum," a "Disabilities Forum," and a "ZD [Ziff-Davis Publishing Co.] Education Forum." These nicely managed forum resources, perhaps relatively provincial, surely complement the thousands of topic-specific listservs and bulletin boards that may be found on the Internet.

Other chapters in this series of books cover well the special benefits that computer-mediated communications afford speakers of English as a second language (see Volume IV) and people with physical and sensory challenges. See, for example, Sheryl Burgstahler's "Students with Disabilities and the Online Classroom" (in Volume I) and Leisa Winrich's "Improving Communications Skills in Learning Disabled Students Through Immersion in a Science/E-mail Based Curriculum" (in Volume II). As a hard-of-hearing person myself, I especially appreciate the Volume II chapters by Cathy Brandt, Joy Kreeft Peyton, and Martha French pertaining to accomplishments of students who are deaf.

Information Retrieval

My conception of information retrieval is multifaceted: parts are based on first-hand experience, others on the philosophies of Alfred North Whitehead, John Dewey, Jerome Bruner, and others. From Whitehead we were granted an initial romantic stage in our quests for knowledge. Dewey emphasized active hypothesis creation and testing—"trying and undergoing." Bruner formalized the concept of a spiral curriculum, the systematic and cumulative acquisition of knowledge within and across disciplines.

My dissertation studies essentially entailed trying to make sense out of what it might mean to "integrate cognitive and affective dimensions of learning." Thus, I derived a tentative conception of what some then called "confluent education," in which students are engaged in spirited, creative, reflective recapitulations of the social construction of knowledge. An update of this analysis now is available in a book edited by Joel Brown (Hackbarth, 1996a) .

In all these aspects of more or less systematic inquiry, commercial online services have much to contribute. All have vast stores of information—news, references, and file libraries. AOL features "Reuter's Hourly News Summary" as well as electronic versions of *The New York Times* and the *Chicago Tribune*. Its "Newsstand" also has a host of magazines, from *Consumer Reports* to *Multimedia World*. Can you search your stack of back issues by keywords? Here you can! AOL also regularly identifies "Top Internet Sites" and provides links to the Internet-based *The Daily News World Wide*, *Electronic Newsstand*, the *San Jose Mercury News*, *TIME World Wide*, and *Web Review*. Prodigy offers *Access Atlanta*, *Gateway Virginia*, the *Houston Chronicle Interactive*, *Newsday Direct*, *On Wisconsin*, and *Tampa Bay Online*, plus *Newsweek Interactive* (with photos and sound), *Sports Illustrated for Kids*, *ZD Net*, and links to magazines on the Web such as *Life*, *People*, *Smithsonian*, and *U.S. News & World Report*.

CompuServe is the only true international commercial service among the three. There you'll find the *Jerusalem Post, Le Monde, Neue Zuercher Zeitung, UK Newspaper Library,* along with *News Source USA* and magazines galore. CompuServe's "Executive News Service" collects articles continuously according to criteria we specify. We download our personalized "newspapers" at our convenience. Again, where AOL and Prodigy offer keyword searchable dictionaries and multimedia encyclopedias, CompuServe has (extra charges apply) the *Knowledge Index, Magazine Database Plus, Newspaper Archives, Government Publications, Magellan Geographix Maps,* and *Books in Print.* Where AOL has (no extra charge) "Homework Help" and Prodigy has (monthly fee) "Homework Helper," CompuServe provides (for a fee) access to the Educational Resource and Information Center (ERIC) database, and to its own "IQuest," with its (for a fee) access to thousands of periodicals and live, interactive research assistance.

Other sources of current information abound on all three services. AOL's "Academic Assistance Center," for example, has "Online Courses," "Career Center," "The Congressional Quarterly," "The Discovery Channel," the "Electronic University Network," "Financial Aid/Grant Info," and "National Public Radio Outreach," just to name a few. Its "Teacher Information Network" includes the "Access Excellence—Biology" program, "Educational Software Libraries," "Lesson Plan Libraries," "The Exam Exchange," and "The Multimedia Exchange." AOL's "Kids Only" area has "Club KidSoft," "Scholastic Kids World," and "Computer Stuff!!" with its "*HomePC* Software Reviews," "PC Programming—Tutorials," and a "Graphics Library." Prodigy's "Kids Zone" features "Learning Adventures," "Reading Magic," "Sesame Street," "Film Reviews," "Nova," "Science News," "National Geographic," and "Television." Its "Teen Turf" has "Beyond Belief," "Carmen Sandiego," "Computers," "Cultures," "People News," and links to such Web sites as "Planet Teenager," "Teens Web Page," and "Virtual Library." Again, CompuServe has three separate student forums—kids, teens, and adults. Each has its own chat areas and file libraries. Messages posted on each forum's bulletin boards (and downloadable text, graphics, and computer program files) can be searched by keyword, author, and date.

Prodigy's ever-expanding list of "Interest Groups" take the form of "interactive Web pages for whatever you're into." Among the 200 topics available are "Artist Resources," "Black Experience," "Books," "Distance Learning," "Education/K-12," "HIV/AIDS," "Latin America," "Native American," "Service Clubs," "Spanish-Speaking World," "Women's Connection," and "Writing Workshop." Each has current information, references, and links to other Web resources across the Internet. For example, the "Education/K-12" Web page table of contents lists "Curriculum Areas," "Teachers' Center," "References," "Arts

Enrichment Center," "Guide to Colleges & Universities," "Parents' Resources," "Schools K12 on the Internet," "Contests & Hot Deals," and "Prodigy's Educational Resources."

Prodigy Webmaster Rita Laws predicted that the second edition of my textbook for teachers will be about Web-based learning from cover to cover, rather than merely the present single chapter. In that book (call it a "Gutenberg home page," filled as it is with references and the phone numbers, e-mail addresses, and URLs of sources), I echo the concerns of many about the "mix of gold and litter" along the information superhighway, reminiscent of earlier technologies that have been held up as panaceas.

The fresh layers of rich and original resources available on the Internet are intermingled with the whimsical postings of "newbies," the "roadkill" of vandals, and the opinions of self-proclaimed "experts." Imagine what the Library of Congress would look like if everyone over the age of eight published whatever came into their heads! The more I hear about the blossoming of Web home pages, the more I wonder if we are entering an "Age of Neo-Scholasticism," where encyclopedic rendition passes for the Classics. Thus, teachers and students need to exercise considerable skill in locating information related to their research topics and good judgment in assessing its validity.

On a much darker side, the Internet abounds with hate mongering and pornography. To date, there are no sure ways to block children from being exposed. Let's face it, they seek out such sites eagerly, if not in your home, at the latch-key kid's house, where my own daughter long ago used to indulge thoroughly her tastes for sweets and television, and where later her friends talked to passing truckers via CB radios. Teachers and parents alike will want to study and apply with care the informative, timely chapter in this volume by Lynne Schrum and Kay Day, "The Internet and Acceptable Use Policies: What Schools Need to Know." Because children cannot be fully protected, they need to be guided in the taking of personal responsibility.

I am an advocate of commercial online services for school use in part (that is, aside from high quality of resources and ease of navigation) because: (a) contributors to forum libraries and chat sessions can be identified, (b) parents and teachers can block access to selected features, (c) bulletin board postings are monitored (some would say "censored"), (d) members are held to a code of conduct (under threat of account termination), and (e) corporations are legally liable. Take the case of CompuServe, which blocked its members' access to the most offensive Internet sites. Although the threat of legal action originated in Germany, the blockage took effect worldwide. In an apparently related action, CompuServe concentrated its vast collection of nude images to "just" three forum libraries, where members must claim to be at least 18 years of age to gain access. With some 20,000 downloads each for many nude images, compared with dozens of downloads for other types, do not expect these to disappear any time soon. AOL and Prodigy are relatively restrained in this area (no frontal nudity), and all three services are quite tame (no acts of violence nor sexual activity are depicted) compared to what goes on via the Internet (the most "graphic" of language and of still and moving images).

Information Sharing

Once information has been collected systematically and pieced together into illuminating, dynamic mosaics we call "knowledge," teachers and students typically share what they have learned (or constructed). We might produce illustrated written reports, video scripts, or multimedia portfolios. Commercial online services and the Internet open up new avenues of sharing among teachers and students worldwide.

Considerable sharing of information takes place in chat rooms and on bulletin boards. Here questions are posed, and everyone can take a shot at providing answers or more questions. Works in progress can be uploaded into the appropriate forum library for review by peers. My own uploading of the preface to my book about educational technology resulted in scores of requests for prepublication diskettes from members of each of the three services. Several members provided helpful suggestions that I incorporated into the final draft. My posting on a leading organizational Internet gopher site resulted in comparatively few responses.

Teachers have uploaded into forum libraries everything from lesson plans and exams to instructional programs. The resultant field testing and feedback is an instance of what constitutes the very essence of educational technology as an iterative process. Students, too, are able to exchange samples of their writing, drawings, and photos and to receive comments from peers. Such opportunities for sharing really energizes effort and encourages critical self-assessment prior to "publication."

A special advantage of commercial online services is that members are able to construct and display (at no additional charge) their own Web home pages. Crafting an attractive, informative, multimedia personal Web page can be an extension of students' putting together their classroom portfolios. These evolving products permit drawing on diverse resources, selecting what is most expressive of one's self and sharing that with others (see Lamb, 1996). Also valuable are projects in which students collaborate in constructing a Web page for their school. Wentworth Worldwide Media (connect@wentworth.com) hosts such pages on its server free of charge.

RECOMMENDATIONS

Today's students and teachers have access to vast resources. Classrooms are filled with books, audiotapes, and videos. Nearby libraries and computer labs offer more opportunities for learning. The virtues of commercial online services need be assessed in relation to what they offer more effectively or efficiently than more traditional sources. Educators need to reflect on merits and costs of e-mail versus snail mail and telephone, online browsing versus opening a book or viewing a video, singing and dancing versus sitting, hands-on experiences versus simulated ones.

Getting the most out of online services requires much offline effort. First, we have to become familiar with the hardware, features, and navigation tools. Then we have to engage our students in planning. Problems need be found and defined and hypotheses proposed before decisions about the best sources can be made. Inquiries need to be discipline-based, not random. Interdisciplinary study at its best evolves out of knowledge of how historians, economists, mathematicians, artists, and scientists conduct their distinctive enterprises. Except during "chat," written communications need to be first drafted by hand. The process-writing activities of brainstorming, prioritizing, outlining, elaborating, editing, sharing, and revising are no less important in online communications than in producing term papers and newsletters (Hackbarth, in press; Rowland & Kinnaman, 1995).

In their use of online services, teachers need to exercise caution. Although the services permit restricting access to the "pink" bulletin boards with their racy content, the Internet abounds with pornographic, sexist, and racist material. The commercial bulletin boards are monitored, but students could subscribe to listservs of every conceivable persuasion. Worst, unless they are warned, students could be enticed to meet adult strangers posing as peers.

Much random exploration of online services can be justified in terms of students gaining familiarity with an exciting and empowering medium. However, as we focus on achievement of higher aims of education, time spent online needs to be made at least as productive as activities it displaces.

BUILDING BRIDGES TO THE INFORMATION SUPERHIGHWAY

I began this chapter with illustrations of gaps that appear between teachers' perceptions of their proper roles and what contributions computer technology might be able to make, and between some of their apprehensive attitudes toward this technology and their students' unbridled enthusiasm. As a computer specialist teacher in Manhattan, it has been my job to integrate computer technology into elementary school classrooms. Students generally react to "computer time" with glee. Teachers' attitudes span the range, and I mean from enabling to *dis*abling. Larry Cuban (1995), in his analysis of why many teachers reject computers, as they did television before, identified perceived efficiency as a core criterion. He rightly gave teachers credit for setting justified priorities and for devising effective means of achieving both the mundane and highest aims of education. The truth of Cuban's observations has been revealed to me over the past few years in my daily encounters with bright, dedicated, and knowledgeable teachers.

In every case, I assure teachers that what they value, and how they perceive their roles, will not be violated. Teachers generally value oral and written expression, collaborative learning, interpersonal skill and character development, information literacy, and creative expression. I observe how they translate these values into classroom activities and coordinate my lessons to fit in. They cherish process writing. I engage their students in drafting and editing prior to keyboarding. They want their students to collect information and data. I suggest print, video, human, CD-ROM, and Internet sources.

The Internet itself is vast and raw. Yet surely there are treasure troves of information for those with the skills to determine both what is needed and where to find it. Commercial online services evolved rich features long before they connected to the Internet and its World-Wide Web. Navigating these features has been made transparent to ensure commercial success. Disconnects are less frequent than encountered on the Internet, access to features generally is assured, areas of interest are easily located, and content generally is current (and most likely will remain so long after many Web sites become cobWebs). Thus, for the industry standard of five hours per month of connect time for about 10 dollars, and about three dollars per hour thereafter, teachers quickly can gain expertise and confidence. High usage options permit about 20 hours of access a month for about 20 dollars; schools get annual rates.

Skills gained while exploring areas of personal interest readily translate to making productive professional use of both commercial and Internet resources. Thus armed and assured, we all can better collaborate with our already eager students in efficiently exploiting features of the ever evolving information superhighway to achieve the most ambitious of educational aims.

REFERENCES

Cuban, L. (1995). Déjà vu all over again? *Electronic Learning, 15*(2), 34-37, 61.

Hackbarth, S. (1996a). Confluent education: An analysis from the perspective of Merleau-Ponty's philosophy. In J. H. Brown (Ed.), *Confluence in education: Integrating consciousness for human change* (pp. 17-42). Greenwich, CT: JAI Press.

Hackbarth, S. (1996b). *The educational technology handbook: A comprehensive guide—process and products for learning.* Englewood Cliffs, NJ: Educational Technology Publications.

Hackbarth, S. (in press). Web-based learning in the context of K-12 schooling. In R.C. Branch & B.B. Minor (Eds.), *The educational media and technology yearbook 1997.* Englewood, CO: Libraries Unlimited.

Lamb, A.C. (1996). *Spin your own Web site using HTML.* Evansville, IN: Vision To Action.

Rowland, R., & Kinnaman, D. (1995). *Researching on the Internet: The complete guide to finding, evaluating, and organizing information effectively.* Rocklin, CA: Proma Publishing.

Tsikalas, K. (1995). Internet-based learning? *Electronic Learning, 14*(7), 14-15.

SUGGESTED READINGS

Albinus, P., & Blumenfeld, J.R. (1995). Ride the wave with graphical online services. *Windows Magazine, 6*(10), 228-236.

Armstrong, S. (1995). *Telecommunications in the classroom* (2nd ed.). Eugene, OR: International Society for Technology in Education.

Banks, M. (1994). *Welcome to . . . CompuServe for Windows: From mystery to mastery.* New York: MIS Press.

Berge, Z.L., & Collins, M.P. (Eds.). (1995). *Computer-mediated communication and the online classroom* (Vols. I, II, and III). Cresskill, NJ: Hampton Press.

Boe, T., Graubart, C., & Cappo, M. (1995). *World desk: A student handbook to Gopher and the World Wide Web.* Santa Cruz, CA: Learning in Motion.

Burbules, N.C., & Callister Jr., T.A. (1996). Knowledge at the crossroads: Some alternative futures of hypertext learning environments. *Educational Theory, 46*(1), 23-50.

Campbell, D., & Campbell, M. (1995). *The student's guide to doing research on the Internet.* Reading, MA: Addison-Wesley.

Clark, D. (1995). *The student's guide to the Internet.* Indianapolis: Alpha Books.

Cornish, M., & Monahan, B. (1996). A network primer for educators. *Educational Technology, 36*(2), 55-57.

Cotton, E.G. (1996). *The online classroom: Teaching with the Internet.* Syracuse, NY: ERIC/EdInfo Press.

Crawford, L. (1995). Kids in cyberspace: A smart, safe guide to online services. *The Computing Teacher, 22*(6), 12-14.

Cummins, J., & Sayers, D. (1995). *Brave new schools: Challenging cultural literacy through global learning networks.* New York: St. Martin's Press.

Davidson, H. (1996). Casting the Web. *Technology & Learning, 16*(6), 22.

Descy, D.E. (1995). Making a World-Wide Web page. *Tech Trends, 40*(5), 9-11.

Descy, D.E. (1996). NCSA Mosaic, Netscape, and Java/HotJava!! *Tech Trends, 41*(1), 6-8.

Descy, D.E. (in press). The Internet and education: Privacy and pitfalls. *Educational Technology.*

Dyrli, O.E. (1995). Personalizing politics. *Technology & Learning, 16*(3), 10.

Dyrli, O.E., & Kinnaman, D.E. (1995). Connecting classrooms: School is more than a place. *Technology & Learning, 15*(8), 82-88.

Dyrli, O.E., & Kinnaman, D.E. (1996a). Part 2: Energizing the classroom curriculum through telecommunications. *Technology & Learning, 16*(4), 65-70.

Dyrli, O.E., & Kinnaman, D.E. (1996b). Part 3: Teaching effectively with telecommunications. *Technology & Learning, 16*(5), 57-62.

Dyrli, O.E., & Kinnaman, D.E. (1996c). Part 4: Connecting with the world through successful telecommunications projects. *Technology & Learning, 16*(6), 57-62.

Dyrli, O.E., & Kinnaman, D.E. (1996d). Part 5: The changing face of telecommunications: What's next for schools? *Technology & Learning, 16*(7), 56-61.

Elliot, G.J., Jones, E., Cooke, A., & Baker, P. (1995). Making sense: A review of hypermedia in higher education. In H. Maurer (Ed.), *Educational multimedia and hypermedia, 1995: Proceedings of ED-MEDIA 95.* Charlottesville, VA: Association for the Advancement of Computing in Education.

Ellsworth, J.H. (1994). *Education on the Internet: A hands-on book of ideas, resources, projects, and advice.* Indianapolis: Sams Publishing.

Ellsworth, J.H., & Ellsworth, M.V. (1994). *Using CompuServe.* Indianapolis: Que.

Fetterman, D.M. (1996). Videoconferencing on-line: Enhancing communication over the Internet. *Educational Researcher, 25*(4), 23-27.

Flynn, C.E. (1995). *The unofficial Macintosh guide to America Online.* New York: Wiley.

Frazier, D., with Kurshan, B., & Armstrong, S. (1995). *Internet for kids.* Alameda, CA: SYBEX.

Frazier, G., & Frazier, D. (1994). *Telecommunications and education: Surfing and the art of change*. Alexandra, VA: National School Boards Association.

Gardner, D.C., Beatty, G.J., & Sauer, D. (1995). *Internet for Windows: America Online edition*. Rocklin, CA: Prima Publishing.

Giagnocavo, G., McLain, T., & DiStefano, V. (1995). *Educator's Internet companion—Classroom Connect's complete guide to educational resources on the Internet*. Lancaster, PA: Wentworth Worldwide Media.

Halliday, C.M. (1995). *The trail guide to Prodigy: A rapid-reading reference to using and cruising the Prodigy online service*. Reading, MA: Addison-Wesley.

Harmon, C. (1996). *Using the Internet, online services, & CD-ROMs for writing research and term papers*. New York: Neal-Schuman.

Harris, J. (1995a). Educational telecomputing activities: Problem-solving projects. *Learning and Leading with Technology, 22*(8), 59-63.

Harris, J. (1995b). *Way of the ferret: Finding and using educational resources on the Internet* (2nd ed.). Eugene, OR: International Society for Technology in Education.

Harris, J. (1995-96). Telehunting, telegathering, teleharvesting. *Learning and Leading with Technology, 23*(4), 36-39.

Heide, A., & Stilborne, L. (1996). *The teacher's complete & easy guide to the Internet*. Buffalo, NY: Trifolium Books.

Hill, J., & Buerger, B. (1996). Hypermedia as a bridge between education and profession. *Educational Technology Review, Winter*(5), 21-25.

Johnson, N.B. (1995). *Navigating the Internet with Prodigy*. Indianapolis: Sams.net Publishing.

Joseph, L. (1995). *World Link: An Internet guide for educators, parents, and students* (2nd ed.). Columbus, OH: Greyden Press.

Junion-Metz, G. (1996). *K-12 resources on the Internet: An instructional guide*. Berkeley: Library Solutions Press.

Kaufeld, J. (1995). *America Online for dummies*. Indianapolis: IDG Books.

Kearsley, G. (1996). The World Wide Web: Global access to education. *Educational Technology Review, Winter*(5), 26-30.

Kimeldorf, M. (1995). Teaching online—techniques and methods. *Learning and Leading with Technology, 23*(1), 26-31.

Krol, E., & Klopfenstein, B. (1996). *The whole Internet, academic edition*. Sebastopol, CA: O'Reilly & Associates.

Kurshan, B. (1996). Virtual communities: The Web of life and learning. *MultiMedia Schools, 3*(3), 24-26.

Lamb, A.C., & Johnson, L. (1995). *Cruisin' the information highway: Internet and the K-12 classroom*. Evansville, IN: Vision To Action.

Landeck, T. (1995). Curriculum and technology: Levels of integration. *Windows K-12 Classroom Resource, 1*(1), 14-15.

Laughton, S., & Hanson, W.R. (1996). Potholes on the Infobahn. *MultiMedia Schools, 3*(3), 14-23.

Leshin, C.B. (1995). *Internet adventures: Visiting virtual communities: A step-by-step guide for educators*. Phoenix, AZ: XPLORA Publishing.

Leshin, C.B. (1995). *Netscape adventures: Step-by-step guide to Netscape Navigator and the World Wide Web*. Phoenix, AZ: XPLORA Publishing.

Leshin, C.B. (1996). *Internet adventures: Step-by-step guide for finding and using educational resources*. Boston: Allyn & Bacon.

Lichty, T. (1994a). *America Online's Internet: Easy, graphical access—the AOL way, Macintosh edition*. Chapel Hill, NC: Ventana Press.

Lichty, T. (1994b). *America Online's Internet: Easy, graphical access—the AOL way, Windows edition*. Chapel Hill, NC: Ventana Press.

Lichty, T. (1994c). *The official America Online for Windows membership kit & tour guide* (2nd ed.). Chapel Hill, NC: Ventana Press.

Linn, M.C., & Muilenburg, L. (1996). Creating lifelong science learners: What models form a firm foundation? *Educational Researcher, 25*(5), 18-24.

Margolis, P.E. (1996). *Random House personal computer dictionary* (2nd ed.). New York: Random House.

McClain, T. (1995). *Educator's Internet companion*. Lancaster, PA: Wentworth Worldwide Media.

McClain, T., & DiStefano, V. (1995). *Educator's World Wide Web tour guide*. Lancaster, PA: Wentworth Worldwide Media.

McClain, T., & DiStefano, V. (1996). *Educator's essential Internet training system*. Lancaster, PA: Wentworth Worldwide Media.

McKenzie, J. (1995). Beforenet and afternet. *MultiMedia Schools, 2*(3), 6-8.

Meyers, E., & McIsaac, P. (1996). *Teachers guide to cyberspace*. New York: Impact II-The Teachers Network.

Miller, E.B. (1996). *The Internet resource directory for K-12 teachers and librarians* (95/96 ed.). Englewood, CO: Libraries Unlimited.

Miller, M. (1994). *Using CompuServe* (2nd ed.). Indianapolis: Que.

Milone Jr., M.N., & Salpeter, J. (1996). Technology and equity issues. *Technology & Learning, 16*(4), 38-47.

Moody, G. (1995). *The Internet with Windows*. Newton, MA: Butterworth-Heinemann.

O'Loughlin, L. (1995a). *Free stuff from America Online: Your guide to getting hundreds of valuable goodies*. Scottsdale, AZ: Coriolis Group Books.

O'Loughlin, L. (1995b). *Free stuff from CompuServe: Your guide to getting hundreds of valuable goodies*. Scottsdale, AZ: Coriolis Group Books.

Peters, M., & Lankshear, C. (1996). Critical literacy and digital texts. *Educational Theory, 46*(1), 51-70.

Pfaffenberger, B. (1995). *Que's computer & Internet dictionary* (6th ed.). Indianapolis: Que.

Pfaffenberger, B. (1996). *Publish it on the Web! Macintosh version*. Boston: AP Professional.

Pivovarnick, J. (1995). *The complete idiot's guide to America Online.* Indianapolis: Alpha Books.

Place, R., Dimmler, K., & Powell, T. (1996). *Educator's Internet yellow pages.* Englewood Cliffs, NJ: PTR Prentice Hall.

Polly, J.A. (1996). *The Internet kids yellow pages special edition.* Berkeley, Osborne McGraw-Hill.

Powell, N. (1996). Ready to be a cybernaut? In E. Meyers & P. McIsaac (Eds.), *Teachers guide to cyberspace* (pp. 65-75). New York: Impact II-The Teachers Network.

Price, J. (1995). *The trail guide to America Online: A rapid-reading reference to using and cruising the America Online service.* Reading, MA: Addison-Wesley.

Quinlan, L. (1996). Customizing Web documents for the classroom: An example from Lakeville High School's advanced composition class. *Tech Trends, 41*(2), 27-30.

Quinlan, L. (in press). Creating a classroom kaleidoscope. *Educational Technology.*

Roblyer, M.D., Dozier-Henry, O., & Burnette, A.P. (1996). Technology and multicultural education: The "uneasy alliance." *Educational Technology, 36*(3), 5-12.

Salpeter, J. (1995). Quit blaming teachers. *Technology & Learning, 16*(3), 6.

Salpeter, J. (1996). Why NetDay? *Technology & Learning, 16*(7), 5.

Sanchez, B., & Harris, J. (1996). Online mentoring: A success story. *Learning and Leading with Technology, 23*(8), 57-60.

Schofield, J.W. (1995). *Computers and classroom culture.* New York: Cambridge University Press.

Shafran, A. (1995). *The complete idiot's guide to CompuServe.* Indianapolis: Que.

Shotsberger, P.G. (1996). Instructional uses of the World Wide Web: Exemplars and precautions. *Educational Technology, 36*(2), 47-50.

Simpson, C.M. (1995). *Internet for library media specialists.* Worthington, OH: Linworth Publishing.

Starr, R.M. (in press). Delivering instruction on the World Wide Web: Overview and basic design principles. *Educational Technology.*

Steen, D.R., Roddy, M.R., Sheffield, D., & Stout, M.B. (1995) *Teaching with the Internet: Putting teachers before technology.* Bellevue, WA: Resolution Business Press.

Steinberg, G. (1995). *Special edition using America Online.* Indianapolis: Que.

Tyre, T. (1995). Commercial online services: Benefits for educators. *T.H.E. Journal, 23*(1), 44-45.

Valauskas, E.J., & Ertel, M. (1996). *The Internet for teachers and school library media specialists: Today's applications, tomorrow's prospects.* New York: Neil-Schuman.

Wagner, R. (1995). *Inside CompuServe* (3rd ed.). Indianapolis: New Riders Publishing.

Warschauer, M. (1995). *E-mail for English teaching: Bringing the Internet and computer learning networks into the language classroom*. Alexandria, VA: TESOL Publications.

Wentworth Worldwide Media (1996). *Educator's Internet companion: Classroom Connect's complete guide to educational resources on the Internet*. Lancaster, PA: Author.

Wentworth Worldwide Media. (1996). *Educator's World Wide Tourguide* (Rev. ed.). Lancaster, PA: Author.

Wiggins, R.R., & Tittle, E. (1995). *The trail guide to CompuServe: A rapid-reading reference to using and cruising the CompuServe online service*. Reading, MA: Addison-Wesley.

Williams, B. (1995). *The Internet for teachers*. Indianapolis: IDG Books.

12

TELECOMMUNICATIONS IN THE CLASSROOM IN AN OVERSEAS AMERICAN SCHOOL—INFORMATION SUPERHIGHWAY OR ROCKY ROAD?

Shabbi Luthra

Telecommunications technologies have opened up new and dynamic learning environments, providing creative and unlimited contexts for learning. For overseas American schools the idea of bringing telecommunications into the classroom is attractive. But beyond the initial excitement of participating in a project lie technical and logistical problems that turn the "information highway" into a rather rocky road. An increased awareness of the potential frustrations can make the experience of communicating with other schools educationally beneficial.

THE NEED

I teach at an overseas American school located in the capital of a developing nation. Overseas American schools generally serve the educational needs of children of diplomats and international businesspersons and follow an American curriculum. I teach a unique, culturally rich, and diverse student body. Our school is always searching for opportunities to extend ongoing, curriculum-related classroom activities through interaction with students from other parts of the world and the United States. The words electronic mail have become common vocabulary in today's world. Our children were interested in the process of how telecommunications takes place and how messages are sent and received. Telecommunications networks and projects served both our objectives: (a) to learn about telecommunications, and (b) communicate with children from other schools.

THE PROMISE OF TELECOMMUNICATIONS IN THE CLASSROOM

Our school participated in an exciting project that would link classrooms around the world via telecommunications. We were lured into the project's promise of an educational computer network that would bring together teachers and students from geographically and culturally diverse classrooms to work as a team to enhance teaching and learning. In theory the project's philosophy was educationally sound. The project's organizers, a commercial company, provided us, the participants, with both the direction and support necessary to creatively integrate communications technology into the classroom. The idea is attractive—integrating telecommunications with the school curriculum.

OUR EXPERIENCE

Information in these types of network projects is exchanged among the schools using a telephone line, modem, and software provided by the parent network. Messages are sent to a central computer, which then sorts and delivers them into electronic mail boxes from which they can be retrieved and read by schools who are participating in the project. Over a period of three years, three grade levels participated in these projects. Project lengths varied from six to nine weeks. One can say that we have had a significant amount of experience with commercial telecommunications networks to be able to opine about them.

What Worked

Students communicated information about their host country. Other schools found this information fascinating. It also enabled our students to learn more about and appreciate their host country's culture. Both teachers and students liked interacting with students from different parts of the United States. American students were able to learn a little more about their home country through this interaction because they have not lived in the United States for a long time.

Technical Cautions

I believe that integrating telecommunications is valuable if students are online and have easy access to electronic mail. Students in an overseas American school based in another country and culture would have benefited invaluably from an interactive experience with schools elsewhere in the world. Due to the technical difficulties associated with using telecommunications in developing nations, children were frustrated when they were unable to open their mailboxes.

The infrastructure in the country did not provide direct and easy access to electronic mail. In addition, the telephone costs were extremely high, and we felt were inconsistent with the promised educational value of the network. As one of the teachers who participated in a semester-long project noted: "I didn't feel like it was all that hands-on for the kids. They didn't *really* send emails and they didn't *really* receive emails. They couldn't do that. . . . Sometimes they'd be there a long time waiting to get a phone line to download. I know a lot of this was just insurmountable. There's just nothing you can do about that."

BEYOND THE PROMISE

Coordination

Another word of caution: Make sure that the network project's objectives and implementation plans are clearly and practically interwoven with its philosophy. In our experience, we were told that we would get much more than the technical links between classrooms; there would be a network of human resources for learning how to use telecommunications as an instructional tool. This, we hoped, would be done through the efforts of a project coordinator. Unfortunately, the coordinators are not consistently competent. At any given time our school was participating in two to three projects. This gave us first-hand experience in comparing the styles of different coordinators. There was a wide variance in the initiative and responsible attitude of each project's coordinator.

Participating Classes

At the heart of a network project is the interaction between students and teachers of different schools. Five to eight geographically diverse classrooms communicate with each other during the period of the project. The grade levels and classes are not chosen by the participating schools. They are matched by the parent network. The theoretical goal is to match teachers and students with other classrooms with common academic interests but from geographically and culturally diverse settings. Although the second criteria is generally easy to meet, the participating classrooms always seem to be randomly selected. For example, one of the fourth-grade classes at our school interacted with eight classes: Four of these were second- to third-grade classes, whereas the other four were fourth- or fifth-grade classes.

So what is the problem? The interaction between students revolves around a research or study project that each participating school sponsors. For any telecommunicating experience to be educationally valuable, we recommend that the classes are at the same grade level. The older grades, for example, grades 5 and 6, asked questions that were too difficult for younger grade students from grade 3. The questions required too lengthy and sophisticated an answer and/or were too complicated for third graders to answer without a lot of time and preparation. It might also be more manageable to have a smaller number of classes interacting with each other at any given time.

THE ROAD AHEAD (NO PUNS INTENDED)

We have not written off participation in telecommunications projects. The next time we do this, it will be very different. Electronic mail, which was basically the type of communication we indulged in, was an incredibly valuable tool, and many teachers noted that it had the potential to revolutionize the way we exchange information. Teachers and students enjoyed the idea of being able to contact this huge network of people who are, or at least seem to be, paying attention. Teachers found it valuable for research. For example, one of the classes conducted research on rivers. Students sent a survey requesting information, collected the data, and worked with the data by comparing/contrasting charts, and presenting it in a published format.

As an overseas American school we have to bear in mind that there are technicalities that we have to overcome. The logistics of time management go hand in hand with the technical cautions. As a result, we will be a lot more selective about the types of activities in which our children will be involved. Instead of organized network projects sponsored by a company, we would prefer independent projects sponsored by a classroom somewhere on this planet requesting participation. That would be exciting and interesting. If working in a group is required, it will be advisable to form our own group with no more than three classrooms, all of which are at the same grade level. If the grade levels are different, then just one classroom is enough.

CONCLUSIONS

Did we achieve our objectives of integrating telecommunications with the curriculum? Not in the manner we had hoped. But we learned a lot from the experiences. Students became aware of the real-world problems associated with using telecommunications in the developing world, an education in itself. Integrating the technology with the curriculum was exciting but became a challenge because of the profile of the participating schools. We are a lot wiser now about the need to weigh the costs, in terms of both time and money, against the benefits. Once the technical glitches are overcome, we can begin to provide students with new and dynamic learning environments for their projects—an exciting development.

13

UPDATING OUR MENTAL MODELS TO TAKE ADVANTAGE OF MODERN COMMUNICATION TECHNOLOGY TO PROMOTE CMC

Michael Szabo

This chapter reflects what I have come to understand as a significant, inhibitory issue in the use of Computer-Mediated Communication (CMC) and other innovations for educational purposes. Although on the surface, the complexity of learning how to use the technology effectively and access to it are certainly inhibitors. But a deeper problem exists with respect to how educators view teaching and learning with CMC. Over the years, we have built up belief systems and ways of knowing about this and other aspects of our real world. In this chapter, I refer to these as mental models.

I believe many of our mental models are stagnant and need to be rethought and reevaluated. In this chapter I discuss the concepts of mental models from the point of view of constructivism (do not let the term scare you) and why they should be reviewed. At the end of the chapter, I have selected several topics that relate to mental models possessed by educators based on my years of work with CMC at university, college, high school, and training levels. These topics were chosen because they have particular import to the use of CMC.

If by reading this you come to review, rethink, and update your mental models of learning with CMC, I will have met my goal in preparing this document. I will use the definition of *Computer Mediated*

Communication provided by Santoro in Chapter 3 of this book. Data are used to refer to isolated bits of information, which by themselves mean little or nothing. Data become information when, in the mind of the receiver, they have relevance or a relationship to some concept, principle, or model. For example, data may indicate that a car is traveling at 50 miles per hour. When it becomes evident that this car is heading for a stop sign and the road is icy, the data become important and perhaps life-saving information!

MENTAL MODELS: WHAT ARE THEY?

Education is about knowing and ways of knowing. It has been estimated that the mammalian eye can receive information at the rate of 10 billion bits per second! This volume of information would quickly build and overpower the most sophisticated computer networks available today. In addition to the many natural protective devices we possess to protect from information overload (perception, restricted field of vision, short-term memory, and sleeping during class), we also actively limit volumes of information by categorizing that which does not get discarded and forming principles or ideas that explain or help us make sense of the world we live in. These entities are referred to as mental models and have much to say about how we come to know.

Mental models are fluid constructs that explain how things work or exist in the form they do. We create them and have built them up over long periods of time through activities such as reading and through interacting with people and things and ideas and facts. We are limited in our model formation by many complex factors, such as perceptions that influence how we interpret facts and new information and color our thinking, inferences that we make during learning and store along with information learned, and the current state of our mental models.

Although there may be one true picture of the way the world "really is," there are probably as many different mental models of the world as there are people. As educated human beings, we hope and trust that there exists a high degree of congruence between the way the world "really is" and our mental model(s) of the world. As professional educators in the information age, we are particularly concerned with those mental models we hold that help us understand how our students learn and of the activities we have created to enable that learning to take place.

MENTAL MODELS AND CONSTRUCTIVIST LEARNING THEORY

Constructivism is an idea that has been around for centuries and is being reborn in expanded form with great vigor, often bordering on a "secular religious" following (Phillips, 1995). Constructivism has a direct bearing on the formation of mental models. In general, it proposes that perfect knowledge of the world is impossible. An example from everyday experience suggests it is impossible to perfectly know the length of the shoreline of an island. An example from theoretical physics states it is impossible to know precisely both the position and velocity of a subatomic particle (electron) at any given time. The latter concept apparently gave Albert Einstein some difficulty, causing him to exclaim that God does not play at dice.

Because perfect and complete understanding and knowledge about our world is not obtainable, according to the constructivist viewpoint (von Glasersfeld, 1988), a person's mental model of how the world works is more important than incomplete knowledge gleaned from other sources. Thus the constructivist argues that our best knowledge of the world is not absorbed or assimilated, but is actively constructed by the learner, showing up in the form of mental models. That is, knowing is not a spectator sport but one in which each individual must become actively and perhaps aggressively involved. As educators, we must lead our students into the process as well.

Although the evidence for constructivism is not strongly convincing, and there are major problems with its implementation and assessment, the idea is spreading and becoming so overwhelmingly popular it appears to be developing a life of its own. That is not to say that someday the research may or may not confirm the validity of the constructivist model.

The predominant literature focuses heavily on the creation of mental models as a way of knowing our world and those selected aspects of our world which we may have an intrinsic or other compelling interest to explore. Often constructivist literature takes a negative view of some forms of instruction, such as review and practice, objectives-driven curricula, and so forth. Rarely, however does it promote the idea that mental models can be quickly outdated and become erroneous. The chief implication of this shortcoming is the need to continuously review and revise our current and key mental models, while at the same time creating or shaping new ones. The purpose of this chapter is to inspire you to begin a never-ending process of explicating your mental models about the role of CMC in instruction and learning and then revise those models with the latest evidence you can find or create.

THE CARE AND FEEDING OF MENTAL MODELS

Initially we rely on common sense, supplemented by limited experience and internal and external controls to know our world and all that is in it. As we move into a university, we are impressed with the rational, scientific, logical, and empirical approach to the study of the world and begin to adopt it, while questioning our previous reliance on common sense that was limited by lack of experience. Finally, we move to the intuitive approach that combines both the intuitive and the rational into an integrated composite, elevating the common sense to its previously high position, but supplementing it with extensive scientific and logical analysis. Each iteration of this process tends to "reject" the previous models, but implicitly builds upon them.

In the ideal situation, we continuously seek new data, extract its information content, and test the results against our extant models. If the information we receive and our mental models are in agreement, we incorporate that information into our models. Otherwise we may reject new information or file it away for further processing, either consciously or unconsciously, or we may question the validity of our models. At times the new information is so compelling that we are forced to rethink and revise our models of various components of the world. It is this process that Piaget must have been talking about when the terms *assimilation* and *accommodation* were used. We assimilate information by reconciling it with our current model and incorporating, or accommodating, it into that model to expand upon and hopefully render our views of the world more accurately than before.

Consider, for example, the receipt of mounting evidence linking health problems with smoking by the smoker whose mental model of the act of smoking makes him or her look sophisticated, or calms nerves, or maintains a certain level of body weight. This new information about health risks may cause the smoker to expand his or her mental model of smoking to include health effects and their importance relative to the previously mentioned benefits within that model. Another issue beyond the scope of this chapter is the change in behavior, if any, of the smoker as a result of the changed mental model.

Often our behaviors are not consistent with our mental models. Frequently models are formed so naturally and inconspicuously that their presence is rarely obvious, much like the ring on your finger of which you take no conscious notice the vast majority of the time. Furthermore, our actions are strongly influenced by these "invisible" models. Some models are highly important and used frequently. For example, our model of what causes students to learn (or fail) is a staple in the models of professional educators. Other models are remote and very rarely used. The former are the main concern in this chapter.

One problem with models is that we are unaware of the models we may possess, even though they strongly influence our actions. Another problem is that we rarely coherently reconstruct how we arrived at our models (e.g., where did you form your model of how students learn or fail?). This act of reconstruction could lead to a validity check on the model formation process and its results. It is also possible that we consciously or unconsciously avoid seeking new information to test our models, or alternatively fail to relate the information we do perceive to our models. In the worst case, we may bend our interpretation of contradictory facts and information to fit our model of the world (e.g., students fail because they are not motivated). We may lose touch with reality in order to stay in touch with our faulty world models. Of such a person it might be said, "His/her narrow waist and broad mind have reversed positions!"

Mental models should not be confused with attitudes. The latter consist of beliefs or feelings that are not supported by data and information. Mental models on the other hand, are supported by sound and valid evidence.

The lack of testing and refinement of personal mental models is detrimental for us as educators in the best of times, but is made worse in times when significant and rapid changes that will affect our profession are occurring. Information technology and CMC are being swept along in the headlong plunge in which society is being transformed from the industrial age to the information age. As you read this, what is your model's voice saying to you? "I've heard it all before but nothing significant every happened in the past," or "Where is the evidence that all this new stuff is effective?" or "How can kids learn anything these days from sound bite, rapid fire, superficial presentations of information? That's not how I learned." If your model is speaking to you, whatever its message, you have begun to reassess it. Read on.

CMC AND THE NEED TO RETHINK OUR MENTAL MODELS OF LEARNING AND INSTRUCTION

Society and governments may still hold strong feelings about inadequacies of school reform. In the face of global competition, there is a widespread willingness to pursue improved efficiency and effectiveness of education at all costs. Those who do not have ready access to CMC are making their voices heard. In the late 1980s, in the Province of Alberta, a prominent government official became concerned that students in distant reaches of the province were unable to access quality high school mathematics training. As a result, all the high school math courses in the four western provinces became available in computer-based instruction format, deliverable on CD-ROM in 1996.

There are four major factors that should compel educators and other decision makers to reexamine and perhaps reformulate their mental models of the way people learn. These factors are heavily driven by CMC and include work in the information society, improved learning, wider access to education, and cost control.

Work in the Information Society

The nature of work was relatively stable during the Industrial Society and since the end of World War II. The nature of work in the Information Society is predicted to be radically different from that of the Industrial Society. There are numerous predictions of how that difference will be manifested; many of these differences are already prominent or visible. First, there will be different organizational patterns as people, things, and technology interact. The industrial assembly line, in which each person completes one task repetitively, has already been radically altered by the use of robots, causing workers' jobs to be radically altered. Even an assembly line that cannot be changed easily to accommodate new product variations is outmoded. More often than not an assembly line worker employs some form of computer to assist in the work, and workers interact more and more with one another to resolve problems, maintain and improve production, and so forth. Some have argued that the conventional classroom with rows of seats, rigid curriculum, and limited intercommunication does a better job of preparing students for the Industrial than the Information Society.

For some time there has been a trend toward corporate downsizing in which middle-level managerial positions are eliminated in favor of having lower level employees take more authority and assume greater and greater responsibilities for decisions. The remaining employees now have to make more decisions in addition to being craftspersons in their chosen field.

To assist them in this process, employees have access to a wider range of data than just what the supervisor wanted them to know in the past. They need to know production-run data, customer order information and inventory, and have access to a host of data and know how to transform those data into useful information. Modern telecommunications and computer equipment are providing these data and in many cases the analytical tools to assist in the decision-making process.

Beyond that, the Information Society employee will be expected to develop and use new ways of finding, evaluating, and processing information as well as communicating ideas and concepts. A major difference from the Industrial Model is that the multimedia computer will require communication skills of more than just inputting text; it will expand to include communicating with audio, video, animation, graphics, and a whole host of new technologies that are just being developed (e.g., virtual reality) or are just beginning to appear in somebody's mental models (e.g., the data communication suit; Tiffin & Rajasingham, 1995). In the 1980s, technology has contributed to the escalating wage gap between skilled and unskilled workers. It is unlikely that trend will magically come to a grinding halt overnight.

A more recent and for some, disturbing, trend is beginning to appear. The trend is away from life-long employment with one organization to several career changes. Some have even suggested that many "jobs" (career positions) will disappear, and workers will be hired on a temporary basis to perform certain tasks or functions for an organization. People will continuously have to upgrade their skill set and move from organization to organization without benefit of health care insurance, pension plans, and other fringe benefits currently afforded to many.

A convincing argument can be made that schools should do more than simply prepare individuals for the world of work. A key phrase in that sentence is "more than" because it suggests it is important for schools to prepare students to work in an information society.

Improved Instruction Through CMC

CMC has been with us for nearly four decades. Early ventures to use computers to teach, called computer-based instruction, began in the early 1960s. Since that time, two major trends have developed. First, the effect of CMC has been heavily evaluated more than any other form of instruction. Second, although evaluation has taken place, the technologies of CMC have changed so dramatically that evaluation must be continuously updated.

The research on the effectiveness of computer-based instruction (CBI), one component of CMC, strongly supports the conclusion that CBI results in consistently and moderately better achievement gains when compared with conventional instruction. Furthermore, the effects on the efficiency of learning suggest CBI learning is accomplished in anywhere from 10% to 30% less time than conventional instruction. Although some would argue that the medium, that is, the computer, is not responsible for the improvement (e.g., Clark, 1983), others contend that the superiority of CBI has been established, and that further research should be aimed at finding out why it is superior rather than on comparing CBI with conventional instruction.

This line of reasoning should cause us to rethink the power of our present models of how people learn. And the finding that students can learn faster using technology has implications for our models of school and curriculum organization.

Wider Access to Education

Although the quality of the mass education systems of North America is questioned when compared with those systems that selectively educate the more elite, no system of mass education is as good as that of North America. Indeed, there have been stronger cries to make education more widely accessible than it is now; accessible to those who are disabled, geographically dispersed, unable to accommodate a rigid time schedule, or are otherwise unable to partake of high-quality education. In this arena there is ample evidence that CMC is successfully permitting such access.

Although one could argue that the present telecommunications facilities are hardly in any shape to foster high-quality and widely accessible instruction to the far-flung corners of the earth, we have historical evidence that such instructional delivery can make a difference (Szabo, 1994). By the time our rapidly developing, loose affiliation of CMC networks such as the World-Wide Web become capable of supporting a wide range of effective instructional alternatives, we should have developed mental models capable of dealing with the new opportunities.

A related matter revolves around the alleged failure of CMC to make a significant impact on education and its delivery. Critics are quick to point out that the "promises" have not been fulfilled, and therefore we should forget CMC and go on about our business. I would like to remind these individuals that there is a natural time lag between the time something is initially discovered and when it becomes widely used. The industrial revolution, which started with the invention of a simple engine to pump water out of mines, has had a far-reaching effect on society, but we often forget that it took 150 years for that effect to become widespread.

On the whole, technology takes about 20 years from discovery to widespread application (e.g., the mouse appeared in about 1964, but did not become widely used until the Macintosh computers of 1984). Educational innovations take about 50 years to become widely adopted in the classroom. Given that CMC may be viewed as a hybrid educational and technological breakthrough, one might predict that widespread acceptance and use might occur between 20 and 50 years after it appeared. Since its appearance in the form of CBI occurred in the early 1960s, one might predict widespread acceptance no earlier than 1980 and probably more like 2010. By this reasoning, we are still well within the time period characterized by learning and exploration of CMC and have not yet reached the optimum time for wide usage.

Cost Control

It is clear that education is expensive when measured in terms of outlay of money. Most would argue that it is money well spent, that it pays solid returns on the investment. This sentiment is expressed in a popular bumper sticker of the 1980s that read: "If you think education is expensive, try ignorance." Unfortunately, the return on investment is hard to demonstrate, but outlay of money looms large when governments come to the simple realization that they cannot continue to spend more than they earn. Beginning in the 1980s, many governments around the world began to recognize this fact and to do something about it. Of course, the item that accounted for the largest portion of the already high education expenses (expenses, not return on investment, mind you) is salaries, and salaries have been targeted through cutbacks and increased student-teacher ratios. Interestingly enough, the budgets for CMC hardware, software, and telecommunications are also subject to severe restrictions.

In summary, the task we are facing is to provide more relevant preparation for work in the information society, better and more efficient instruction, and wider accessibility to all members of society while keeping costs under control. Many segments of society have seen significant gains in productivity that can be attributed in large part to technology and it is only natural for society to assume that some form of technology (CMC) will enable similar gains in educational productivity. Although some of these benefits have been demonstrated in numerous educational research environments, there is not yet a widespread successful demonstration of such hoped-for gains that we can point to and say: "This is the future."

Nevertheless, there is the explicit assumption that these goals can only be reached through massive reliance on CMC. Although there is a clear danger of knowingly or unknowingly sacrificing some things of value in a move to more CMC (Postman, 1992), resistance is not the answer and will be swept aside. A more prudent course of action is to begin a careful reassessment of our individual and collective mental models of education with respect to, among other things, CMC.

A SAMPLING OF MENTAL MODELS HELD BY EDUCATORS

This chapter was designed to set the stage to initiate in educators and administrators a personal investigation of the mental models that may have been formed regarding how we gain knowledge and cause others to gain knowledge, as well as the role of CMC in knowing. It is the author's assumption that numerous mental models held by some educators prohibit or inhibit rather than advance open dialogue and honest experimentation in the use of CMC.

As you examine these mental models, reflect on the corresponding models you may hold about how we come to know and impart knowledge to others and how they were formed. What evidence, assumptions, and conflicts led you to formulate the particular models that you hold? Then consider what kinds of evidence of information you would need in order to critically examine, validate, and modify or discard each model.

Note that this collection of mental models is only a starting point. Undoubtedly you will think of many more that might have been included. Furthermore, time and space do not permit an in-depth treatment of each model, nor should it happen, if the constructivist position is valid. Hopefully there is a sufficient amount of detail about each model to stimulate your personal consideration of the ones you hold as well as the ones you may never have thought about or perhaps have thought about in a somewhat different light, viewpoint, or time. The mental model topics that are described here include subject-matter specialization, monopolies, technology is inherently good, socialization, equality, teaching as a human activity, speed of disseminating information, emphasis on learning, and innovation.

Subject-Matter Specialization

Is your view of the use of CMC influenced by the effect of the culture of your subject matter specialty on your mental model of teaching and learning? We have frequently heard educators state that they see how CMC could be used in some subject fields, but not theirs, and then they are unable to explain why. There is research to indicate that strong subject-matter subcultures exist in both secondary schools (Grossman & Stodolsky, 1995) and universities (Clark, 1987). These subcultures affect the work of educators and their response to reform and innovation efforts (e.g., CMC).

Take a hypothetical group of teachers whose subject-matter specialty seems to have relatively higher status, is perceived as inherently sequential, and is drawn from narrow rather than diverse disciplinary backgrounds (e.g., mathematics or foreign language teachers). Such teachers may be resistant to multi-ability grouping on the grounds that their subject matter would not allow it (Ball, 1981) and more often believe in the transmission perspective of learning rather than the interpretation perspective (Grossman & Stodolsky, 1995). If CMC applications were perceived to promote multi-ability grouping and sequential transmission of basic factual or conceptual data, one might see how members of a subject subculture could accept or reject "disengage from" CMC opportunities. To put it another way, instructional policy is usually mediated through individual teacher's mental models (Cohen, 1990).

Involvement of Students in the Goals, Activities, and Outcomes of Implementing CMC

In your mental model that considers changing to instruction that utilizes more CMC, what is the role of the student in implementing CMC? Will students adjust to change in the way they function? Fullan (1991) observed:

> When adults do think of students, they think of them as the potential beneficiaries of change. They think of achievement results, skills, attitudes and jobs. They rarely think of students as participants in the process of change and organizational life. (p. 170)

Alternatively should students "have the opportunity to anticipate and to experiment with the role changes before they are expected to demonstrate the results of having made the change?" (Corbett & Wilson, 1995, p. 13).

Of what consequence is the involvement or lack of involvement of students in the implementation of CMC? First, many students are far more comfortable and capable with CMC than are their teachers. Second, there may be a discrepancy between the old and new roles that students can help identify and satisfy. For example, if a student is instructed to use CMC to search for data that can be turned into information and integrated into personal mental models, but that student is subsequently examined and evaluated based on memorization of information and replication of standard problem solutions, there is a contradiction that many students will recognize. Corbett and Wilson (1995) argued that the issue is not whether students know how to do what they are expected to do, but whether they view those expectations as valuable and appropriate.

Given that adults are expert in pretending that reform is taking place without vesting any ownership in the process, especially when there are sanctions for not changing (Rossman, Corbett, & Firestone, 1988), would not students also give the "appearance of reform" and misuse or not use CMC?

Monopolistic

Do educators, in the broadest sense of the profession, perceive they have a monopoly over the process of instruction and learning? Is it a growing or weakening monopoly? If the role of educator is strongly oriented toward the dispensing of information, where will the advantage be when (or if) the day comes that students can access all the information in the world via CMC and telecommunication?

Instructing and coaching students to access data, sort out the credible information from the erroneous, and apply the results to solving problems may provide a role for educators that will allow them to work hand in hand with CMC and maintain a monopoly, or at least provide a unique function in education.

Several efforts to break the monopoly have been tried but have not met with great success. Home schooling and private schools seem to have made some inroads as have for-profit education providers. How would we restructure and reform schools if we thought the monopoly might be threatened? Do we take comfort in knowing that education represents one of the largest organized labor bodies in the world and is therefore unassailable? Will the day come when students will earn credit for competencies, rather than courses; competencies that can be obtained through CMC, independent of organized educational systems?

If It Is Technology, It Must Be Good

At the risk of being labeled a Luddite, is it fair to ask what CMC can and cannot do in relation to the accepted goals of education? Have we come to understand something of the powers and limits of CMC? Education has a long history of limiting or restricting information flow (Postman, 1992) as a major activity. For example, do we not wish to restrict access to information that may be generally accepted as pornographic or information that has not been validated or authenticated? Much information of these types is already available through existing CMC providers, and it will grow. Will the MTV—sound-bite, rapid-fire, topic-jumping form of communication used in the broadcast industry—set a standard that results in rapid assimilation of incomplete information without depth of processing, reflection, or construction of defensible mental models?

Is CMC limited to review and practice applications that can often be boring and unmotivating to students? Or can the computer

> offer students the possibility of becoming inquisitive, the possibility of exploration, and the possibility of recovery from failure that is free from embarrassment. Computer systems can free schools to follow the course prescribed by the process of natural learning. Schools are hampered in their ability to leverage natural learning because of the amount of individual attention it requires. The shortcuts schools take are partially a result of how learning is accomplished but more the result of economic necessity. (Bracco, Petersen, & Dill, 1990, p 57)

Is there a danger in that the act of facing the often daunting task of learning how to use the technology will crowd out asking the more important question of what should be the goals of education and can technology assist (and how do we know)? Proponents of technology would have us believe it will increase our standards of living and position in the highly competitive global economy. Is that our reason for existing?

Finally, we must constantly change and update our mental model of technology. Computer technology began with large single-user machines and moved to large multiple-user machines. At that point CMC made an early and serious appearance on the scene (Szabo, 1994). Along came the microprocessor, and the stand-alone desktop computer with built-in memory appeared. That machine soon evolved into the linked network machine and more recently reappeared as a multimedia device, complete with audio, CD-ROM, high-resolution graphics, and color. We are now witnessing the further transformation into a personal communication device that will link everyone's computer with everyone else's computer in the world in an instant. What will technology mean in three years from now? In five years? in fifteen years? We can say with equal certainty that we do not know, but that it will be different from what it is today.

Postman (1992) warned against technopoly, the subversion of culture and worthwhile goals to the demands of technology. He argued for technopoly controls in several ways. First, it is nonneutral; people are used by technology, and not vice versa. Second, it creates its own imperatives and wide-ranging social systems to reinforce them. Finally, it redefines what professionals are, where they focus their attention, and how they reconceptualize their clients.

Might we be served well by considering the analogy of the archer when planning to use technology? With one hand, the archer pulls toward him- or herself and, with the other hand, pushes away. If only one hand is used, it fails. There needs to be a natural tension put in place. So, too, we must embrace technology, find out as much as we can about it, but at the same time find what it cannot or should not do, and above all not bend our purpose and goals in life to enable technology to fit in.

Socialization

Does CMC conjure up images of students working alone in cubicles, cut off from the interaction needed to develop communication and other important socialization skills? Adams and Hamm (1990) report that computers have been found to increase socialization among kids, and software that provides for social interaction are among the most popular. It has also been observed that insufficient numbers of computers (more than one student per computer) has led to the practice of having several students share computers. This indirectly forces them into cooperative learning and increased social interaction, and the research on cooperative learning strongly suggests better learning and socialization.

Nespor (1994) argued that learning and knowledge are largely the products of our participation in social activity, such as family life, work, course work, academic programs, apprenticeships, and peer associations. These activities are largely carried out in a face-to-face environment, but can the effects be obtained over distances? Knowledge can be spread throughout computer networks spread across time and space. Individuals learn and change as they move across these networks as well as in the local settings (Eisenhart, 1995).

Students may have to develop new or different communication skills as they deal with individual peers rather than a classroom of peers. CMC changes communication in many ways, including changing or removing the visual cues and body language components of communication. It also presents the opportunity to employ graphics, audio, video, and animation into receiving and producing communication. The predicted appearance of full-motion videoconferencing implies yet another set of communication skills that may be needed for success in schools and employment. Teachers may have to identify and provide instruction in these new skills.

Teachers may require new communication skills as they find themselves in charge of dozens of students who are located at several different physical locations.

CMC and Equality

Does CMC reduce or increase equality? And what do we mean by equality? Is access to CMC now unequal across groups, and can nothing be done to change that? Some data from the 1980s provide information to challenge our mental models on computer use and equality. Becker and Sterling (1987) used data from a 1985-86 National Assessment of Educational Progress study and found that at the high school level, 89% of Whites, 81% of African-Americans, and 80% of Hispanics had used a computer. The percentage spread was wider for elementary-level students.

Sutton (1991) concluded that evidence on computer use during the 1980s "maintained and exaggerated existing inequalities in education in input, processes of computer learning, and output" (p. 494). She also observed that teachers held attitudes (mental models?) that hindered access, believing that better behaved students deserved computer time, and the primary benefit for low achievers was mastery of basic skills. The finding that minority, poor, female, or low-achieving students were likely to be further behind after introduction of computers into schools was corroborated in the United States, Great Britain, Australia, Canada, and New Zealand.

There was a high degree of variation in equality of computer usage across schools, suggesting an examination of why some schools are successful whereas others are not when it comes to achieving equality. Edwards (1990) concluded that special teacher intervention resulted in gains in computer literacy and problem-solving among poor and African-American middle school students. The intervention was accompanied by special training and technical support.

Teaching and Learning is (Exclusively) Human Activity

Often implied in this statement is the caveat that learning that does not take place at a single location with face-to-face contact is less than adequate. Do you hold this model of teaching/learning, and if so what is the basis or evidence for it?

Presently teachers come to one location for educational and social and work experiences in which direct contact with students constitutes a significant portion of activities. Compare this with a model of the future hinted at by Tiffin and Rajasingham (1995). In this vision, teachers work from home or anywhere with computer, modem, and Internet access to school servers. In the transition, there will be banks of terminal rooms in the old school buildings to bridge the gap.

Administrators who currently run the operation, set policy, manage space, register students, and oversee safety, parking, and library materials will choose and keep the servers and telecommunications operational. They will market and expand their service to the community, control their budgets, and become more entrepreneurial in function, perhaps like the school district in northern Canada, which is considering selling advertising space on its school buses.

Education is Doing an Adequate Job at Disseminating Information

Society is clamoring for more data and information to maintain its progress and freedoms. Coombs (1985) saw the biggest problem in education as the slow trickle down of new knowledge through the system. New information takes a long time to get into the curriculum through the conventional process of publishing, and it is now cheaper to disseminate information electronically than by the printed word. Faltis and DeVillar (1990) concluded that between 6,000 and 7,000 scientific articles are written everyday, and information doubles every five and one half years.

Can placing this new knowledge on the information highway servers increase the trickle down to a torrent? And at what costs? How do people now effectively search out the information, validate its accuracy and authenticity, and apply it to improving our quality of life in its broadest sense (Postman, 1992)? What new role does placing information on the highway imply for educators?

New and Renewed Emphasis on Learning

Are different learning practices made possible by CMC? Swan and Mitrani (1993) found that teaching and learning in computer-based classrooms is significantly more student-centered and individualized than teaching and learning in conventional classrooms. On the contrary, Finkel (1991) observed that some believe teachers are the center of the teaching-learning system and because of their teaching style are reluctant to use much of the teaching resources available to them.

Are students passive receptors of information, complaining along the way? Or are they apprentices in learning and learning how to learn, with teachers who model, coach, scaffold, help students articulate, discuss and reflect on what they know and what they are knowing (Jonassen, 1996)? Data and information on the role and effectiveness of CMC in bringing about changes like these are scarce at present but will grow dramatically in the next few years and must be consulted to validate our mental models.

Do students learn best by being homogeneously grouped and taught in a competitive environment, as opposed to heterogeneous grouping from different age, cultural, linguistic, social, or geographic groups? Which model better prepares for the work world of the next century? Can the latter arrangements be accomplished without CMC?

At what point has a learner acquired sufficient data to be able to begin critically interpreting and creatively applying information? What are the appropriate and complementary roles of the teacher and CMC in these different endeavors?

Nobel scientist Polanyi (1994) painted a bright picture of a possible consequence of using CMC wisely

> The fact that the necessary information comes to the student on demand, rather than as part of a forced diet, will have the consequence that it is more keenly desired. In addition, the flow of information will be matched to the capability and appetite of the student. Furthermore, there can be an open invitation to the student to apply newly encountered principles at an early stage, without fear of ridicule. Even partial success in this game of simulating understanding can be counted on to reinforce the learning process in a spectacular way. Taken together, these developments present an unparalleled opportunity for education. (p. 33)

CMC is an Innovation

CMC clearly is an innovation that appeared in the 1960s in the instructional system known as PLATO (Szabo, 1994). Do educators handle innovation well? Clearly most educators speak positively and glowingly about the need to continue to innovate and move forward, leaving the old behind and improving teaching and learning. We feel innovation can be integrated easily with little or no preparation, training, lead time, or buy-in by those affected. If you are confident about the innovative aspects of CMC, check your mental model of innovation and change.

Scholars of change point to the fact that innovations rarely become integrated into systems, whether they are education, manufacturing, government, or other systems. The reasons that have been identified in the literature are too numerous to list. A few examples suffice. Administrators have every reason to praise innovation verbally and every reason to do all they can to avoid disruption to a smoothly functioning system. Innovations inherently carry risks of failure that can cause serious disruptions.

Educators are neither trained nor expected to identify and overcome the major sources of resistance to change (Fullan, 1991). Resistance is a natural reaction or defense mechanism that always arises when one's situation and routine is changed or change is proposed. It is my contention that successful adoption of CMC will require a solid knowledge of the factors that resist change and a good plan to overcome or bypass those factors.

SUMMARY

This chapter has been an attempt to address a real but hidden problem that stands in the way of implementation of CMC, the mental models that educators have developed from the industrial society and their lack of applicability to the information society. Through a discussion of mental models and their formation plus the current situation with respect to the rapid change being experienced by all aspects of society, it is hoped that we will carefully but quickly rethink our mental models. A further hope is that we will take decisive actions to update and operationalize our mental models, particularly where emerging forms of CMC are involved.

REFERENCES

Adams, D. M., & Hamm, M. E. (1990). *Cooperative learning: Critical thinking and collaboration across the curriculum*. Springfield, IL: Charles C. Thomas.

Ball, S. (1981). *Beachside comprehensive: A case study of secondary schooling*. New York: Cambridge University Press.

Becker, H. J., & Sterling, C. W. (1987). Equity in school computer use: National data and neglected considerations. *Journal of Educational Computing Research, 3*, 289-311.

Bracco, J., Petersen, P., & Dill, W. (1990). *Engines for learning*. Hillsdale, NJ: Lawrence Erlbaum & Associates.

Clark, B. R. (1987). *The academic life: Small worlds, different worlds.* Princeton, NJ: Carnegie Foundation for the Advancement of Teaching.

Clark, R. E. (1983). Reconsidering research on learning from media. *Review of Educational Research, 53*, 445-459.

Cohen, D. K. (1990). A revolution in one classroom: The case of Mrs. Oublier. *Educational Evaluation and Policy Analysis, 12*, 327-345.

Coombs, P. W. (1985). *The world crisis in education: The view from the eighties.* New York: Oxford University Press.

Corbett, D., & Wilson, B. (1995). Make a difference with, not for, students: A plea to researchers and reformers. *Educational Researcher, 24*, 12-17.

Edwards, C. (1990, April). *Assessing success in analytical thinking skills: PROJECT MiCRO and schools.* Paper presented at the annual meeting of the American Educational Research Association, Boston.

Eisenhart, M. (1995). Learning as movement in networks of knowledge and power. *Educational Researcher, 24*, 35-36.

Faltis, C. J., & DeVillar R. A. (Eds.). (1990). *Language, minority students and computers.* New York: Haworth Press.

Finkel, L. (1991). *Technology tools in the information age classroom.* Wilsonville, OR: Franklin, Beedle & Associates.

Fullan, M. (with S. Stiegelbauer). (1991). *The new meaning of educational change* (2nd ed.). New York: Teachers College Press.

Grossman, P. L., & Stodolsky, S. S. (1995). Content as context: The role of school subjects in secondary school teaching. *Educational Researcher, 24*, 5-11.

Jonassen, D. H. (1996). *Computers in the classroom: Mindtools for critical thinking.* Englewood Cliffs NJ: Prentice Hall.

Nespor, J. (1994). *Knowledge in motion: Space, time and curriculum in undergraduate physics and management.* Washington, DC: Falmer Press.

Phillips, D. C. (1995). The good, the bad, and the ugly: The many faces of constructivism. *Educational Researcher, 24*, 5-12.

Polanyi, J. C. (1994). Education in the Information Age. *Northern Telecom 1994 Annual Report: A World of Networks*, pp. 32-33.

Postman, N. (1992). *Technopoly: The surrender of culture to technology.* New York: Alfred A. Knopf.

Rossman, G., Corbett, D., & Firestone, W. (1988). *Change and effectiveness in schools: A cultural perspective.* Albany: State University of New York Press.

Sutton, R. E. (1991). Equity and computers in the schools: A decade of research. *Review of Educational Research, 61*, 475-503.

Swan, K., & Mitrani, M. (1993). The changing nature of teaching and learning in computer-based classrooms. *Journal of Research on Computing in Education, 26*, 40-54.

Szabo, M. (1994). Enhancing the interactive classroom through computer-based instruction: Some examples from PLATO. In Z.L.

Berge, & M.P. Collins, (Eds.), *Computer-mediated communications and the online classroom: Overview and perspectives* (pp. 165-192). Cresskill, NJ: Hampton Press.

Tiffin, J., & Rajasingham, L. (1995). *In search of the virtual class: Education in an information society*. London: Routledge.

von Glasersfeld, E. (1988). *The construction of knowledge: Contributions to conceptual semantics*. Seaside, CA: Intersystems.

14

CREATING SHARED UNDERSTANDING THROUGH DISTRIBUTED LEARNING*

Esther L. Tiessen and Douglas R. Ward

The processes and patterns of classroom communication can be significantly altered from their traditional forms through the use of computer-based communication technologies (Hawkins, 1993). In this chapter we describe some specific ways in which computer-mediated communication (CMC) technologies can afford nontraditional communication patterns and directly support educationally valuable activities that would be difficult through traditional media. We also describe some ways in which educational activities must change in order to take advantage of the new communication media.

*We wish to thank David Shaffer and his students at Castilleja School, Palo Alto, CA, for allowing us to participate in planning and executing the unit in their classroom. Also, thanks go to Marlene Scadamalia for allowing us the opportunity and freedom to work at the CSILE research site. Funding for the field portion of this work was provided by the James S. McDonnell Foundation through grants to the Schools for Thought and CSILE projects.

THE POTENTIAL OF CMC FOR CLASSROOM DISCOURSE

The form of CMC that is considered here falls within the first two categories of CMC described by Santoro (this volume): the computer acts as a simple conduit for human-human communication (conferencing), and the computer has a facilitative role in organizing and retrieving information (informatics). This form of CMC allows for a shift away from one-to-one and one-to-many communication patterns and toward many-to-many patterns, in which multiple individuals can simultaneously contribute to a classroom discourse (Kaye, 1992). In traditional classroom settings, the teacher sets the means, patterns, and content of classroom discourse and is typically involved in all communication interchanges (Sinclair & Coulthard, 1975). In these cases, communication is limited to one-to-one or one-to-many by the nature of face-to-face interaction. In face-to-face, group-based learning activities, where students begin to take more active communication roles, communication is still only manageable and productive if one student (at a time) takes the traditional teacher role of focusing communication. With CMC software, many-to-many communication can be manageable and productive, and we will show here that this has the potential to shift the onus for control and content of communication to the students, making them more responsible, active learners.

This raises serious management problems for teachers: How does one turn over the processes of classroom communication to students and still promote educationally valuable activity? Similar problems are faced by all educators trying to establish learner-centered models of instruction. We suggest that CMC offers some powerful options for solving the problems of developing these new educational models, by requiring and supporting participation by members of a class or group and by removing the teacher as the central figure in classroom discourse.

In the next section, we describe an example of an instructional unit in which CMC technology was used to support many-to-many communication. The example is not intended to be a "how to" manual, but to illustrate, in practical terms, the issues that are discussed in the sections that follow.

EXAMPLE UNIT: 100 YEARS TO CIVIL RIGHTS

During a three-week period, three eighth-grade history classes met separately for 40 minutes daily. Their shared goal was to create an answer to the question, "Why did it take 100 years from the end of the Civil War until the passage of the Civil Rights Act of 1964, giving African Americans effective legal protection against discrimination?"

To construct an in-depth answer to the assigned question, one would require a deep understanding of the relationships between a broad range of historical events. The general structure of the unit was that individual students became "experts" in a subset of particular events in the 100-year time frame, then expanded their expertise by finding and relating "their" events to others. By working in small and whole-class groups, the students' expertise was pooled to build a shared artifact (knowledge representation) and a shared understanding of the whole time period.

In addition to meeting face to face and exchanging print materials, students used Computer Supported Intentional Learning Environments (CSILE) as a communication and collaboration tool. CSILE is a hypermedia database system that allows students to create text or graphic notes, either individually or by group authorship, and to contribute to group discussion notes with computer conferencing facilities (Hewitt & Webb, 1992; Scardamalia & Bereiter, 1992a; Scardamalia & Bereiter, 1992b; Scardamalia & Bereiter, 1993; Scardamalia et al., 1992; Scardamalia, Bereiter, McLean, Swallow & Woodruff, 1989). Students' CSILE notes are stored in a communal database and are accessible through various search and retrieval mechanisms—notes can be retrieved by author or topic or searched by student-assigned keywords. As well, students can create and follow hypertext links between notes of all types in the database. Much of the activity in the unit focused on creating and using a CSILE database to support the construction of shared understanding and ultimately an answer to the assigned question.

Information about the events, people, and organizations important to the 100-year time frame was selected by the teacher and presented to students as 78 short texts (100-200 words), which were seeded into a CSILE database. During the first week of the unit, each student was assigned two of the texts. The students' first assignment was to read the text notes and assign keywords to the notes (in CSILE) that would describe the main ideas of the texts. In total, 575 unique keywords were assigned to notes in the database (average 12 keywords per note). The keywording activity created a searchable index of all the content in the database.

During the second week, students focused on establishing conceptual connections between the text notes in the database. Students searched the database (by these student-assigned keywords) to find additional notes related to the ones they had originally been assigned. They created hypertext links between these notes; the links explained the important relationships between the chunks of information in the database. The result was a database of highly interconnected notes with explicitly labeled relationships. As the "web" of notes was being created in CSILE, a large map of the notes and interconnecting links was created on the classroom wall. Printed copies of notes were arranged in chronological order on the wall, and at the end of each day, all the links in the database were represented by drawing chalk lines between the notes. Theoretically this representation could have been created within CSILE, but given the number of links and notes, it was impractical on small computer monitors.

An impressive knowledge web emerged from the students' collective work—a total of 229 explicit links was generated, with an average of three links originating from each note. This web became a communal, shared knowledge object upon which students reflected and worked to refine and expand their understanding of the issues in the content of their database. Once all the links had been pooled, students spent a class period working in small groups to create simplified webs that contained what they thought were the most important events and connections. Rich discussions emerged around the web as students attempted to consolidate, share, and reconcile their understandings.

The teacher led whole-class discussions about these simplified webs and a list was constructed of what students agreed were the most important events and/or people represented in the database. In some cases, multiple chunks were consolidated into single items. A graphic organizer note was then created in CSILE that contained labels for each of the 11 student-selected important items. The organizer was chronological, like before, but no connections were drawn between these labels, as students had not discussed specifically what they should be. A CSILE discussion note was created for each of the key events and people and linked to the corresponding label in the organizer note.

During the final week, students worked in the CSILE discussions, sharing their explanations and understandings of the importance of the events and people in the 100-year process. As well, they continued to work at creating, exchanging, and discussing simplified knowledge webs, focusing on formulating answers to the original question. As a culminating activity, each student wrote a short in-class essay to answer the original question.

REALIZING THE EDUCATIONAL POTENTIAL OF CMC

Distributed Learning Activities

In traditional classrooms, learning activities are structured to facilitate one-to-many and one-to-one communication: The teacher presents information and activities to the students, who communicate their finished assignments back to the teacher. In such a model, students all do essentially the same tasks—the only variations are due to student ability and effort. Clearly, this type of structure does not translate well to a CMC environment, where many-to-many communication is to be encouraged; there is no reason to communicate one's work to someone who has done essentially the same thing (imagine how dull this volume would be if all the authors had been required to write the same essay). For successful implementation of CMC in the classroom, learning activities need to be structured so that students' contributions are worth receiving. This will give everyone an opportunity to make a real and meaningful contribution to the class's discourse, and to learn from everyone else.

The strategy of distributing expertise (Brown, 1994; Brown et al., 1993) among the students created an authentic need for communication in our example unit. Responsibility for the 78 texts was distributed between students in three different classes. Students were able to make unique and meaningful contributions to the CSILE database through their keyword assignments, links, and discussion note entries. Conversely, students used each other's contributions to explore and build connections within the subject matter, thus developing and enriching their understanding.

The ability of CMC to facilitate many-to-many communication can help teachers address the age-old problem of depth versus breadth. By distributing responsibility for a collection of issues to be explored among many students, each student can develop unique depth of knowledge, and breadth is covered in the knowledge distributed among the students. This is only profitable, though, if there is some eventual pooling or interchange of ideas among the students that broadens each student's perspective on the subject.

Shift from Teacher Control to Student Ownership

From a learner-centered perspective, it is particularly important that students develop a sense of ownership of their knowledge and understanding. For our example unit to be successful, students needed to have the sense that what was important was the answer they constructed, not some "correct" answer that the teacher or some other authoritative source might have in mind. It may seem that it would be more efficient for students to simply find and learn to replicate someone else's answer to difficult questions than to figure out their own. However, being able to successfully replicate a specific answer does not mean that one has understanding, and conveying to students that their goal should be to replicate someone else's answer reduces their responsibility for constructing the best understanding that they can. Hence, our approach was to turn over the process of creating understanding to the students. For example, when asked by a student if two notes should be linked, the teacher turned the question back to the student, asking what she thought. The CSILE database, and the discourse it supported, was where students expressed their own understanding and ideas, and this allowed students to become deeply committed to their individual and shared ideas.

Many-to-many CMC implicitly supports student ownership of learning processes. In traditional classroom discourse, the teacher can control the means for generating student contributions and what happens to these contributions. In many-to-many CMC, the teacher can no longer have this control: More than one student can respond to the teacher's question or task, and students can respond to and build on each other's contributions instead of waiting for feedback from the teacher. As well, the CMC medium maintains an accessible record of students' contributions, which allows students to revisit, revise, and build on their own ideas and those of their peers, without the teacher mediating these interactions.

In our example, the use of many-to-many CMC required students to write to express their own understanding and share and explore each other's understanding. The teacher did not have the central role in the discourse. Although the teacher maintained the flow of activities and provided focus for the tasks and content, it was the students' contributions that drove the discourse. Students assigned the keywords that they thought were important, searched for related issues on the basis of their own understanding, expressed their own ideas about the relationships among the chunks of information when forming hypertext links, and discussed and summarized what they collectively agreed were key ideas in the content.

Shift from Focus on Tasks to Focus on Understanding

It can be a struggle to get students to focus on understanding rather than on tasks. For example, when students were first assigned their texts and asked to keyword them, some of the students put keywords on their notes without first trying to understand the text. Their lack of understanding became evident to them when it came time to finding connections for their notes because they realized that they were unable to find related ideas without understanding the original ideas. They eventually had to rethink and redo the original task and focus on the understanding. Although it is important to let students know what the tasks are that they need to accomplish, it is also important to work out ways to maintain understanding as the central focus—to make learning an intentional outcome of school activities (Bereiter & Scardamalia, 1989). Tasks need to be framed in terms of how their completion will aid and contribute toward building understanding, and it must be made clear that understanding, not task completion, is the goal. One way to facilitate this is to put the problem or principles that students are to work toward understanding up front and to refer to them as much as possible.

CMC can help shift the focus of students' work to understanding. If the teacher's knowledge is no longer central in a discourse, and the goal of the discourse is to create and express understanding, then students' contributions must take on this responsibility. Mindless completion of tasks is not a viable strategy for students when their knowledge is at the center of classroom discourse. In the keywording example, when students realized that keywording without understanding did not help them advance their own knowledge, and that there would be no way to contribute to the collective discourse of the database without advancing their knowledge, a new strategy was adopted.

Creating Shared Understanding Through Collaboratively Constructed Artifacts

CMC has the potential to support more than just communication—it can facilitate the collaborative construction of artifacts, which can be used to help students further their building of a shared understanding. By "collaboratively constructed artifacts" we mean the representations of students' individual or collective knowledge that are created in the process of communicating students' understanding. The CSILE database itself is a collaboratively constructed artifact that includes representations of students' collective understanding. The keyword index, the explicit hypertext links, the discussions about particular events in history, and the knowledge web of important events and people are all persistent artifacts created through group communication processes. As such, they represent something of the collective knowledge of the students.

The key aspect of using many-to-many CMC that advances the creation of shared understanding is simply that the discourse is between students about their own ideas. In teacher-led discussions, the teacher often adds to or adapts students' responses to direct the discussion toward eliciting the teacher's own understanding, rather than allowing students to build on their own understanding . In these cases, it is often the teacher who does most of the work and, hence, takes ownership, whereas the students do not. Through the use of CMC, students' knowledge and representations become central, not that of the teacher.

Students' collective knowledge representations offer an impressive potential for further collaborative work if they are available through a shared communication medium. They can, themselves, become the basis for further inquiry—we refer to this process as "progressive inquiry." Progressive inquiry is a powerful educational approach in that students' knowledge and understanding are central to further instruction. This fosters students' ownership and responsibility for their own knowledge and lends purpose to students' constructive acts. For example, the web of linked information that emerged through students' individual keywording, searching, and linking activities became an object of reflection and further inquiry. The web represented the contributions of all of the students, and it would have been impossible for any one student to have created it. Once created, discussions and negotiations about which events and connections were more important offered a means of sharing ideas and building shared understanding. What started off as distributed and divergent knowledge about the subject matter became shared and highly interconnected knowledge. This happened as students shared and reflected on their own understanding of the subject matter and progressively discussed and improved their shared knowledge.

CONCLUSION

The use of CMC to shift away from one-to-one or one-to-many and toward many-to-many communication patterns offers new possibilities for classroom discourse. The most significant affordance of many-to-many CMC is that it is not necessary (nor, by definition, possible) for a single individual to be a focal point of communication. The focus and content of communication would typically be directed by the teacher, but with many-to-many discourse, the onus for control and content of communication shifts to the students, and classroom discourse can become about student ideas and understanding. Furthermore, it can be expected (and supported) that all students participate in the communicative processes of building understanding.

The example unit described here illustrates how distributed knowledge—in which each student is initially responsible for learning something different—can be turned into shared, collective knowledge of a large group. This is not something that requires CMC (e.g., the "jigsaw classroom"; Aronson, 1978), but CMC can support it in powerful ways. In fact, CMC requires some such group activity structure, in which different students can make different contributions to the discourse or there will be no authentic reasons to communicate.

Given that students in our example had an authentic purpose and a means for communicating between each other, they took ownership of the classroom discourse and the understanding they were creating. The collaboratively constructed representations of their individual and collective understanding were available as objects of progressive inquiry within the communication medium, allowing them to reflect and focus discussion on further refining and developing their understanding. Through this particular use of CMC technology, the patterns of classroom communication were fundamentally altered, allowing for a strong learner-centered approach to active learning.

REFERENCES

Aronson, E. (1978). *The jigsaw classroom*. Beverly Hills: Sage.

Bereiter, C., & Scardamalia, M. (1989). Intentional learning as a goal of instruction. In L. B. Resnick (Ed.), *Knowing, learning, and instruction: Essays in honor of Robert Glaser* (pp. 337-360). Hillsdale, NJ: Lawrence Erlbaum Associates.

Brown, A. L. (1994). The advancement of learning. *Educational Researcher, 23*(8), 4-12.

Brown, A. L., Ash, D., Rutherford, M., Nakagawa, K., Gordon, A., & Campione, J. C. (1993). Distributed expertise in the classroom. In G. Salomon (Ed.), *Distributed cognitions: Psychological and educational considerations* (pp. 188-228). Cambridge: Cambridge University Press.

Hawkins, J. (1993). Technology and the organization of schooling. *Communications of the ACM, 36*(5), 30-35.

Hewitt, J., & Webb, J. (1992, April). *Designs to encourage discourse in the OISE CSILE system*. Paper presented at the Computer and Human Interactions Conference (CHI 92). Monterey, CA.

Kaye, A. (1992). Learning together apart. In A. R. Kaye (Ed.), *Collaborative learning through computer conferencing* (Vol. 90, pp. 1-24). Berlin: Springer-Verlag.

Scardamalia, M., & Bereiter, C. (1992a). An architecture for collaborative knowledge building. In E. D. Corte, M. C. Linn, H. Mandl, & L. Verschaffel (Eds.), *Computer-based learning environments and problem solving* (Vol. 84, pp. 41-66). Berlin: Springer-Verlag.

Scardamalia, M., & Bereiter, C. (1992b, April). *Computer support for knowledge-building communities*. Paper presented at the Annual Meeting of the American Educational Research Association, San Francisco, CA.

Scardamalia, M., & Bereiter, C. (1993). Technologies for knowledge-building discourse. *Communications of the ACM, 36*(5), 37-41.

Scardamalia, M., Bereiter, C., Brett, C., Burtis, P. J., Calhoun, C., & Smith Lea, N. (1992). Educational applications of a networked communal database. *Interactive Learning Environments, 2*(1), 45-71.

Scardamalia, M., Bereiter, C., McLean, R. S., Swallow, J., & Woodruff, E. (1989). Computer-supported intentional learning environments. *Journal of Educational Computing Research, 5*(1), 51-68.

Sinclair, J. M., & Coulthard, M. (1975). *Towards an analysis of discourse.* London: Oxford University Press.

15

WHAT DO USERS LEARN FROM "WEB" TECHNOLOGIES?

Amy Shapiro

WHAT ARE "WEB" TECHNOLOGIES?

Innovations such as the World-Wide Web (WWW) and hypermedia have received much attention in journals, conferences, and trade publications over the past decade. Such systems are collectively referred to here as "web" technologies because multiple links between items form a rich web of thematically related information. The technology allows large collections of text, graphics, sound resources, demonstrations, and video to be displayed by a desktop computer. Whereas the WWW interconnects the resources of universities, research institutes, museums, and libraries across the country, hypermedia programs tend to be much smaller collections programmed into an independent piece of software. Both types of systems are striking in the flexibility they offer programmers and users to interconnect or link conceptually related pieces of information with electronic "buttons" that move the user from one document to another when "clicked" with a mouse.

THE DEBATE OVER UTILITY

When Vannevar Bush first wrote of the technology in 1945, he hypothesized that learning from a source with multiple links between ideas would be more effective than learning from linear text because "the human mind . . . operates by association. With one item in its grasp, it snaps instantly to the next that is suggested by the association of thoughts, in accordance with some intricate web of trails carried by the cells of the brain" (pp. 31-32). Since Bush's time, cognitive psychology has found evidence for the contention that human's do learn associatively (Collins & Quillian, 1969; McCloskey & Glucksberg, 1978; Smith, Rips, & Shoben, 1974). Furthermore, evidence has been found that the structure of information to be learned largely influences the structure of learned material in memory (Shavelson, 1972, 1974; Thro, 1978). It is perhaps due to such evidence and Bush's early statements finding their way into the common repertoire of psychologists and educators that web technology was widely embraced for its potential in the classroom.

There are those, however, who question whether classroom use of the technology will do more harm than good. Charney (1994) states that evidence from rhetorical theory, cognitive psychology, and document design suggests that "hypertext may dramatically increase the burdens on both readers and writers" (p. 241). She goes on to write that "if the goal is to ensure that readers consider a specific set of associations, then a highly organized text format is more likely to achieve that aim than an amorphous network" (p. 243). The contradiction between this perspective and the evidence supporting Bush's (1945) intuitively appealing statements to the contrary can be somewhat daunting for the educator faced with the decision to use the technology.

The fact is that, despite the arguments posed by the opposing sides presented here and the interest shown by educators and psychologists, little is known about the educational benefit of using the technology in educational settings. We do know that efforts to improve education through this technology have not met expectations (Cohen, 1989; Cuban, 1986; Kerr, 1989). As several researchers have noted, this failure is largely due to the difficulty of applying basic psychological research to practical problems (Clark, 1989; Landa, 1983; Reigeluth, 1983). Schank and Edelson (1990) observe that "in current educational practice, technology overpowers theories of learning and understanding in determining methods of instruction" (p. 23).

Clark (1989) has provided a reasonable voice in the midst of a furious debate on the use of technology in the classroom. Recognizing how little we understand about the impact of the technology and about its effective use, he suggests that "if we seek a technology for instruction (or for planning, delivery, organization, and access to education), we must apply all existing, relevant, robust scientific principles to the problem." A theoretical case can be made for each side of the debate, and Clark has suggested that our efforts may be better spent studying the problem in a principled fashion. Only such directed study will flesh out the reality of the technology's impact on learning. The next section describes work directed at that goal.

RECENT RESEARCH

Over the past seven years, my approach to the question of web technology's educational effectiveness has been to create small models of the WWW in the form of independent hypermedia systems. This method allowed me to evaluate the learning outcome from such systems in a controlled setting. One component of this program has involved presenting students with hypermedia systems of various structures in order to explore whether multiply linked systems promote better learning than a linear presentation of the same material (as in a book).

Learning from Complex Versus Linear Information Structures

To control for possible effects of any single interface, students in one study worked with one of four systems designed to teach about ecology (Shapiro, under review). Three of these systems had a complex structure, containing multiple links between documents. Differing interfaces, however, created distinct structures: a hierarchy, a collection of thematic clusters, and an unstructured web of connected ideas. In all cases, links were present between documents containing information about particular geographical regions and the animals living there. Further links were placed between animals of the same family or sharing symbiotic relationships.

For example, a particular bird's document in the hierarchical system contained superordinate links to a general category of birds, subordinate links to more specialized species, and lateral links to members of its ecosystem. In contrast, the clustered system contained a "bird" cluster that contained all the links present in the hierarchical system, but the system was not structured around a hierarchy. In this way, the same links were presented, but the hierarchy was not emphasized. The unstructured system also contained the same links, but the interface offered no organizing features to impose a particular structure. The links were simply placed in random order on each document, marked with only a one-word topic label. The fourth (control) system was presented as an electronic book with no link buttons except "previous" and "next document" buttons. This system only allowed users to move through the system by "turning pages" as in a book. The document content was identical across the four conditions.

After working with one of these systems, students were tested on their general knowledge of the system material, the associations they acquired between concepts in the system (tested with a cued-association task), and their ability to use their knowledge of the associations to solve novel problems involving inferences. As evidenced in students' performance on the test of general knowledge, all subjects learned the same amount of factual information. This result is unsurprising, as all the declarative information probed by this test was identical across conditions.

Data from the cued-association task, however, were provocative. The book (nonlinked) group almost exclusively reported links between ideas presented within single documents of the text. Not only did the three linked groups report as many of these text associates as the book group, but they also reported a significant number of associations presented to them via the link structure. In other words, the system links helped them to obtain a significantly more integrated understanding of the concepts in the system. In spite of their increased knowledge, however, the three linked groups performed comparably to the book group on the inference problem-solving task. They were unable to apply their acquired associations in a meaningful way.

It appears that pointing to associations between ideas and giving students the opportunity to use links to move between documents is enough to impart shallow knowledge of thematic associations. However, simply working with such systems does not appear to be enough to convey a creative or flexible understanding of conceptual associations. This outcome is consistent with the large body of literature on learning from traditional text. Specifically, many have found that inference making beyond that necessary to create textual coherence is rare (Britton & Gulgoz, 1991; Graesser, 1981; McCoon & Ratcliff, 1992; Millis & Graesser, 1994).

How Well Integrated is the Knowledge Acquired from Web Systems?

Although the learning was not flexible, the previous study did show that complex, linked systems offer some advantage over linear systems in that they imparted knowledge of conceptual relationships. How well integrated is this knowledge? To address this question, students participated in a study similar to that just described. They were presented with one of three systems designed to present material on American history: hierarchical, unstructured, and linear (Shapiro, in press). After working with one of these systems, students were tested on their (a) general knowledge of the surface information contained in the system documents, and (b) ability to display an integrated and deep understanding of the material through an essay.

Again, the general knowledge test revealed that all subjects learned the same amount of surface information. The essay test was coded by a content expert who was asked to rate students' essays on a variety of dimensions.[1] Interestingly, subjects in the unstructured group wrote essays of significantly greater depth and quality than the hierarchical and linear groups. The hierarchical group's performance was statistically comparable to the linear group on these measures. It appears that in the process of working through the more ambiguous links in the unstructured system, students were put in a position to elaborate on the material and develop a deeper understanding than those who were given very explicit information about link relations. Analysis of users' navigation patterns supports this interpretation. Those in the hierarchical systems tended to use links closest to the end of the document. They were able to be more cavalier because they were assured of remaining oriented in the highly structured system. Those working with more ambiguous systems, which more closely resembled WWW, appeared to navigate more thoughtfully, choosing topics with more conceptually based criteria.

Another important point to emerge from the essay analysis, though, is that both the unstructured and hierarchical groups' performance was statistically equivalent to the linear group on a measure of integration. This result suggests that web systems, even those whose designs have been shown to promote some elaborative processing, may fail to augment the coherence of users' understanding. In other words, the information contained in the web of system links was not well incorporated into users' understanding of the material, as these systems promote no more integration than one with no links at all. Consistent with results from the study described previously, merely presenting students with a multiply linked system is not enough to promote conceptual integration.

Conclusions Drawn from the Research

W. Kintsch (personal communication, March 21, 1995) has suggested that merely moving through linked systems provides students with a shallow understanding of the surface form of the information, which he calls a text base. A more meaningful understanding is derived when that information is elaborated on and incorporated with one's prior

---

[1]Interrater reliability was established by a second independent rater.

knowledge. The integration of a text base with one's prior knowledge results in the creation of a larger structure called a situation model. Kintsch has proposed that the experience is too passive if the student is given the opportunity to "ride through" the system with little effort, so a situation model is not well developed. Indeed, McNamara, Kintsch, Songer, and Kintsch (1996) have shown that texts with low coherence may promote a better learning outcome because the student must exert effort to comprehend it, developing a situation model in the process. The unstructured system in the second study described here is analogous to a low coherence text in that work on the part of the user is necessary to make sense of the content. It also closely resembles the WWW. In spite of some improvement resulting from use of that system, however, it failed to provide users with a highly integrated understanding.

It is clear that some of our knowledge of text processing may be transferred to the processing of web links. Comparing results from my laboratory with those of McNamara et al., it appears that extracting information from web links is akin to learning from traditional text in that active processing improves learning. However, it has also been shown that mere presentation of system links is not enough to promote flexible and creative use of knowledge (as revealed in problem-solving tasks) or an integrated understanding (as revealed in essay writing performance). The relevant question is, what will?

SUGGESTIONS FOR IMPROVING LEARNING FROM WEB TECHNOLOGIES

In spite of the fact that there is still much unknown about learning from web systems, the literature does offer information about productive interaction with the technology. This section draws from that literature to suggest ways in which instruction delivered via online web systems may be augmented. The focus is on the development of user skills. In the studies described here, untrained users displayed a consistent inability to develop a well-integrated or flexible understanding of the material, regardless of system structure. As developing such an understanding is a major goal in virtually any educational setting, it is clear that user skills must be addressed. Suggestions for fostering such skills follow.

Recognize Links as Content-Laden

Users tend to see the links as mere conduits between items that they believe will contain the information they seek. The reality is that, if implemented wisely, a system link contains a great deal of information. By overlooking this hidden information, the user may be missing something important being conveyed by the link's author. Indeed, results of the second study described here showed that a user who is able to stay oriented in the system without having to think deeply about navigation choices is less likely to engage in meaningful learning. The challenge, then, is to teach users to see the links as important pieces of information in and of themselves, rather than as mere conduits between facts. The solution may be to foster elaboration about the conceptual links between documents. Suggestions for achieving this goal follow.

Develop Metacognitive Abilities

Theorists and researchers have repeatedly argued that achieving a level of mastery of a body of material requires elaborative processing (Craik & Lockhart, 1972; Haviland & Clark, 1974; Kintsch, 1988). Indeed, programs based on this contention have been implemented to improve skills as varied as reading (Baker & Brown, 1984; Brown & Day, 1983; Brown, Palinscar, & Armbruster, 1984) and computer programming (Bielaczyc, Pirolli, & Brown, 1995) with no small amount of success. As Brown (1984) points out, educational psychologists have been aware for almost a century of the role played by activities that are now referred to as metacognitive (Dewey, 1910; Huey, 1908/1968; Thorndike, 1917).

Given the wide acceptance of the importance of these skills to reading, it is sensible to acknowledge them when approaching the topic of computer-based learning. Indeed, in a study of the effects of navigation strategy on hypertext-based learning, Gay, Trumbull, and Mazur (1991) conclude that "users need adequate learning and study skills preparation to be successful navigators in hypertext systems" (p. 7). There is every reason to believe that the same activities that have been shown to foster metacognitive skills for text-based learning should do the same for computer-based learning. In this volume, Eastmond has noted that "effective instructional design models may be transferred from other contexts."

What sort of activities from other contexts are appropriate within the context of CMC? Relevant activities include reciprocal teaching (Palinscar & Brown, 1984) and the "comprehension fostering activities" described by Brown (1985). In brief, users must learn to summarize what they have read in a document, question which link to travel next, and then clarify the relationship between the two linked documents. The ultimate goal is to gain a deep and integrated understanding of the richness of information contained in documents and embedded in a web system's link structure.

Guide Early Sessions

Although users must eventually become independent consumers of the technology, they will require the guidance of a skilled user on the way to becoming skilled themselves. Initially, the instructor's role should be to summarize the material of a given document and ask the group questions about it. He or she may then model a principled navigation decision by instructing which link to follow and providing an explanation for that choice. Once the new document is reached, its content should also be summarized and questioned. In addition, the link's relevance should become a topic for discussion (e.g., What is the author conveying through placement of the link? What is the relationship between these topics?). The relevance of the system content to the overall class unit must also be made clear, and this should become part of the discussion.

Lead Students through Zones of Proximal Development

The Vygotskian concept of leading students through a zone of proximal development toward mastery is important. That is, responsibility for the activities described here should gradually shift to the users as they become able. This move simultaneously shifts the role of the instructor to that of facilitator, a suggestion also endorsed by Eastmond in this volume. The timing and magnitude of each shift must be determined by the teacher. As more time is spent working with the system and students become more comfortable, the skill level and readiness of individuals will progress. Teachers may offer assignments requiring written explanations of linked documents' relationships to one another and the class unit as a way of monitoring users' development.

Take Advantage of Orienting Tools

A final (and basic) suggestion is to ensure that students are comfortable and familiar with the tools offered by their network provider. All the systems created for the research discussed here provided orienting and navigation tools. One difficulty with the WWW is that it is authored by many hands, so a consistent and easily understood organization is not likely to emerge on a global scale. For this reason, the well-documented problem of getting lost must be addressed if learning is to be profitable (Marshall & Irish, 1989; Nielsen, 1990; Thuring, Hannemann, & Haake, 1995).

The most widely used providers offer the user a chronological listing of the documents visited within a session. Users are even offered the possibility of creating a record of their own "paths" through the system. In this way, the user may create his or her own organization within the enormous and sometimes unwieldy web of information.

Becoming skilled at using search engines will also prevent aimless wandering through the system, which wastes time and may ultimately disorient the user.

REFERENCES

Baker, A.L., & Brown, A.L. (1984). Cognitive mentoring in reading. In J. Flood (Ed.), *Understanding reading comprehension* (pp. 21-44). Newark, DE: International Reading Association.

Bielaczyc, K., Pirolli, P., & Brown, A. (1995). Training in self-explanation and self-regulation strategies: Investigating the effects of knowledge acquisition activities on problem solving. *Cognition and Instruction, 13*(2), 161-188.

Britton, B.K., & Gulgoz, S. (1991). Using Kintsch's computational model to improve instructional text: Effects of repairing inference calls on recall and cognitive structures. *Journal of Educational Psychology, 83*, 329-345.

Brown, A. (1984). Metacognition, executive control, self-regulation, and other more mysterious mechanisms. In F.E. Weinert & R.H. Kluwe (Eds.), *Metacognition, motivation, and learning* (pp. 60-108). West Germany: Kuhlhammer.

Brown, A.L. (1985). *Teaching students to think as they read: Implications for curriculum reform* (Reading Education Rep. No. 58). Champaign: Center for the Study of Reading, University of Illinois.

Brown, A.L., & Day, J.D. (1983). Macrorules for summarizing texts: The development of expertise. *Journal of Verbal Learning and Verbal Behavior, 22*(1), 1-14.

Brown, A.L., Palinscar, A.S., & Armbruster, B.B. (1984). Inducing comprehension-fostering activities in interactive learning situations. In H. Mandl, N. Stein, & T. Trabasso (Eds.), *Learning and comprehension of texts* (pp. 255-287). Hillsdale, NJ: Lawrence Erlbaum Associates.

Bush, V. (1945). As we may think. *Atlantic Monthly, 176*, 101-108.

Charney, D. (1994). The effect of hypertext on processes of reading and writing. In C. Selfe & S. Hillgoss (Eds.), *Literacy and computers: The implications of teaching and learning with technology.* New York: Modern Language Association of America.

Clark, R. (1989). Current progress and future directions for research in instructional technology. *Educational Technology, Research and Development, 37*, 57-66.

Cohen, D. (1989). Teaching practice: Plus ca change . . . In P. Jackson (Ed.), *Contributing to educational change: Perspectives on research and practice* (pp. 27-84). Berkeley, CA: McCutchan

Collins, A.M., & Quillian, M.R. (1969). Retrieval time from semantic memory. *Journal of Verbal Learning and Verbal Behavior, 8*, 240-247.

Craik, F.I.M., & Lockhart, R.S. (1972). Levels of processing: A framework for memory research. *Journal of Verbal Learning and Verbal Behavior, 11*, 671-684.

Cuban, L. (1986). Teachers and machines: The classroom of technology since 1920. New York: Teachers College Press.

Dewey, J. (1910). *How we think.* Boston: Heath.

Gay, G., Trumbull, D., & Mazur, J. (1991). Designing and testing navigational strategies and guidance tools for a hypertext program. *Journal of Educational Computing Research.*

Graesser, A.C. (1981). *Prose comprehension beyond the world.* New York: Springer-Verlag.

Haviland, S.C., & Clark, H.H. (1974). What's new? Acquiring new information as a process of comprehension. *Journal of Verbal Learning and Verbal Behavior, 13*, 512-521.

Huey, E. (1968). *Thinking: An introduction to its experimental psychology.* New York: John Wiley. (Original work published in 1908).

Kerr, S. (1989). Technology, teachers, and the search for school reform. *Educational Technology, Research and Development, 37*, 5-17.

Kintsch, W. (1988). The use of knowledge in discourse processing: A construction integration model. *Psychological Review, 95*, 163-182.

Landa, L. (1983). Descriptive and prescriptive theories of learning and instruction: An analysis of their relationships and interactions. In C.M. Reigeluth (Ed.), *Instructional design theories and models.* Hillsdale, NJ: Lawrence Erlbaum Associates.

Marshall, C.C., & Irish, P.M. (1989). Guided tours and on-line presentations: How authors make existing hypertext intelligible for readers. In *Hypertext '89 Proceedings.*

McCloskey, M.E., & Glucksberg, S. (1978). Natural categories: Well defined or fuzzy sets? *Memory & Cognition, 6*, 462-472.

McCoon, G., & Ratcliff, R. (1992). Inferences during reading. *Psychological Review, 99*, 440-466.

McNamara, D.S., Kintsch, E., Songer, N.B., & Kintsch, W. (1996). Are good texts always better? Interactions of text coherence, background knowledge, and levels of understanding in learning from text. *Cognition & Instruction, 14*(1), 1-44.

Millis, K.K., & Graesser, A.C. (1994). The time-course of constructing knowledge-based inferences for scientific texts. *Journal of Memory and Language, 33*, 583-599.

Nielsen, J. (1990). The art of navigating through Hypertext. *Communications of the ACM, 33*, 296-310.

Palinscar, A.S., & Brown, A.L. (1984). Reciprocal teaching of comprehension-fostering and monitoring activities. *Cognition and Instruction, 1*(1), 117-175.

Reigeluth, C.M. (Ed.). (1983). *Instructional design theories and models.* Hillsdale, NJ: Lawrence Erlbaum Associates.

Schank, R., & Edelson, D. (1990). *A role for AI in education: Using technology to reshape education* (Tech. Rep. No. 1). Evanston, IL: Northwestern University Institute for the Learning Sciences.

Shapiro, A.M. (in preparation). *Meaning and associativity: A study of the relevance of hierarchies to learning.*

Shapiro, A.M. (in press). *Learning from hypermedia: The effect of information structure on complex concept acquisition.* To be published in *Human-Computer Interaction.*

Shavelson, R.J. (1972). Some aspects of correspondence between content structure and cognitive structure in physics instruction. *Journal of Educational Psychology, 63,* 225-234.

Shavelson (1974). Methods for examining representations of a subject matter structure in a student's memory. *Journal of Research in Science Teaching, 11,* 231-249.

Smith, E.E., Rips, L.J., & Shoben, E.J. (1974). Structure and process in semantic memory: A featural model for semantic decisions. *Psychological Review, 81,* 214-241.

Thorndike, E. (1917). Reading as reasoning: A study of mistakes in paragraph reading. *Journal of Educational Psychology, 8,* 323-332.

Thro, M. (1978). Relationships between associative and content structure of physics concepts. *Journal of Educational Psychology, 70,* 971-978.

Thuring, M., Hannemann, J., & Haake, J.M. (1995). Hypertext and cognition: Designing for comprehension. *Communications of the ACM, 38*(8), 57-66.

16

STUDENTS WITH DISABILITIES AND THE ONLINE CLASSROOM

Sheryl Burgstahler

Other chapters in this volume document the value of online resources for promoting the best education for all students. If provided access, students with disabilities can receive all of these benefits along with their non-disabled peers. In addition, however, computer and network access delivers unique benefits to students with disabilities in the areas of increasing independence, productivity, learning, and support.

This chapter summarizes the specific benefits of technology to students with disabilities (see Appendix A). Approaches to overcoming the barriers to standard computer input, output, and documentation for people with a variety of disabilities are also summarized. The chapter concludes with a description of project DO-IT (Disabilities, Opportunities, Internetworking, and Technology), which promotes the education and employment of people with disabilities through extensive use of computers, adaptive technology, and the Internet network.

THE BENEFITS OF TECHNOLOGY

Independence

Randy, blind since birth, was a bright high school student who loved to participate in sports. However, all printed materials needed to be produced on tape or in Braille or read to him by another human being—all slow processes. He wondered how he would be able to keep up with academics if he went to college. Then, through project DO-IT, Randy gained access to a portable computer system with voice output, a scanner with optical character recognition, a Braille printer, and the wealth of human and information resources on the Internet. On the Internet, he read a "newspaper" independently for the first time in his life; he used an encyclopedia; he met practicing engineers and scientists and college students, some of whom were blind, too. Randy reported, "Getting access to the Internet was the best thing that ever happened to me. In a way, my computer and access to the Net have become my eyes to the world."

Randy provides an example of how access to network technology can provide students with disabilities independent access to information resources. Without such access, they are often provided with accommodations that involve extensive assistance from other people, which only reinforces dependent behavior. In order for students to achieve the level of independence necessary to succeed in college programs and challenging careers, access to technology that can support this goal should be provided.

Productivity

Katharine has a learning disability that makes it difficult for her to read and to complete writing tasks. Through DO-IT she obtained access to a computer that read to her aloud what was on the screen. She was given access to the Internet. For materials available on the Internet or installed on her hard disk she can use her voice output system to read to her, dramatically improving her reading speed and comprehension. Her writing skills are enhanced by using word processing and spell-checking software. Some students with disabilities have the skills to complete reading and writing tasks, but, because of their disabilities, they need much more time than their disabled peers. Katharine provides an example of how computer and network access can increase a student's level of productivity. Such access can help a student better compete in college programs and reach levels of productivity expected of a potential employer.

Learning

Ben has muscular dystrophy. His learning opportunities have been limited because he cannot walk and has very limited use of his hands. Access to educational software and Internet services through DO-IT provides him with learning opportunities not available to him in other ways. For example, he can carry on discussions with scientists around the world and access NASA databases without leaving his bedroom and without the assistance of other people.

Computer and network technologies can be powerful learning tools for students with disabilities. Educational software that enables the computer to provide multisensory experiences, interaction, positive reinforcement, individualized instruction, and repetition can be useful in skill building. Some students who have difficulty processing written information can also benefit from completing writing assignments, tutorial lessons, and drill-and-practice work with the aid of computers. Word processing and educational software can also help hearing-impaired students develop writing skills. In addition, speech syntheses provided on a portable computer can act as substitute voices for students who cannot speak, allowing them to participate in class discussions.

Support

Lloyd, a hearing-impaired student who lives in a remote area on an Indian reservation, "talks" to a deaf professor of computer science at the University of Edinburgh about his academic interests. He has also made friends on the Net; some are hearing impaired and some have common social, academic, and career interests. He accesses the Internet network with a computer that provides visual feedback instead of the typical computer beeps and other sounds.

The Internet provides opportunities for peer support and mentoring between people with similar disabilities who do not live in the same region and who cannot get together because of their disability, location, or schedule. Such access can help overcome the social isolation that many students with disabilities face. It also can be used to give them access to role models who are successful in college and careers and who also have disabilities. Such communication can provide encouragement as well as practical suggestions for overcoming barriers associated with their disabilities in the classroom or workplace.

DO-IT SCHOLARS

The DO-IT Scholars program at the University of Washington, funded primarily by the National Science Foundation, provides examples of how computers, adaptive technology, and the Internet network can increase the independence, productivity, learning, and support of students with disabilities. It offers students with disabilities, beginning in their sophomore or junior year of high school, opportunities to study science, engineering, and mathematics; experience campus living; develop self-advocacy skills; interact with mentors; and use technology to pursue academic interests. The only comprehensive program of this type in the nation, it includes Internetworking, mentoring, and summer study activities for DO-IT Scholars.

Internetworking

DO-IT Scholars learn to use computers and the Internet to explore academic and career interests. Computer and adaptive technologies are selected for each participant; local Internet connections are established; and in-home training is provided. A DO-IT industry partner reported, "Network communication is a liberating experience for many of these kids, since their disabilities aren't visible in their email. They have been quick to exploit the technology, both to communicate among themselves and also to explore worlds that were previously inaccessible to them."

Electronic tools on the Internet allow DO-IT Scholars to reach a large and growing audience of thousands worldwide. Electronic discussion lists and gopher and World-Wide Web information servers promote the inclusion of individuals with disabilities in science, engineering, and mathematics fields and the use of access technologies to level the playing field for individuals with disabilities in the information age.

A Scholar with muscular dystrophy talked about how the Internet has changed his life: "It has made my world seem a little bigger, and little more within my grasp. I think bigger with my life goals. Before I didn't share my thoughts at all; now there are many people with whom I can discuss them" Although Duchenne muscular dystrophy has slowly taken away his ability to walk, dress himself, and manipulate a fork, adaptive technologies have allowed him to continue to interact on the Internet, first with a mini-keyboard and now with a head-controlled system. Without rolling his wheelchair an inch, he can reach hundreds of people. "I don't see myself as disabled," he continued. "I see myself as playing football and baseball even though I don't. Sometimes when I'm e-mailing somebody, I think of myself as being normal. It kind of puts you on equal footing."

Mentoring

Through electronic communications, DO-IT Scholars are brought together with postsecondary student and career Mentors to facilitate academic, career, and personal achievements. DO-IT Mentors study and/or work in a variety of fields including computer programming, postsecondary education, statistics, physics, engineering, computer science, computer consulting, and biology. One Scholar described mentors as people who "provide us with useful contacts in academics, career, and personal areas. They help participants find their talents, interests, and confirm their goals." A professor who sustained a stroke, summarized, "I think the DO-IT program is a really wonderful thing."

It seems to be really helping the kids in achieving their goals, and from a mentor's point of view it has given me a chance to use my experience in a positive way, and help these kids out. It's a win-win game! . . . The key to this program is the use of computers and the Net. With the mobility problems many of us have, it's the only way we could ever meet!"

Experienced Scholars practice communication and leadership skills as peer Mentors for new Scholars. Scholars and Mentors are encouraged to reach out and help others. For example, they communicate with patients at a children's hospital through an electronic mail account established at the hospital through DO-IT. A parent reports that her son, a Scholar with attention deficit disorder (ADD) and a learning disability, "has already passed on some of what he got to another ADD child, by taking a boy to register for high school and showing him around so he will know where things are the first day of class."

Summer Study

During live-in programs held during two consecutive summers at the University of Washington, each Scholar studies science, engineering, and mathematics by participating in lectures and labs and using computer applications and the Internet network. Subjects include oceanography; heart surgery; chemistry; virtual reality; geophysics; material sciences; civil, mechanical, and electrical engineering; mathematics; biology; physics, and astronomy.

Accommodations are made in each activity to ensure that all participants remain as active as possible. "It was interesting to watch these students when they first arrived," observed an instructor. "They were just like any group of campers—a little tentative in a new situation where they didn't really know how they would fit in. As they started to bond as a group they discovered that there were things they shared in common. Across disabilities there were some very exciting things to see, where students realized they could complement each other."

After observing two summer programs, a corporate partner and advisory board member noted, "We repeatedly hear the comment that these kids have never experienced a situation like this before—where the focus is on their abilities (rather than their disabilities), and yet everyone else has their own challenges to overcome. The combination seems to produce an almost immediate sense of community and an extremely supportive intellectual environment." A mother of one of the Scholars with a learning disability pointed out how the summer study program boosted her son's "belief in himself and his abilities. . . . This experience has changed the course of his life."

Scholars learn self-advocacy skills as part of the summer curriculum. One parent reported her son's plans to "talk to the math department head about challenging the math class he has been put into. . . . He says it's too easy and he wants a more difficult class where he can learn something new. He is not asking for me to help. He has the courage to go and work on this on his own. Him being his own advocate has been coming, but this jump in ability is a direct result of the DO-IT experience."

The important role that computers and the Internet play in the summer study sessions is evidenced by a few "snapshots" of the Scholars in a special equipped computer lab where students with a wide variety of disabilities were actively engaged in sending electronic mail:

- A Scholar with a learning disability uses screen enlarging software and voice output to help with reading electronic mail messages.
- A Scholar who lost both arms in a farming accident pushes the keys of his keyboard with a device attached to his one remaining elbow, at 20-25 words per minute.
- One student with no use of his hands types electronic mail by talking into a microphone on his headset.
- One student with no functional use of his hands and limited speech uses an on-screen keyboard controlled with a foot switch and says with a wide grin, "I can express my ideas to other people!"
- "Their boundaries are no longer the chair they're in or the room they're in," observed a summer study instructor. "They have the whole world at their call."

Thanks to the Internet, DO-IT does not end the day the on-campus program is complete. From their home systems, Scholars log on the next day to continue their conversations. Friendships continue, electronically. "It's kind of like going to summer camp, but to a certain extent I don't ever have to go home," said one Scholar.

The most effective way DO-IT improves access and attitudes toward students with disabilities is to invite University faculty to teach in the summer study program for DO-IT Scholars. Staff provide assistance in making presentations and make labs accessible to all Scholars. "People need to realize that," advises a DO-IT Scholar with a mobility impairment, "yes there is a brain in there. So people may look different, but that doesn't mean they can't think just like anyone else." Without exception, instructors come away with a positive impression of the capabilities of students with disabilities and a better understanding of access requirements. Disability awareness presentations are delivered regularly to faculty.

Special Projects and Events

Throughout their involvement in DO-IT, Scholars have opportunities to pursue projects of special interest, using Mentors and staff as resources. Options include collecting scientific resources on the Internet, administrating systems, editing the newsletter, teaching about Internet resources in the summer program for new Scholars, and helping with other DO-IT events. The Internet plays a key role in coordinating and implementing these projects.

DO-IT Scholars participate in special events throughout the year. For example, some Scholars demonstrate adaptive technology in a booth at the UW Computer Fair and participate in a panel discussion about the value of computer and Internet access for people with disabilities. Such activities allow Scholars to develop leadership skills and to encourage other children with disabilities to use technology to help them reach their educational and career goals. DO-IT Scholars, through their participation in project activities and work internships, have an impact on potential employers as well. A Microsoft representative stated, "I sincerely hope and expect to someday count DO-IT graduates among my colleagues at Microsoft." For Battelle Pacific Northwest Laboratories, involvement in the DO-IT project has "provided a way for our staff scientists and educators to learn first hand what we can do to ensure that our working environment welcomes students of diversity, including those with disabilities. The overarching goal of our participation is to enrich science and technology by opening the door to a diverse, highly talented work force. . . . Through DO-IT, we have been able to link students to our scientists via Internet."

DO-IT Scholars and Mentors have formed the nucleus of an electronic community of people who share both a love of science, engineering, and mathematics, and the challenges of a disability. DO-IT helps students with disabilities transition to postsecondary studies and careers in science, engineering, and mathematics and helps teachers and employers create positive and accessible learning and working environments. Technology plays a key role in these efforts.

CONCLUSION

The historical impact of technology on people with disabilities cannot be overestimated. Computers and networks can help them access resources, communicate with others, and perform academic tasks independently. Such tools are required if individuals with disabilities are to compete with their nondisabled peers in academics and careers. Educators should make sure that facilities and programs are accessible to people with a variety of disabilities, and that students with disabilities begin to use computers, electronic communications, and network resources to increase their independence, productivity, and learning at an early age.

Programs like DO-IT help educators, employers, and co-workers appreciate the potential contributions of people with disabilities and create flexible learning environments, in which skills are developed, independence is promoted, productivity is maximized, and encouragement is found. The payoff of such efforts is greater opportunities for full inclusion of people with disabilities in all life experiences.

As summarized by a DO-IT Mentor who is blind: "In the beginning, when they let us work, persons with disabilities were pigeonholed into positions involving basic manual skills such as basket weaving and chair caning; then we got computer smart and the application of this technology led to augmentation and adaptations that expanded our employment opportunities into all aspects of clerical, administrative, legal and scientific office work; now we have the information superhighway and we reach out to connect with each other and with the world."

For more information about DO-IT contact:

DO-IT
University of Washington
4545 15th Avenue NE
Seattle, WA 98105-4527
(206) 685-DOIT
doit@u.washington.edu

APPENDIX A: ADAPTIVE TECHNOLOGIES

In order to gain the educational and career benefits of computer and network technologies, people with disabilities need to be able to operate them fully. People with specific disabilities face a variety of barriers to reading documentation, providing computer input, and interpreting output. For example, students who are blind or who have low vision cannot read a standard computer screen. People who cannot use their hands cannot type on a standard keyboard. Furthermore, students with some learning disabilities have trouble interpreting output.

Adaptive hardware and software have been developed to provide functional alternatives to standard operations. Some computer adaptations assist individuals with a variety of disabilities. For example, products that allow monitors, keyboards, documentation, and tabletops to be positioned in a variety of ways are useful for many disabled users. When computer components are plugged into power outlet strips with accessible on/off switches, individuals with a variety of disabilities can also turn equipment on and off independently. The access solutions for people with specific disabilities described in this appendix demonstrate the wide variety of approaches that can help students use computers.

Visual Impairments

People with visual impairments may not be able to read material as it is typically presented on monitors, in computer printouts, and in printed documentation.

Input. Most individuals who are visually impaired can use standard keyboards. Large print and Braille key labels assist with keyboard use. Braille input devices are available as well. They allow individuals to type in Braille instead of use standard keyboards.

Output. Special equipment for students with visual impairments can modify display and printer output. Computer-generated symbols, both text and graphics, can be enlarged on the monitor or printer, thereby allowing individuals with low vision to use standard word processing, spreadsheet, educational simulations, electronic mail, and other software applications.

For individuals with some visual impairments, the ability to adjust the color of the monitor or change the foreground and background colors is also of value. For example, special software can reverse the screen from black on white to white on black for people who are light sensitive. Antiglare screens can also make screens easier to read for some students with visual impairments.

A combination of screen reading software and voice synthesizers can be used to read text to students who are blind. The availability of earphones for individuals using voice output systems reduces distractions to other students.

Refreshable Braille displays allow line-by-line translation of the screen into Braille on a display area where vertical pins move into Braille configurations as screen text is scanned. Braille displays can be read quickly by those with advanced Braille skills and are good for detailed editing (e.g., programming and final editing of papers). Braille printers provide hard-copy output for blind students.

Speech and Braille technologies work best with text. The general movement toward more graphical user interfaces on stand-alone and networked computer systems is problematic for those who are blind.

Documentation. Document scanners with optical character recognition that are connected to computers can be used to read printed material and store it electronically on computers. Then it can be read using voice synthesis or printed with Braille translation software and Braille printers. Such systems can provide independent access to journals, syllabi, and homework assignments for blind students. Some hardware and software vendors also provide Braille, large print, or ASCII versions of their documentation to support visually impaired users of their products.

Hearing and/or Speech Impairments

Students with hearing and/or speech impairments benefit greatly from the communication capabilities that computer and network technologies provide.

Input. Students with hearing disabilities generally do not have special problems inputting information with a standard keyboard and mouse.

Output. Although most hearing-impaired students can use computer applications without special adaptive technology, alternatives to audio output can assist the hearing-impaired computer user. For example, if the sound volume is turned to zero, a Macintosh computer will flash the menu bar when audio output is normally used. It is important that software used in the classroom provide text alternatives to voice output so that deaf students can participate equally.

Documentation. Individuals with hearing impairments typically do not have difficulty using standard written or on-screen documentation.

Specific Learning Disabilities

The computer, with or without modification, can enhance the learning environment for students with learning disabilities.

Input. Quiet work areas and ear protectors may make computer input easier for learning-disabled individuals who are hypersensitive to background noise. Software that aids in efficient and accurate input can also assist. Those who have high rates of input errors can benefit from using spell checkers, thesauruses, and grammar checkers. In addition, word prediction programs (software that predicts whole words from entered fragments) have been used successfully by students with learning disabilities. Macro software that expands abbreviations can reduce the necessity to memorize keyboard commands and can ease the input of commonly used text.

Output. Some learning-disabled individuals find adaptive devices designed for those with visual impairments useful. In particular, large print displays, alternative colors on the computer screen, and voice output are useful for some individuals with visual or reading disabilities. People who have difficulty interpreting visual material can improve comprehension, speed, and the ability to identify and correct errors when words are printed in large fonts or spoken.

Documentation. Some individuals with specific learning disabilities find it difficult to read. Computer documentation provided in electronic forms can be used by enlarged character and voice synthesis devices to make it accessible to those with reading difficulties. These accommodations can improve comprehension and increase reading speed.

Mobility Impairments

A wide variety of adaptive hardware and software products make it possible for students with a wide range of mobility impairments to operate computers.

Input. Some products help individuals with little or no use of their hands in operating a standard keyboard. Individuals who have use of one finger, a mouth- or head-stick, or some other pointing device can control the computer by pressing keys with the single finger or pointing device. Software utilities can create "sticky keys" that electronically latch the shift, control, and other keys. They allow those who are typing with single fingers or pointing devices to input commands by typing several keys sequentially that would normally be pressed simultaneously. Another useful accommodation is to deactivate the key repeat function for those who cannot release keys quickly enough to avoid multiple selections. In addition, keyboard guards (solid templates with holes over each key to assist precise selection) can be used by those who lack fine motor control.

Sometimes repositioning the keyboard and monitor can enhance accessibility. For example, mounting keyboards perpendicular to tables or wheelchair trays and at head-height can assist individuals who use head- and mouth-pointing devices to press keys.

Some hardware products completely replace standard keyboards and computer mice for people who cannot operate these devices. Expanded keyboards have larger keys, spaced far apart; they are useful to those who lack fine motor control. Mini-keyboards provide access to those who have fine motor control but lack the range of motion required to use a standard keyboard. Some people with mobility impairments use track balls and/or specialized input devices instead of computer mice. Some individuals have the use of only one hand. For them, special left- and right-handed keyboards are available. They provide more efficient key arrangements than standard keyboards designed for two-handed typists.

Some students with mobility impairments cannot use standard or modified keyboards and mice. For them, keyboard emulation is available, including scanning and Morse code input. In each case, special switches make use of at least one muscle over which the individual has voluntary control (e.g., head, finger, knee, mouth, eyebrow). In scanning input, lights or cursors scan letters and symbols displayed on computer screens or external devices.

To make selections, individuals use switches activated by movement of the head, finger, foot, breath, and so on. Hundreds of switches tailor input devices to individual needs. In Morse code input, users input Morse code by activating switches (e.g., a sip-and-puff switch registers a dot with a sip and a dash with a puff). Special adaptive hardware and software translate Morse code into a form that computers understand so that standard software can be used.

Voice input provides another option for individuals with disabilities. Speech recognition systems allow users to train the systems to recognize their voices. They can control computers by speaking words and letters into a microphone.

Special software can assist those with mobility impairments regardless of whether they use other adaptive technology.

Abbreviation expansion (macro) and word prediction software can reduce input demands for commonly used text and keyboard commands. For example, macros allow abbreviations to be used in place of larger strings of characters and word prediction software that anticipates entire words after several keystrokes can increase input speed.

Output. Individuals with mobility impairments may have difficulty obtaining output from a printer because of limited hand use. Reading materials on the computer screen and obtaining the assistance of others can be useful. Those who have multiple disabilities including visual impairments, hearing impairments, or learning disabilities, can benefit from the technology discussed in earlier sections of this chapter.

Documentation. On-screen help can provide efficient access to user guides for individuals who are unable to turn pages in books. The proliferation of instructional materials on the Internet is a positive development for people with mobility as well as for those with other impairments.

IV

INSTRUCTIONAL DESIGN

17

INSTRUCTIONAL DESIGN FOR CMC IN THE K-12 ENVIRONMENT

Dan Eastmond

Despite the many recent publications about computer-mediated communication (CMC), very little has been written about instructional design for this medium. Much of what exists primarily addresses the delivery of CMC for distance education in a higher education setting (Davie, 1995; Eastmond & Zeighan, 1995; Murphy, 1995), and not in support of regular classroom instruction in the K-12 environment. Moreover, instructional design at the micro or media level is continually changing with the profusion of new environments becoming available as computer network technology matures. This growth and widespread use of the Internet permits implementation of the creative innovations that could only be dreamed about previously. This includes the World-Wide Web (WWW), gophers, listservs, computer-conferencing environments, and the plethora of resources that are becoming available to support learning and teaching. These resources continually challenge educators to shift from the role of teacher—the source and transmitter of knowledge to passive students—to that of facilitator—directing active student-participants to appropriate CMC resources for further interaction, dialog, and exchange.

As Murphy (1995) notes, much of the good design of CMC takes place when educators explore Internet resources and borrow effective strategies or incorporate resources into their own instructional contexts. Stout and Thompson (1995) suggest exemplary, general, and discipline-specific WWW sites for educators to browse in collecting design ideas for their courses. Many of these ideas can also be gleaned from reading about Internet activities in K-12 settings in journals and magazines. For example, a recent article describes a host of such activities: e-mail exchanges with classroom partners in foreign countries for language instruction, student access to current law cases online to judge their outcome in a business law class, linkage of students by e-mail to scientists who conduct radio astronomy experiments for them, students involvement in creating their school's home page, and an invitation of a guest CMC lecturer from abroad to discuss online the cultural and historical issues in his country with a social studies class (Wilson & Utecht, 1995).

However new these CMC environments may be, teachers are not without guidance as they strive to create successful learning experiences for students. Effective instructional design models can be transferred from other contexts, many of which share similar media characteristics (e.g., text, graphics, sound, conferencing) from past media of computer-assisted instruction, interactive video, as well as audio and video production. In fact, most instructional technology product development activities remain the same, regardless of the media being employed for delivery.

Before attempting to describe instructional design for CMC for the K-12 classroom, it is important to briefly define what activities this entails. Instructional design refers to the systematic analysis, planning, design, and subsequent development, delivery, evaluation, and revision of an educational system to maximize learning. Although design influences all phases of course delivery, the lion's share of it occurs up front, before the students engage in the educational experience, because the teacher has anticipated decisions and tasks, having made plans to effectively address them ahead of time. Instructional design, like education itself, is both a science (i.e., research-driven) and an art (i.e., creativity-driven).

Much of what happens in a CMC classroom is the result of the instructional designer's own educational philosophy about what constitutes an effective learning experience. This can range from an outcomes-oriented perspective, such as the ability of learners to increase their performance of some externally defined task to a criterion level of mastery, to one that views learning as an activity that emphasizes process—that students need to interactively engage in dialog with content, the teacher, other learners, and their own conceptions in order to construct an individual interpretation of knowledge. My own approach to instructional design is eclectic, a belief that the designer should borrow from the tools, activities, and possibilities of the behaviorists, cognitivists, humanists, and constructivists, depending on the context, audience, and instructional need.

This chapter presents a series of design activities, through which most educational projects progress, that can guide educators in developing successful CMC materials and activities.

INSTRUCTIONAL SYSTEMS DESIGN MODELS

Instructional systems design (ISD) models have been used effectively as heuristics to guide the development of a wide variety of educational programs and materials, including classroom instruction, on-the-job training, and distance education using a variety of media. Romiszowski (1981), Dick and Carey (1996), and Mager (1988) are among the authors who have provided useful texts outlining uses of these models. Each of these models contains similar stages and steps. Although the ISD model proposes a sequence of design, development, implementation, and evaluation activities, many of the steps are iterative or anticipated in advance, so the process is not strictly linear. Using the steps of the ISD model as a guide, the K-12 educator can anticipate and make the decisions at each stage of course development and come out with a CMC project that works effectively.

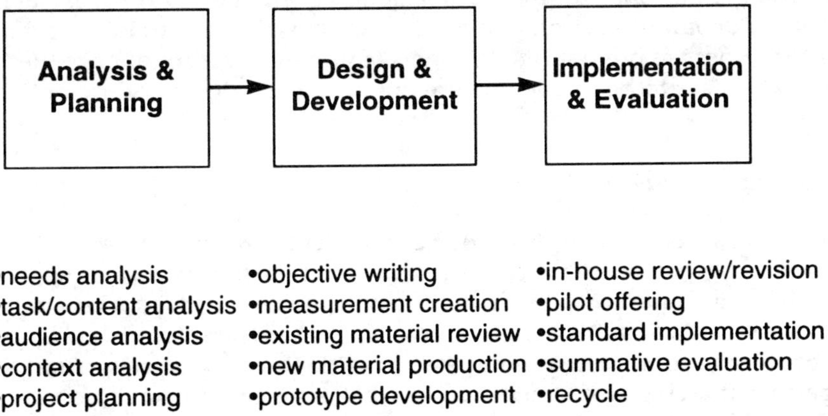

Figure 16.1. Instructional design sequence

PHASE 1: ANALYSIS AND PLANNING

The analysis and planning phase of the instructional design is the time to consider all the parameters, clearly define what is to be accomplished, and make plans to successfully complete the CMC project.

Needs Analysis

Determining the gap between the actual situation and the ideal and the causes for the discrepancy is the purpose of a needs analysis. In an educational setting the difference between the knowledge or skills of the student without CMC experience versus those anticipated by the student who participates in CMC usually defines this need. The needs may not be driven entirely by the subject matter being learned through the activity; rather, the initiative may be directed toward students gaining important information acquisition and computer network skills as well.

Task/Content Analysis

In this step you determine how the various topics of the subject fit together within content that you are trying to teach through CMC; part of this content analysis should also be a determination of how the CMC content fits into the overall unit you are teaching. For example, in a science course, if you plan to have students access the Internet for hurricane data or query an expert meteorologist, you will need to decide how this fits into the weather unit. In the task part of this analysis step, you may need to analyze the knowledge and skill of someone proficient in using a personal computer to acquire information and participate in network communication to determine what skills need to be taught and which ones are prerequisite to others (e.g., being able to manage files on the PC needs to be learned before uploading and downloading network files).

Audience Analysis

You will next want to examine your students: What characteristics do they have that bears on the learning activities that you plan for their CMC engagement? Subject matter considerations predominate. For example, in a Spanish penpal relationship over the Internet, you might consider your students' competence with the language in arranging partner matches and determine in what ways English may be used in the CMC exchange. Do you have shy or gregarious students? How will you accommodate their personalities? What computer competencies do they have or will they need to obtain prior to the CMC activity? The audience analysis addresses these types of questions.

Context Analysis

During this step, you must decide the features, advantages, and limitations of the educational context within which you are developing your CMC project. You may need to consider the capability of your equipment for the CMC tasks you envision. For instance, you will not want to make use of WWW resources that rely upon lots of visual attributes if your school computers are not equipped with hardwire connections, or high-speed modems, or do not support a graphical user interface. Perhaps there are text-based resources that will work instead (or you can make equipment upgrades as part of your plan). What support does your project have from the administration for personnel assistance, additional funding, workspace, recognition, and the like? These are the items to investigate during context analysis.

Project Planning

The need, task/content, audience, and context analyses circumscribe the scope and goals of the project so that you can determine tasks, timelines, staff, and resources in developing a project plan. Establishing tasks and timelines for the project commonly involves thinking backward from the final desired outcome and CMC delivery date to identify all the intermediary steps and dates necessary for project completion. Because this CMC project probably involves exploration into new territory for you and the others involved, allowing perhaps 30% more time for development to cover unanticipated tasks is a good idea. Likewise, estimate longer for students to participate in CMC because they will likely be groping with the technology as well as interacting with the content.

Much of the CMC literature describes development teams for CMC instructional materials and activities, but the reality is that a solo teacher, perhaps with some assistance, usually builds and carries out the CMC course (Murphy, 1995). Even if you are doing this alone, it is a good idea to identify and gain support from others with interest and vital interface with the project, such as a computer support person and your principal or superintendent or computer specialist. Some of the "hats" you may find yourself wearing include project manager, instructional developer, technical trainer, and moderator/teacher. In a large CMC project separate people perform these roles, playing more substantive or diminished roles, depending on the stage of the project.

Developing a budget by task in your plan is often a useful means of estimating costs. Each task may be divided up into budget categories, such as personnel, equipment and software, overhead expenses, etc., for more detailed specificity. Other items to consider are computer access and telephone dial-up charges, photocopies of guides or instructional materials, as well as travel and facilities expenses for training or meetings.

DESIGN AND DEVELOPMENT PHASE

During this phase of the ISD model you move from the conceptual outlines about the subject of your CMC activity into the specifics of material and activity development. Here is where you combine the various online activities—e-mail exchanges, participation in a online discussion group, database searches, or virtual laboratory learning on the WWW—with offline activities—classroom presentations, reports and papers, or perhaps a field trip activity. The steps in this phase of the CMC project further clarify learning expectations and culminate in a prototype instructional product.

Objective Writing

As a first step you may want to write objectives at two levels: overall course goals and more specific lesson objectives. Specifying student performance as a result of the CMC activity can guide you in developing the instructional activities and materials to meet those objectives. If you are more inclined to create an optimal process and environment for learning, you may wish to describe what that entails—the opportunity for students to develop or choose their own objectives in relation to the content or to describe how you will facilitate emergent objectives during the course (Hiemstra & Sisco, 1990).

Measurement Creation

Based on the objectives you then structure the assignments, activities, and tests so that you can observe and grade student work to ascertain whether these objectives were met or the process provided the learning you expected.

Existing Material Review

If an appropriate CMC unit or module exists in your subject area, why produce a new one? Having analyzed your needs and drawn up objectives, you now have the criteria for judging whether various CMC instructional materials you come across are worth adopting or adapting.

New Material Design

To adapt existing materials or develop a course from scratch, your analyses and objectives will guide the design of CMC activities and materials. In this step you select media, determine instructional strategies, and sequence topics. Depending on the media you select to be a part of your CMC exchange, you may need to be involved in graphic design, scripting, or storyboarding during this stage.

If CMC discussion takes place in a computer conference or mail list, you may want to incorporate a number of online activities to add variety and interest to the course, such as role plays, guest presenters, case studies, small group discussions, and so forth (Eastmond & Zeighan, 1995). You will also want to include activities that are interactive, collaborative, reflective, and learner-centered for increased learning (Murphy, 1995).

Perhaps your online class is designed to take advantage of various network environments. For example, a writing course could permit students to exchange e-mail, search databases of writing resources, access a "virtual writing center" on the WWW, or post writings in a computer conference for critique and discussion.

Prototype Development

Finally, in development, you combine new and existing elements, write and produce student materials, and complete the draft of the CMC module or unit. This is the time to attend to "micro" design considerations, such as screen layout, instructional cues, and information organization on a WWW page (Stout & Thompson, 1995).

IMPLEMENTATION AND EVALUATION

During the next phase of the instructional design process, you refine the prototype CMC materials and activities as part of the larger educational system by soliciting and incorporating the input of colleagues and students.

In-House Review/Revision

After a personal review of the course materials, you may wish to share the CMC materials and activities with other teachers and select students who may be familiar with the subject matter or online technology for their critique. Based on their input, you revise the instruction accordingly.

Pilot Offering

During a small-scale tryout of the online activities with the first group of students, you will want to pay particular attention to formative evaluation, such as how you can improve the instruction so that it is as effective as possible. Where do the CMC materials and activities fail? How can they be improved? Do the students achieve the objectives, or are they having the experience that you designed? (Can you tell this adequately from the measures you set)? Is the online work too demanding, or can it be addressed comfortably by all students? In your instruction, have you addressed both the subject matter, as well as help students gain the technological skills to access and effectively utilize the CMC resources as you had envisioned? You will want to use this input to revise the course before offering the section or unit again or sharing the instruction with other teachers.

Standard Implementation

At this point the CMC components you have developed can become a regular part of your class when you offer the unit again. If you have developed this CMC project for wider distribution, you will proceed to share the instruction with other teachers in your school, district, or state. Certainly you should still be seeking feedback from other faculty members and classes about its effectiveness and revising various elements as necessary, especially during first offerings.

Summative Evaluation

At some point in the classroom or at a wider level, educators will decide whether the CMC instruction should become the preferred way of teaching the unit or course for the subject matter. This is the goal of summative evaluation, to decide to make the CMC innovation the standard, revert to the old way of doing things, or seek some combination of old and new, or an entirely different, more effective educational alternative. Because of your effective instructional development of the CMC component, it should become the preferred choice. However, on some regular cycle it is essential for educators to assess whether the need for the CMC instruction still exists and if the materials and activities are still effective.

Recycle

When the answer to the summative evaluation is "no" (i.e., the online instruction, or parts of it, no longer works), the course will require a major overhaul, beginning again with the analysis phase of the ISD model.

CONCLUSION

This excursion through the instructional development process is complete, and hopefully this brief discussion of the use of an ISD model in the context of CMC design will provide a guide for developing activities and support materials for your online classroom. However, many of the creative ideas to give your project life are waiting to be discovered:

> The Internet is an ocean and we don't know yet where in that ocean all those islands of learning are for teachers and students. . . . As more and more schools go online with Internet, others on the network will start paying more attention to K-12 education and will develop additional "islands" to meet the needs of that group." (Wilson & Utecht, 1995, p. 77)

With effective instructional design, the online experience that you create can become one of these "islands" for other teachers to emulate in creating successful learning environments and resources for their students—a synergistic process possible now through the marvels of the Internet.

REFERENCES

Davie, L.E. (1995). Times of turbulence and transition in distance education: Needed research in computer-mediated communication (CMC) course design. In M.A. Koble (Ed.), *Discussion papers of the invitational research conference in distance education: Towards excellence in distance education* (pp. 197-206). University Park, PA: The American Center for the Study of Distance Education.

Dick, W., & Carey, L. (1996). *The systematic design of instruction* (4th ed.). New York: HarperCollins.

Eastmond, D.V. & Zeighan, L. (1995). Instructional design for the online classroom. In Z.L. Berge & M.P. Collins (Eds.), *Computer mediated communication and the online classroom, Vol. 3: Distance learning* (pp. 59-80). Cresskill, NJ: Hampton Press.

Hiemstra, R. & Sisco, B. (1990). *Individualizing instruction: Making learning personal, empowering, and successful.* San Francisco, CA: Jossey-Bass.

Mager, R.F. (1988). *Making instruction work: Or skillbloomers.* Belmont, CA: Lake Publishers.

Murphy, K. (1995). Designing online coursework mindfully. In M.A. Koble (Ed.), *Discussion papers of the invitational research conference in distance education: Towards excellence in distance education* (pp. 221-237). University Park, PA: The American Center for the Study of Distance Education.

Stout, M.W., & Thompson, J.L. (1995). Instructional design issues and the world wide web. *Educator's Tech Exchange, 3*(1), 24- 35.

Romiszowski, A.J. (1981). *Designing instructional systems: Decision making in course planning and curriculum design.* New York: Nichols Publishing.

Wilson, T.F., & Utecht, G. (1995). The Internet at Eagan High School. *Technological Horizons in Education Journal, 22*(9), 75-79.

18

GROUPS, TASKS, AND CMC: DESIGNING FOR OPTIMAL PARTICIPATION

Terence C. Ahern

Achieving quality instruction requires a designer to use a variety of skills and knowledge. First and foremost is an understanding of the group's dynamics, that is, the audience and its culture. Second, it is paramount that the designer understand the outcomes required for the task. Once these essential elements are understood, the designer can make an informed decision concerning the appropriate delivery media.

The correct choice of the delivery system is therefore the result of an understanding of the relationship between task and group dynamics. This chapter is designed to help teachers understand the various elements of culture and the task in order to choose effectively the appropriate computer-mediated communication (CMC) systems. First, this chapter explores the group dynamics of the classroom in order to understand the interaction requirements. Second, it outlines an overview of task outcomes along with a simple model that teachers can use to choose appropriate and effective CMC technologies for use in their classrooms.

THE CLASSROOM

There is an inherent misunderstanding of the true nature of the classroom. On the one hand, the public views the school simply as an assembly-line, where students enter as raw material, receive skills and knowledge, and are supposed to come out educated, productive members of society. There is a clash of both perceived and real cultures that has resulted in a mistrust of innovative teaching techniques. Misunderstanding the true nature of the classroom has led more to a clash in expectations than to any formal resistance to change.

The classroom is not a factory but functions as a large, well-structured hierarchical group with the teacher in charge. If a student in the traditional classroom wants to be recognized by the teacher, the student must raise a hand in order to gain access to the floor, much in the same way as any large meeting. Consequently, it is not surprising to find more orderly interaction patterns in the upper grades than in the lower. As individual students move through school they are better equipped to understand the dynamic process of group behavior and conduct themselves according to developed norms.

Nonetheless, research tells us that other types of social interaction can have important benefits and are critical variables in learning and cognitive development (Cazden, 1986; Johnson & Johnson, 1990; Sharan, 1990; Webb, 1982). The advantage of multidimensional interaction is not only that it encourages individual cognitive development, but it also creates important social environments with far-reaching consequences.

Collaborative interaction provides significant opportunities for individual learning because a student must confront different points of view that require the need to either accommodate, challenge, reject, or integrate the new information (Daiute & Dalton, 1988). These other interactive environments create experiences in which schoolwork is perceived as an authentic opportunity to engage a community of peers on issues of personal importance. These experiences provide an important building block for learning because one major function of group interaction is the opportunity to validate one's concepts in the absence of any objective criteria (Stasser & Davis, 1981). Learning, therefore, is accomplished when individuals test their perception against a collective authority and can argue for a new understanding or accommodate the standing view.

The problem with schools is a lack of understanding of how to interact in groups. Students learn how to read, write and compute but not how interact in groups. It is assumed that, because we can speak a language by the time we enter school, we know how to behave in large and small groups. However, many studies point out that public speaking is one of the most feared tasks an adult or anyone can do.

By teaching teachers not only how groups function but also how to manage large- and small-group dynamics, we will be able to design better instruction for the whole classroom. Additionally, teachers will be better equipped to understand and use other technologies such as computer-mediated systems by designing more appropriate activities given the nature and purpose of the group. Consequently, to encourage and to improve participation in online communication understanding the nature of groups is essential.

GROUP DYNAMICS

In this section, we explore the type of structure that is essential for groups to achieve optimal learning. Group structure creates and regulates expectations concerning individual behavior in the group. Shimanoff (1988) sees structure as a guideline that "indicates what behaviors a group considers appropriate or inappropriate" (p. 50). The structure of groups can be explored along many different dimensions such as size, status, roles, and rules. Structure can either emerge from within or be imposed from outside of the group.

Size

The size of the group is extremely important. Large groups are defined as having more than 12 members. In large groups, individual member participation decreases while the need for leadership increases. A typical classroom can be categorized as "large group" under the leadership of the teacher. Normalized participation patterns require that the chair control the floor in order to maintain order. Consequently, in most classrooms students must raise their hands in order to talk. Small groups usually have no more than five to seven members. Participation is much more dynamic with a healthy disregard for order.

Status

Status within groups provides a controlling mechanism that regulates interaction within groups. Brillhart (1986) reported that status differential creates a disparity in talk such that high status members control the interaction. High status members will also more often interrupt low status members. Additionally, Brilhart (1986) wrote that high status discussants more often than not ignore comments by low status members.

Role

Palazzolo (1988) defines roles within a group environment as "sets of expectations which members in groups share concerning the behavior of each individual who occupies a position within the group structure" (p. 17). For example, in learning groups there are the roles of student and of teacher.

Roles allow us to anticipate the proper behavior for an interaction that Palazzolo (1988) suggests is the basis for "effective interaction" within group settings. Each member assumes that the others will behave according to their assigned role so that we can expect a student to act like a student or a teacher to act like a teacher. Often role definition and adherence is a function of the group goal. The more formal the group in terms of authority and status, the more formal the role structure.

Rules

Rules are the basis for all group interaction because without some rule mechanism for the coordination of interaction normal participation would be impossible. Shimanoff (1988) sees rules as guidelines that "indicate what behaviors a group considers appropriate or inappropriate" (p. 50). For most groups, the most basic of communication rules can be essentially classified as: who says what to whom and when (Shimanoff, 1988).

TASK OUTCOMES

Careful determination of the instructional goal provides the designer with clear guidelines for organizing the course content and determining lesson sequence and pacing. Without a clear understanding of the goal state, instruction becomes muddled and unproductive. There are two types of goal states: well defined and ill defined.

Well defined

A well-defined goal state is one that has a clearly defined solution such as introductory physics or algebra. This type of outcome is well suited for novice learners, which can be presented directly and is easily acquired individually. This type of goal state is well suited for large groups that have a high degree of independence and low cohesiveness and interaction.

Ill defined

An ill-defined goal state is equivocal and normally requires multiple inputs that can lead to different solutions or perspectives such as trying to determine the reason why Lee lost at Gettysburg. There are numerous factors, inputs and perspectives that provide a range of solutions. This type of goal state is better suited for small groups that have a high degree of interdependence, cohesiveness, and interaction.

GROUPS, TASKS AND CMC

The goal of any instruction is to overcome a deficiency of skill or knowledge in a learner. Achieving this state change is accomplished through engagement with delivery media, which can range from teacher, textbook, or electronic media. Given the many different CMC systems, how can a teacher or designer select the most appropriate technology for the task? This is a difficult question because different CMC delivery systems are better suited for particular types of group processes and outcomes.

CMC and Group Dynamics

In order to address the problem of which system is appropriate for which type of group, this section illustrates some of the effects that electronic-mediated communication has had on groups.

Status

Research with CMC indicates that there is a leveling of status such that every member of the group has equal access to the others. Murray (1985) found that CMC relaxed the formal status hierarchy in favor of a familiar style. It seems that CMC limits status as a controlling device and creates more opportunity for traditionally low status individuals to have access to higher status members. However, this breakdown in normative structure can have serious consequences for normative group interaction. Without an implicit social structure, participants in CMC feel a greater sense of personal anonymity with correspondingly less responsibility to the group. This results in group members who are unconcerned with meeting minimal requirements for maintaining interactional structure over time.

Rules

For most groups, basic communication rules can be essentially classified as who says what, to whom, when (Shimanoff, 1988). CMC provides groups the flexibility to communicate with one another unfettered by the normal restrictions of time and place. One interesting feature of computer-mediated interaction is that turns can be interleaved (Murray, 1989), which means that a sender can send another message before receiving a response from the first one.

This ability to interact whenever can have devastating effects on traditional interaction patterns, especially for small groups. Current group-oriented software such as e-mail or listservs make it difficult to "respond to, incorporate, build on, or modify" previous messages (Hiltz, Dufner, Holmes, & Poole, 1991, p. 149). This can inhibit the capacity of groups to structure exchanges (Ahern, 1993; Hesse, Werner, & Altman, 1988; Hiltz, Johnson, & Turoff, 1991; McGrath, 1990), which is necessary for members to "pick up where they left off from past encounters" (Turner, 1988, p. 121). Consequently, there is a breakdown in the group's cohesion, which leads to "individual reasoning, not collective reasoning" (Hiltz et al., 1991, p. 149).

McGrath (1990) has suggested external intervention as one way to create "the very kinds of social norms that apparently arise spontaneously in natural face-to-face groups" (p. 55; see also Ahern, Peck, & Laycock, 1992). On the other hand, Hesse, Werner, and Altman (1988) suggest that this breakdown in cohesion is a technical problem that could be solved by future software.

CMC AND THE TASK

The question of performance for groups can be a difficult issue to generalize about, as there are many types of groups. McGuire, Kiesler, and Siegel (1987) and Siegel, Dubrovsky, Kiesler, and McGuire (1986) conducted a series of studies that investigated the issue of group performance in CMC by comparing it to face-to-face interaction. Their results indicated that participation within the computer-mediated discussion took longer but produced comparable results to the face-to-face interaction. Siegel et al. (1986) state that even though the participants took more time, they used fewer arguments to reach a decision and produced more task-oriented talk that resulted in more explicit outcomes.

Researchers have also discovered that within computer-mediated, problem-solving groups, an individual is more likely to resist changing his or her personal view of the solution. McGuire et al. (1987)

found that a face-to-face discussion developed more group decisions that deviated from their individually held choice more often than in the computer-mediated environment. They suggest that this may be a potential problem in using CMC in problem-solving groups, in which minority views could hold sway and interfere with the decision-making progress.

CMC has a substantial impact on group structure. What is clear at least from these studies is that, for problem-solving groups, the results of the interaction are essentially no different when compared with real-time, face-to-face communication. Therefore, using CMC within the classroom is one of design and not of technology. Specific design strategies used by a teacher will lead to effective and appropriate use of the new mediating technologies.

DESIGNING CMC FOR OPTIMAL INTERACTION IN THE CLASSROOM

Groups are dynamic and require advance planning to achieve effective results. This is even more important for the classroom and especially difficult given the current state of online technology. I think it will be helpful for teachers in selecting and planning effective online activities to consider the model shown in Figure 17.1.

INSTRUCTIONAL DESIGN

Task

The first question for a teacher to ask of the goal state is: What is the students' deficiency in terms of skill or knowledge? Once the goal state is identified the teacher needs to determine its nature as a well-defined

	BBS/Listservs/E-mail	Conferencing
Task	well defined	ill defined
Group dynamics	external rules, large size, independent	emergent rules, small size, interdependent

Figure 17.1. Selection model for CMC in the classroom

problem or an ill-defined one. A good rule of thumb is to consider the types of verbs a teacher would use to describe the task. For example, having students generate the social and economic impact of the Civil War is an "ill-defined" problem in contrast to having students identify the generals of the Army of the Potomac.

Harasim (1993) describes a series of online activities. For example, in *Ask an Expert* students pose questions to an expert such as an astronaut online. The expert usually responds both to the individual who posed the question along with the whole group. A simple BBS, listserv, or even broadcast e-mail would be an effective technology because there is little need for individual interaction (see Figure 17.1).

Harasim also describes the *Writers in Electronic Residence* program that had professional writers read and comment on students' work. This type of activity is ill-defined and is guided by a high degree of interaction, group interdependence, and emergent rules. The goal of this type of activity is to have the apprentice learn from the experience and wisdom of the mentor.

Conferencing software is better suited for ill-defined goals that require more interaction with a higher group interdependence. Group conferencing software is much better at allowing each member of the group the ability to track the threads of an ongoing interaction (see Figure 17.1). According to the selection model (see Figure 17.1), a small group conference would be the technology of choice for this type of activity. Once the goal state has been determined and the delivery technology determined, the teacher must manage the group structure appropriate for the delivery technology chosen.

STRUCTURAL PLANNING

Size

The size of the group is determined by the group's goal. The more well-defined the goal is, the larger the group will be. For ill-defined groups that have a high level of group interdependence, generally no more than five to seven members per group is recommended.

None of these recommendations is absolute. You could also design a well-defined goal state for small groups of five to seven members if more interaction is desired. For example, a teacher might develop small member teams that could use a BBS as a homework chat board. By specifying that mathematics questions will be answered on Tuesday and English items on Wednesday, the outcome is well defined but would provide high group interaction and thereby increase motivation and performance.

Rules

The performance and behavior of a group are very important to maintain—even online. Just as in the regular classroom, rules provide guidelines for appropriate behavior. Given the lack of time in most classrooms, external rules, even for small groups, provide a simple measure that will improve the success of online activities. One simple rule we discovered is to set clear deadlines. For example, each student must discover the method for developing a series of numbers such as the Fibonacci series. The teacher should clearly indicate the date for final posting an adhere to it.

Another good rule that we have found works well for large online groups is to set closing dates for topics. Typically, because topic discussions are online, it is easy to continue to keep topics open indefinitely. However, we found that students were not able to keep up. Some of the students indicated that wading through all the material was difficult, and because the topic was still active they felt obliged to try. Consequently, it is important that each member be made aware that the topic will only be available for a determinate time.

On the other hand, in small groups, more global deadlines were appropriate. For example, in a small, goal-oriented group, the only requirement was to visit the software on average twice a week over a three-week period. We found this provided enough incentive to maintain interest and to sustain the discussion.

Roles

The final question teachers have to consider when designing an online activity is what role or roles they want to assume. In most typical CMC there is the role of moderator, monitor, or facilitator. These are not exclusive roles and can be combined in various ways. The most restrictive role, and one that requires the most work for the teacher, is the moderator. Typically a moderator reviews all comments prior to posting on the network.

We found that the moderator is well suited for large group interaction. However, most of our students found that the moderator method too intrusive as well as very slow. Nonetheless, a moderator may be necessary in sensitive, highly explosive, or controversial topics discussions, in which the teacher wants to maintain close control over which messages were posted.

The monitor controls the general flow of interaction by controlling and redirecting the global topic (see Berge, 1995, for a more in-depth description of these roles). In a variety of studies we found that even though the topic was moderated by the teacher, the students' interaction was not greatly hampered. In fact, the overall group cohesion and depth of processing was enhanced.

In one study, Ahern (1996) allowed a group of seventh-grade students to set their own topics after the general topic for discussion for both groups was established by the teacher. One group could develop topics on their own while the other group was restricted to the moderator's topics. After two weeks they switched. What we found was that in general the moderated group's interaction was not only more coherent, but the group had better cohesion. Surprisingly, the unmoderated group created topics that in general followed the theme as set by the teacher. The student-generated topics, however, generated less interaction and were less cohesive overall. What is interesting from this study was the impact of the role of teacher as moderator.

The role of facilitator is the most dynamic. In a previous paper Ahern et al. (1992) found that a facilitating role produced the most peer-to-peer interaction with the highest frequency of complex responses for any discourse style. The facilitator manages the interaction, usually in the background, by relating individual comments, by suggesting a different interpretation of an idea, or by clarifying a position and so forth.

Planning for the online experience requires that the teacher pay close attention to the impact of the social issues in the group. Some research has shown for specific types of groups member participation patterns can be higher online than in regular face-to-face encounters. However, this advantage will break down over time simply because it is more difficult in online systems to maintain group coherence and cohesion.

Interaction breaks down in highly salient groups because the members are afraid to risk engagement resulting in more conservative, less complex interaction sequences. One way to encourage more interaction is for teachers from time to time to provide some form of anonymity for members of the group. This allows them the freedom to voice different views without long-term social consequences.

SUMMARY

In general I have argued that in order to achieve optimal participation in online systems a better understanding of the basic nature of the classroom is necessary. The traditional classroom is better understood as a large group. Essential components of the group were discussed briefly as well as the impact CMC has on group dynamics. Finally, a selection model was provided that helps teacher use CMC technology based on their planning for different types of goals, structure, and social factors. To improve interaction online requires a better understanding relationship of task and group dynamics.

REFERENCES

Ahern, T. C. (1993). The effect of a graphic interface on participation, interaction, and student achievement in a computer-mediated small-group discussion. *Journal of Educational Computing Research, 9*(4), 535-548.

Ahern, T. C. (1996). *The effect of topic ownership on the structure of interaction in an online mediated conference.* Unpublished manuscript.

Ahern, T. C., Peck, K., & Laycock, M. (1992). The effects of teacher discourse in computer-mediated discussion. *Journal of Educational Computing Research, 8*(3), 255-273.

Berge, Z. L. (1995, January/February). Facilitating computer conferencing: Recommendations from the field. *Educational Technology,* pp. 22-30.

Brilhart, J. K. (1986). *Effective group discussion* (5th ed.). Dubuque, IA: Wm. C. Brown.

Cazden, C. B. (1986). Classroom discourse. In M. C. Wittrock (Ed.), *Handbook of research on teaching* (3rd ed., pp. 432-463). New York: Macmillan and American Educational Research Association.

Daiute, C., & Dalton, B. (1988). "Let's brighten it up a bit": Collaboration and cognition in writing. In B. A. Raforth & D. L. Rubin (Eds.), *The social construction of written communication* (pp. 249-269). Norwood, NJ: Ablex.

Harasim, L. (1993). Learning to teach online. *TIE News, 5*(1), 22-27.

Hesse, B. W., Werner, C. M., & Altman, I. (1988). Temporal aspects of computer-mediated communication. *Computers in Human Behavior, 4,* 147-165.

Hiltz, S. R., Dufner, D., Holmes, M., & Poole, S. (1991). Distributed group support systems: Social dynamics and design dilemmas. *Journal of Organizational Computing, 1*(2), 135-159.

Hiltz, S. R., Johnson, K., & Turoff, M. (1991). Group decision support: The effects of designated human leaders and statistical feedback in computerized conferences. *Journal of Management Information Systems, 8*(2), 81-108.

Johnson, D. W., & Johnson, R. T. (1990). Cooperative learning and achievement. In S. Sharan (Ed.), *Cooperative learning* (pp. 23-37). New York: Praeger.

McGrath, J. E. (1990). Time matters in groups. In J. Galegher, R. E. Kraut, & C. Egido (Eds.), *Intellectual teamwork: Social and technological foundations of cooperative work* (pp. 23-61). Hillsdale, NJ: Lawrence Erlbaum Associates.

McGuire, T. W., Kiesler, S., & Siegel, S. (1987). Group and computer-mediated discussion effects in risk decision making. *Journal of Personality and Social Psychology, 52,* 917-930.

Murray, D. E. (1985). Composition as conversation. In L. Odell & D. Goswami (Eds.), *Writing in non-academic settings* (pp. 203-227). New York: Guilford.

Murray, D. E. (1989). When the medium determines turns: Turn-taking in computer conversation. In H. Coleman (Ed.), *Working with language: A multidisciplinary consideration of language use in work contexts* (pp. 319-337). Berlin: Mouton de Gruyter.

Palazzolo, C. S. (1988). The social group: Definitions. In R. S. Cathcart & L. A. Samovar (Eds.), *Small group communication* (pp. 6-19). Dubuque, IA: Wm. C. Brown.

Sharan, S. (1990). Cooperative learning: A perspective on research and practice. In S. Sharan (Ed.), *Cooperative learning: Theory and research.* New York: Praeger.

Shimanoff, S. B. (1988). Group interaction via communication rules. In R. S. Cathcart & L. A. Samovar (Eds.), *Small group communication.* Dubuque, IA: Wm. C. Brown.

Siegel, J., Dubrovsky, V., Kiesler, S., & McGuire, T. W. (1986). Group processes in computer-mediated communication. *Organizational Behavior and Human Decision Processes, 37,* 157-187.

Stasser, G., & Davis, J. H. (1981). Group decision making and social influence: A social interaction sequence model. *Psychological Review, 88*(6), 523-551.

Turner, J. H. (1988). *A theory of social interaction.* Stanford, CA: Stanford University Press.

Webb, N. M. (1982). Student interaction and learning in small groups. *Review of Educational Research, 52,* 421-445.

19

DESIGNING EFFECTIVE TELECOMMUNICATIONS PROJECTS

Sally Laughon

A class in Virginia was preparing to exchange paragraphs with another class in New York as part of the Monster Project, moderated annually by a teacher in New Jersey (http://www.intac.com/~brunner/projects/monster.htm). The fifth graders had drawn their monster picture, and one group wrote a description of their creature: "My monster has a round green body and four eyes coming up out of its head." As access to Internet resources becomes more common in the classroom, teachers are finding engaging avenues for bringing the world into their classrooms. Using the Internet as a communications conduit educators began to plan and design projects to enhance their curriculum and connect their classes to others around the globe with a variety of activities that captivate the students.

I have searched for sources of telecommunications activities and collected and printed copies of exemplary projects popular enough to be repeated year after year. I catalogued enticing activities with well-defined plans-of-action and stuffed a filing cabinet until it bulged with projects. After reading hundreds of postings announcing projects on the Internet, a clear pattern for successful designs began to emerge. Some educators are remarkably creative with their ideas for telecommunications projects, and often find they are overwhelmed with requests to join the activity. Others have splendid ideas but have difficulty finding companion classes. What distinguishes a good idea from a good project? What are the key components of a telecommunications project that will appeal to other educators and will be successful?

In this chapter, projects will be examined to determine the features making them appeal to other educators and assure successful completion. The projects discussed here use the Internet for connecting people and classes. The World-Wide Web (WWW) is a source of information for projects but is also a conduit for communication between educators when it invites interactivity. The Web component provides complementary activities as well as an online library of resources for facilitating communication among educators. This chapter also presents information on how to develop a project using other Internet capabilities such as e-mail.

An online telecommunications project has four distinct phases:

1. Planning the project: developing an idea into a workable project
2. Announcing the project to the Internet community and accepting companion classes
3. Coordinating or moderating the activities
4. Evaluating the project

When educators begin to develop a project, one compelling reason should drive the objectives and activities: It must fit into a curriculum with respect to time and content. One reason that projects designed around penpal exchanges (http://www.stolaf.edu/network/iecc/) are often abysmal failures is that they do not directly contribute to the curriculum. In addition, keypal exchanges rarely have a clearly defined deadline for exchanges, so they can easily be moved into a low priority in daily activities.

Although successful projects may have only a few of the components outlined in this chapter, all such projects have the following elements: specific goals or objectives, clearly defined activities, a well-planned timeline with a definite closure to the project, and plans for exchanging information among all the participants in the project.

PLANNING THE PROJECT

Design your project around the current curriculum and what is presently being taught. The project should integrate and enhance the curriculum. Recently, a teacher from New South Wales Australia posted a message titled: Seeking American primary class in English language (http://www.stolaf.edu/network/iecc/iecc-projects.html). He was looking for six other elementary school classes to communicate from September to December. His message stated: "We would like to find out what life is like in other countries." This interest in others could easily be expanded into a series of well-planned, well-focused exchanges.

Set Goals and Expected Outcomes

To design a project that will attract other classes, the goals need to be specific, and there need to be definite tasks with expected outcomes. For example, one activity for New South Wales could be that students write a descriptive essay describing the typical school day. As the student moves from class to class in a typical day, information about special activities that differ from the routine schedule could also be included. This activity, if carefully planned, would serve as a method for exchanging information about school systems in different countries, such as the length of classes and what a typical course load for a student might be. When a class of students shares their daily activities, a pattern emerges for the partner school reading the descriptions. The power of connection emerges from the authenticity of the writers' descriptions.

Include Activities Across the Curriculum

To encourage other educators to join a project, they need enough information to determine if the activities will correspond with the curricular area, age group, and time available to participate. Projects that include more than one discipline area are appealing, especially to middle school educators and schools with large blocks of time for teaching.

Online activities can be categorized into 18 structures according to Judi Harris (http://www.ed.uiuc.edu/Activity-Structures/). Judi identified three major categories of activities: Collaborative Problem-Solving Projects, Information Collections, and Interpersonal Exchanges. All features presented in this chapter may not be necessary for every project, but each element should be given careful consideration when designing a project.

Plan a Preliminary Timeline

Timelines need to be specific, with beginning dates, ending dates, and a schedule for exchanges that is reasonable for the time allocated. For example, New South Wales might plan on exchanges once every other week, concluding by Friday of the second week, recognizing that Australian time is a day ahead of American. For four months, plans are needed for eight exchanges. Students need specific guidelines for writing about their countries. For example, students could write "A day in the life of" journals describing a typical school day, such as activities in each class, subjects, homework. Extracurricular activities such as sports, clubs, publications, and volunteer activities would complete the description.

Another topic for writing could be weekend activities. Students would then need to brainstorm about all the weekend activities that appeal to them and send this information to the partner classes. One weekend will not provide a visual snapshot of what life in this country resembles. But an overview of the activities that interest students, complete with a rating system mutually decided by a class, would provide a comprehensive picture of weekend life.

Plan How the Project Will Be Managed

As a project is designed, the educator should also plan for keeping copies of the exchanges so they can be posted on a bulletin board or assembled into a notebook. In 1992, when KidCafe was new, I printed every introductory letter written by the 10- to 15-year-olds on this list for over four months and made a wall of letters, assembled by country, down the cinder block hallway outside my room. At first there were about 7 countries, but by the end of the year almost 40 countries were represented. I used a graphics package to print signs indicating the origin of the electronic mail. Students, staff members, teachers, parents, and visitors often read the messages from around the world. Educators should think about a product that can result from a particular project.

Plan How Information Will Be Shared

The keystone for any project that will attract a wide circle of participants is the plan to share information throughout the project or at the end of a project. All projects should provide every participant with data from all other participants. For example, a simple "What's for Supper" message asked students from six areas of the United States for their favorite regional supper menu. Participants were promised a compilation of the menus at the end of the project. Others on the Internet should not be considered just a source of information but a cooperator for sharing information. This is a vital and critical component that has doomed many a good idea when the project is designed to be only a one-way flow of information.

CONVERTING A GOOD IDEA INTO A GREAT PROJECT

When posting a project to newsgroups or on sites on the WWW, large and long-term projects may need to be split into two messages: first, a call for collaboration; and second, final details for the project.

Here are the essential and central elements of successful projects based on past postings to the Net and based on my own experiences in the classroom.

Project Components

An inviting title. The educator should choose a clever, eye-catching title and use it in the subject line of the e-mail when the project is announced or as the heading when registering with the Global SchoolNet (GSN) Foundation (e-mail address: proj.register@gsn.org). The e-mail subject line is not the place to cram as much information as possible about the message. A witty title will invite the reader to investigate further. It is best to avoid a plain description or lengthy overview of the entire project. Many educators read an overwhelming volume of e-mail daily, and a mundane title may be easily overlooked. Educators who use the WWW browsing through archives of messages looking for partner classes or a registry of future projects read messages from titles with humor, verbal puns, or twists of words.

The best project titles are short, inviting, and witty. The teacher can ask students for assistance in naming the project by having a brainstorming session, writing all ideas on the board, and allowing the wildest ideas to spark creativity in other students:

Ordinary title	Inviting title
Fourth-grade History Project	Colonial Computing
Science Class Water Exchange Project	Water is Life
High School art class seeks partners (http://www.ed.uiuc.edu/Activity-Structures/Collaborative-Problem-Solving/Sequential-Creations/Art-FAX-Project.html)	Art/Fax Exchange
Middle School Journalism	NewsDay (http://gsn.org/gsn/newsday.home.html)
Geography contest	GEOGAME (http://gsn.org/gsn/geogame.home.html)
Traveling around the world	Where on the Globe is Roger? (http://gsn.org/gsn/roger.home.html)

Al Rogers of the Global SchoolNet created a convention he uses for all projects received from educators that he forwards to educators using e-mail lists. He includes the grade levels at the beginning of each subject line of e-mail messages announcing projects. For example, he would post the "Colonial Computing" invitation with this subject line: "3-5: Colonial Computing." Because schools study state history in different grade levels, the expanded invitation invites all elementary school classes who might be currently studying this topic. This is a simple but extraordinarily effective way to identify project target populations in the United States. However, this convention can be confusing to others for projects inviting international participation.

An age range. One should always provide a student age range as well as grade levels. The American grade classification system is not used around the world, and educators need to be sensitive about other school systems.

As educators design a project, they should be flexible with student ages and encourage everyone who responds to participate, within manageable numbers. I helped design an art/fax project for our high school media art class, ages 16 to 18. Our class exchanged art with a magnet school for the arts in North Carolina, whose students were ages 12 to 14. In spite of the age differences, the North Carolina art was exceptionally creative and provided us with exemplary examples of what comprises collaborative art. A special education class may successfully participate in a project designed for students a bit younger. Likewise, students in an English as a Second Language class may benefit from written exchanges with younger students. Gifted classes may successfully complete projects designed for students older.

Curricular areas. As educators design projects, they should consider all disciplines and ways in which this project could become interdisciplinary. The annual "Global Grocery List" (http://www.gsn.org/gsn/proj/ggl/index.html) price lists have been used to enhance math, science, social studies, health, and writing instruction. These lists can be used to practice calculations, as an information base for drawing conclusions and as a springboard for writing assignments. The most popular projects make connections for the kids in many curriculum areas. With a bit of practice, it is easy to expand a simple project across the curriculum.

For example, a project called "Birthday Graphs" asked students to share data about their birthday. These data were then used for bar, line, stacked, area, and pie charts: one for the month, one for the day of the month. A natural extension would be locating the classes' hometowns on a map, researching the geography of the area, and extending the project to include a language arts activity: "How do you celebrate your birthdays? Do you have a party? What are the special foods you eat at your birthday celebrations? Write a descriptive paragraph about your most memorable birthday or your most recent birthday. Write about the ultimate birthday party!"

An overview. This overview should be short, so when interested participants are reading the message describing this project, the first four components (project name, student age range, curricular areas, project overview) can be viewed on one computer screen. By writing concisely, busy educators can quickly determine whether this project can fit into the curriculum of their school or classroom.

The overview should be a clear, precise, positive, and short paragraph. This overview is a synopsis to encourage the participant to read further and ultimately join the project. Crisp and clear writing is essential here. The following is a project overview of a poetry project designed for 8- to 10-year-olds: "I am" poems are written in a format designed to allow students to express feelings about themselves. Students create a word picture of who they are by finishing sentences in the "poem starter" that are arranged in non-rhyming poetic form.

Objectives or outcomes. As a project is developed, objectives clarify the purpose of the project. Educators can use the format most familiar to them to help define the curricular areas included in the activities. Although objectives or outcomes are optional, it is helpful for potential participants to make certain the activity is designed well enough to incorporate into their own curriculum.

Objectives assist with clarification of activities as well as provide a framework for project evaluation. Were the objectives realistic or too idealistic? Do objectives need revision?

Activity description and template. This section provides a detailed description of all activities for this project. Educators need to be specific about the number and length of class periods devoted to each activity and an estimated time frame for all the project activities. The descriptions should be in the proper sequence for completion.

If the students share data with this project, the educator should design the forms or a template for data entry. These files should be saved as text files, unless the project description specifically lists special equipment or software needed to exchange information. The project provides consistency for participants if every school participating in data collection and exchange uses the same entry format.

For each activity, a template should be provided as well an example of student work. For example, in the "I am" poetry exchange, the activity description provides a pattern for the poem to be composed. Here is the structure of the poem:

I am (two special characteristics that you have)
I wonder (something you are actually curious about)
I hear (an imaginary sound)
I see (an imaginary sight)
I want (an actual desire)

I am (the first line of the poem repeated)
I pretend (something you actually pretend to do)
I feel (a feeling about something imaginary)
I touch (an imaginary touch)
I worry (something that really bothers you)
I cry (something that makes you very sad)

I am (the first line of the poem repeated)
I understand (something you know is true)
I say (something you believe in)
I dream (something you actually dream about)
I try (something you really make an effort about)
I hope (something you actually hope for)

I am (the first line of the poem repeated)

In addition, when the call for participation was posted, several examples of student work were included to provide a model for participating classes:

"I am" by Jennifer—8
I am a wild girl who loves to dream.
I wonder if I'll ever be dead.
I hear silent roars in the night.
I see misty ghosts in my mind.
I want to shout out to everybody!

I am a wild girl who loves to dream.
I pretend I am a helpless child.
I feel like I am a tiny ant in the world.
I touch like a feather on silk.
I worry if the world is going to explode!
I cry about sad songs.

I am a wild girl who loves to dream.
I understand the meaning of life.
I say things about god.
I dream I will live forever.
I try to understand the life of everybody.
I hope a rumble won't ever come.

I am a wild girl who loves to dream.

To provide feedback for the template designed for the project, the educator can ask students in the home school to complete a sample activity using the forms. Students' questions will help clarify any instructions and fine tune the template scheme.

A timeline. Each project should have a realistic timeline, with a beginning date, a reasonable turn-around time between exchanges among participants, and a specific time for closure. Projects that dwindle along do not provide the same enthusiasm from participants as those with clear timelines. A project can be a short exchange, such as the Art/Fax Project (http://www.ed.uiuc.edu/Activity-Structures/Collaborative-Problem-Solving/Sequential-Creations/Art-FAX-Project.html), or one that takes several weeks to complete, such as the Visual Art Project (http://www.ed.uiuc.edu/Activity-Structures/Collaborative-Problem-Solving/Sequential-Creations/Synergy-Visual-Art.html). Long-term projects such as NewsDay (http://gsn.org/gsn/newsday.home.html), extending over a month, need clear objectives for each round of exchanges. NewsDay has clear examples of all exchanges expected. Some projects extend over several months, but each month a new series of activities is expected to be completed by the participants.

Educators designing a project should check their home school calendar for any special events that may interfere with planned exchanges. In addition, throughout the project, the coordinator needs to keep all participants informed of any changes due to school scheduling problems. For example, unforeseen weather closing, building problems such as a lack of electricity, water, or heat may close school and special events such as a guest artist may change the time line. Keep others informed.

Contact information. The originator of a project is often the moderator or manager. Each mail message should have well-organized information about the person who will be managing the project. Every message about your project should contain:

Contact person(s) name
E-mail address
Name of the school
Complete address of the school
Telephone and fax numbers
Home phone number (optional)

Telephone and fax numbers are vital information. During our art/fax project, I had to call one school and request that the phone line be switched to the fax machine prior to our exchange. In addition, novice Internet users may have questions and concerns that are easily addressed in a short phone call. It is optional to include a home phone number, but often educators prefer communicating at home because daily schedules make it difficult to make or receive phone calls during the school day.

The address of the school is included for two reasons. One, if the geographical location of a school is not included somewhere in the project overview, participants may not be able to determine exactly where this project is originating. Often educators are seeking diverse locations to expand the scope of their classroom activities. Second, participants may want to send photographs, art work, or postcards to the organizer of this project.

Plan for a product. It helps future funding and support for Internet activities if a product is produced as the result of your project. The product can be a finished product that has been produced by desktop publishing or a collection of exchanges during the project. If the final product is notebook size or smaller, it can be a good public relations vehicle. The project can be shared with key people in the school district such as the principal, the superintendent, Board of Trustees, Computer or Technology Committee, Library, and local newspapers. Student work should be displayed on a bulletin board display of the project. This provides positive support for student work. Bulletin boards communicate information about the project to parents, other teachers and students, administrators, and visitors to the school.

Plan for evaluation. Too often educators neglect this important step that provides valuable feedback for designing and implementing online projects. The time to establish guidelines for evaluation is when the project is being developed. Without a plan for evaluation, after a project has been completed, it is easy to reflect on the serendipitous learning experiences and the logistical challenges that had to be overcome, but how do the educators know if the objectives of the project were met? If they were not, were there new educational advantages that had not been considered?

ANNOUNCING THE PROJECT TO THE INTERNET COMMUNITY AND ACCEPTING COMPANION CLASSES

If a project has a timeline that extends over several weeks and includes a series of activities, the "announcement" for the project should be brief. This abbreviated announcement to online newsgroups and Web sites is also known as a "Call for Participation" rather than complete project announcement. A short Call for Participation allows the coordinator to choose participants and then e-mail the longer version of the expected activities.

When accepting companion classes or project partners, determine if there is a limit to how many participants can be accommodated. Experience suggests that more participants should be accepted because often schedules, weather, or electrical connections may force a companion class to withdraw. Keep an up-to-date list of all participant information, and share this information with all classes involved with the project.

Often educators will provide a short introduction to their school and classes of other participants, and these introductions should also be shared with everyone else.

COORDINATING OR MODERATING THE ACTIVITIES

As the project designer coordinates and moderates the activity, keeping information not only electronically but also in hardcopy, facilitates managing the information for evaluation. The coordinator should send gentle reminders of all deadlines and acknowledge when information is shared in a timely manner.

If students are corresponding with other individuals, or if student groups are interacting with other groups, stress etiquette and ethical behavior before the project begins. Keep copies of all student correspondence. The paper copies of exchanges provides information for a final product resulting from the project.

When the project is finished, the coordinator should write electronic Thank You notes to the participating classes, and students should be encouraged to do the same. If possible, younger students value Certificates of Appreciation for their contributions and cooperation. These can be mailed to distant classrooms.

EVALUATING THE PROJECT

Evaluation plans are part of an activity design so the final evaluation of the activity should have clear guidelines.

As the project progresses, the educator should keep a journal in a binder with copies of all exchanges sent and received, noting successes and difficulties with the project. These observations can be invaluable for redesigning the objectives, activities, and management techniques needed for a successful replication. In addition, soliciting successes and difficulties with the other participants can provide a rich source of ideas for improvement.

The educator should have the students write about their reflections on their experiences. A successful project finds students learning what had been outlined in the objectives. Serendipitous learning can also occur, making the outcomes much richer than anticipated.

CONCLUSION

Educators furnish a fascinating variety of ideas for collaborating and sharing information using the Internet as a method for communicating. Many people who post their ideas to newsgroups or Web sites designed to facilitate connections find little response to their message. By carefully considering the elements of successful telecommunications projects, good ideas can be turned into great projects that may become classic activities, repeated year after year.

GLOSSARY

Zane Berge, Mauri Collins, and Michael Day

Acceptable Use Policy. A written document setting out the terms and conditions for using internal and external computer networks.

Address. There are two forms of machine addresses that commonly identify any computer connected to the Internet. They appear as either words or as IP numbers in the form of dotted quads (1234.1234.1234.1234). For instance, GUVAX, a VAX computer at Georgetown University, is known as either 141.161.1.2 or guvax.acc.georgetown.edu.

Anonymous FTP. A form of FTP (*see* **FTP**) which allows unregistered users (those without passwords to the account) access to files. When using anonymous FTP, one logs in as "anonymous" and uses one's email address (e.g., BERGE@UMBC2.UMBC.EDU) as the password.

ARPANet. A packet switched network developed in the early 1970s. The "grandfather" of today's Internet. ARPANet was decommissioned in June 1990.

ARCHIE. An internet service which allows users to search the indexes of many FTP sites. Archie tracks the contents of over 800 anonymous FTP archive sites containing over 1 million files stored across the Internet. Two archie sites are archie.ans.net (147.225.1.31) and archie.unl.edu (129.93.1.14). Logon as "archie."

ASCII. American Standard Code for Information Interchange, pronounced "ASKEE." A standard data transmission code which the computer uses to encode alphanumeric and other characters into a binary file.

Asynchronous. Transmission by individual bytes, or packets of bytes, not related to specific timing on the transmitting end. When used to describe computer-mediated communication, it indicates that communication can take place without both parties being logged on at the same time, as messages can be left for subsequent reading (e.g., email).

Backbone. The primary or trunk connection on a distributed hierarchical network system such as the Internet. All systems connected to the backbone are assured of being connected to each other. This does not prevent systems from setting up private arrangements with each other to bypass the backbone for reasons of cost, performance, or security.

Bandwidth. Used generally to refer to the capacity or throughput of a communications link. High bandwidth implies high data throughput, which can provide a very high speed to a few users at a time, or lower data rates to many users.

Bitnet. Acronym for "Because It's Time Network." Begun in 1981, BITnet is a world-wide academic and research network that connects many universities, colleges, and collaborating research centers and is restricted to the noncommercial exchange of information. It is operated by EDUCOM. Bitnet differs from the Internet in the types of services (e.g., FTP and telnet) its users can access. Bitnet uses the RSCS protocol set and provides electronic mail, file transfer, and "Tell/Send" messaging. GATEWAYS are computers that link Internet and BITnet sites.

Bookmark. A navigational shortcut that takes one directly to a resource, often used by WEB browsers to keep track of a user's frequently visited Web sites.

Boolean searching. A method of searching in some electronic databases which allows the searcher to combine terms and/or phrases by using the Boolean operators "and," "or," and "not."

Browser.. A software client program that lets you access the Web (e.g., Mosaic, Netscape) and display and/or retrieve information (text, images, and sounds).

Bulletin-Board Systems (BBS). A network-based file sharing system into which users may enter information, usually in the form of messages, for others to read or download. Many bulletin boards are set up according to general topics and are accessible throughout a network.

Campus-Wide Information System (CWIS). A tool that allows users to navigate through and retrieve data from a variety of campus sources (e.g., library, news bureau, events center, admissions and registrar, computing center), commonly implemented using WWW or Gopher.

Client/Server software. In network terminology, "client" can have two meanings. Sometimes it is synonymous with "user." Other times it is used to denote a relationship between two computers in which one computer is a "host" and serves a "client" machine. In this situation, the client computer requests data or other resources from the host, or server, machine. The program on the client machine that provides the user-interface for those resources is typically called the "client" software.

Client-server interface. A type of computer connection, typically over a network, in which the host computer, or server, provides files or services to remote computers, called clients. An example of this interface is the WWW and it can be found on LANs, WANs, or the Internet.

Client/server network. A Local Area Network (LAN) situation in which one computer acts as a server, or host, for all other client computers on the network. This type of network commonly provides clients with access to services such as common databases, network printers, and so on.

Compression. Files can be compressed to reduce the amount of storage space they occupy on a computer or the amount of BANDWIDTH they occupy when being transmitted across a network. Compatible software is required at compression and decompression locations.

Computer-Based Instruction (CBI) or Computer-mediated Instruction. Refers to using computers to instruct human users. CBI includes Computer Assisted Instruction (CAI; tutorial, review and practice, simulation, etc.); computer-managed instruction (diagnostic and prescriptive testing functions); and electronic messaging, which is generally associated with networked computer classrooms.

CMC. Computer-mediated communication. An acronym that refers to the entire range of electronic networking activities and includes electronic mail, computer conferencing, informatics, and computer-based instruction.

Courseware. Software, including documentation and workbooks, that is marketed for educational purposes.

Cross-Posting. Posting a BBS message to multiple subject groups or conferences.

CU-SeeMe. A desktop video-conferencing software program, available from Cornell University and many NASA sites, that allows users with the appropriate cameras and video equipment to transmit video over the Internet in real time.

Cyberspace. A term for immersive virtual reality, sometimes used to denote the Internet or the area behind one's computer screen in which one interacts with other users, computers, databases, and so on.

Daemons. Small "mainframe" programs that follow what is happening in a system. Mail daemons are often activated when mail is bounced; idle daemons track user's logon time and disconnect sessions with no activity after a predetermined length of time.

DEC VAX Notes. *see* **Vax Notes.**

Domain. Usually the last term in an address (q.v.). Domains are usually functional or national. Functional domains in the United States include EDU for education, GOV for government, COM for commercial, MIL for military, NET for network related, and ORG for nonprofit organizations. National domains are country codes such as CA for Canada, MY for Malaysia, SG for Singapore, and TH for Thailand.

Download. The electronic transfer of information from a remote computer to a local one, or from a personal computer's hard drive to a floppy disk. *see* **UPLOAD.**

EFF. Electronic Frontier Foundation. An organization established as a clearinghouse for open discussion and analysis of the many legal and social implications of the increasing role of computer communications in the world. EFF maintains a Gopher and a WWW server and is based in Washington, DC.

Electronic Bulletin Board. *see* **Bulletin Board Systems (BBS).**

Electronic Emissary Project (EEP). The Electronic Emissary Project is an Internet-based interpersonal resource that has been online since February 1993. The Emissary is a "matching service," based in the College of Education at the University of Texas at Austin. that helps teachers with access to the Internet locate other Internet account holders who are experts in different disciplines, for purposes of setting up curriculum-based, electronic exchanges among the teachers, their students, and the Subject Matter Experts

Electronic Journal (ejournal). An electronically distributed publication which, like a print journal, includes a table of contents, numerically defined issues, and an ISSN number. Recipients can reformat text as they wish and print only those articles or issues they want to read or save in hard-copy.

Electronic Mail (email). Transmitting textual and nontextual messages in machine readable form using an electronic mail program (like Pine, Elm, or Eudora) from one computer terminal or computer system to another. A message sent from one computer user to another is stored in the recipient's mailbox, a file on the host machine where that person receives mail.

Emoticon (smiley). The typical communication style on the internet is "written conversational" and this type of communication does a poor job of expressing emotion, hence "emoticons" were invented.

They are electronic text likenesses of human faces used in mail and news to indicate a variety of emotions and reactions. :-). Tip your head to your left shoulder to read the smile. The most common emoticon is :-) connoting a smile or happiness. One also often sees :- (or :-| meaning sadness or disappointment and ;-) ("winky") meaning irony or sarcasm.

Encryption. The act of making a readable file secure. Used on the World Wide Web for the transmission of credit card numbers or other sensitive information.

FAQ. *see* **Frequently Asked Question.**

Fiber optics. The technology of connecting or networking communication devices such as computers by means of optical fiber (glass) cable instead of copper wire.

File Transfer protocol (FTP). A TCP/IP protocol and program that one can use to transfer files over the network. *see* **Anonymous FTP.**

Finger. A program that identifies a user by name and last login time.

Firewall. A software security measure that helps to limit pirate attacks by preventing access to some locations from other locations on a network or a computer.

Flame. A confrontational, emotionally charged email message usually couched in language that is vulgar, sarcastic, or profane.

FrEdMail Network. Free Educational Electronic Mail. One of the pioneering networks of microcomputer-based BBS systems serving K-12 educators, FrEdMail was begun in 1986 by Al Rogers in San Diego, CA, and has spread to include more than 150 electronic bulletin boards systems across the United States and as far away as Australia and Ireland. FrEdMail offers collaborative activities designed to help students become better writers and learners and promotes the sharing of resources and experiences among teachers. FrEdMail can now be accessed through the internet. For more information, contact Al Rogers, FrEdMail Foundation, P.O. Box 243, Bonita, CA 91908-0243.

Frequently Asked Questions (FAQs). A document containing answers to frequently asked questions about some service, application, or function. These documents are generally updated as users gain experience with the service, application, or function. (Pronounced"fak".)

Freenet. Community-based bulletin board or Gopher information system, some with email and conferencing capabilities. Based on the public television/public radio model of community access and support.

FTP. *see* **File Transfer Protocol and Anonymous FTP.**

Full Text Delivery. The ability of an information server, like Gopher, to deliver the full electronic text of a document to a patron.

Gateway. A computer or device that acts as a connector between two logically separate networks. It has interfaces to more than one network and can translate data so that it can pass from one network to another, possibly dissimilar, network in a way that is transparent to the user.

.gif (Graphics Interchange Format). A platform-independent file format developed by CompuServe, the GIF format is commonly used to distribute graphics on the Internet and especially on the World Wide Web. (Often pronounced "jiff.")

Gopher. An information management tool that allows users to search for specific kinds of information over a wide-area network by using a series of menus. Gopher was developed by the University of Minnesota and is freely available in client and server form for MAC and DOS platforms. Many Gophers serve as useful front-ends to Internet databases, FTP archives, and CWISs.

Groupware (Group Conferencing Systems). A program (often marketed for business) that permits simultaneous work on a common file by more than one networked user. All the users can see the changes made by any other person as they occur.

Home page. The first page of any site on the World Wide Web. This page typically contains links to other pages at the site and may contain links to off-site locations. Each user or account at a Web site may also have their individual home pages.

Host computer. In the context of networks, a computer that provides service to a user who is typically running "client" software which turns their computer into a "terminal" of the host. On the Internet these host computers are known as NODES>.

HTML. Hypertext Markup Language; a document-formatting language used to write World Wide Web "pages." HTML consists of "tags." These are formatting commands read by Web browsers that control the appearance of documents on the reader's screen and the links to other resources they contain. HTML documents are basic ASCII files so they can be read by most word processors and text editors.

HTTP. Hypertext Transport Protocol; the protocol of the Web that allows text, images, audio, and video to be combined into a single document. HTTP also allows the linking of documents and document components.

Hypertext. A method of embedding links into documents that provide connections with related data (text, images, or sound) at either local or remote locations. The World Wide Web is based on hypermedia applications.

Hytelnet. A menu-driven version of Telnet that serves as a guide to online library catalogs and other information sources, updated 2-3 times per year. It can be downloaded by Anonymous FTP and placed on a local machine. Information on Hytelnet is available from: hytelnet.src.

Informatics. A general term describing network-accessible information servers. These include data archives such as anonymous ftp sites, interactive databases such as library OPACs, and client/server systems such as GOPHER and WAIS.

Intelligent Agent. A program that searches the network looking for items that match criteria one specifies; also called KNOWbots.

Internet Relay Chat (IRC). A world-wide synchronous multiuser chat protocol that allows one to converse with others in real time. IRC is structured as a network of servers, each of which accepts connections from client programs, one per user. Jarkko Oikarinen, a Finnish programmer, created Internet Relay Chat. IRC is a free program, which means that anyone with access to the internet can get a client program and use it to talk with others.

internet. A collection of computer networks interconnected by a set of routers that allow them to function as a single, large virtual network.

Internet (note the capital "I"). The largest network in the world consisting of large national backbone nets (such as MILNET, NSFNET, and CREN) and a myriad of regional and local campus networks all over the world. The Internet uses the Internet protocol suite, including the TCP/IP protocol set that includes electronic mail, TELNET, and FTP. To be on the Internet you must have IP connectivity, that is, be able to Telnet to—or ping— other systems. Networks with only e-mail connectivity are not actually classified as being on the Internet.

Interoperability. What allows different computer models from different manufacturers to communicate meaningfully with each other.

IP (Internet Protocol). *see* **TCP/IP.**

IP Address. The numeric address (a dotted quad) of a computer connected to the Internet; also called Internet address. It has the form 255.255.255.255. Guvax.georgetown.edu, to other computers and the network routers, is 141.161.1.2.

IP (Internet Protocol) name. A structured, numeric-based unique name for a computer on a network. The number includes four sections separated by periods. Often there is an alphabetical equivalent to the numeric name. Example: 128.04.12.62 or abc.lib.uma.edu. *See also* domain.

IRC. *see* **Internet Relay Chat.**

.jpeg (Joint Photographic Experts Group). A filename extension used to mark JPEG compressed images.

KIDSNET. Has been renamed KIDSPHERE. *see* **KIDSPHERE.**

KIDSPHERE. The major mailing list for the discussion of K-12 computer networking. It was established in 1989 with the name KIDSNET by Bob Carlitz. In Spring 1993 is was renamed KIDSPHERE with this statement of purpose: "to stimulate the development of an international computer network for the use of children and their teachers. The first pieces of this network have already begun to take shape, and the mailing list now helps to guide its continuing evolution. Subscribers to the list include teachers, administrators, scientists, developers of software and hardware, and officials of relevant funding agencies." To join the list, send your request to Bob Carlitz <joinkids@vms.cis.pitt.edu> and ask to be added to the KIDSPHERE mailing list.

LAN. *see* **Local Area Network**

Listserv. Listserv and its clones are the software that manages electronic discussion groups or computer conference distribution lists. These discussion groups are often called "lists" because, using what is called a "mail exploder" and a subscription list of electronic mail addresses, Listserv sends messages directly to the electronic mailboxes of many subscribers. Participants subscribe by sending a message to the Listserv hosting the list of interest. Eric Thomas originally wrote the Listserv software for IBM mainframes, but he has since migrated it to most available platforms.

Local Area Network (LAN). A network connecting machines at one site, often through a single server.

Logon or Login. A set of commands to gain access to another computer, network, or online service that often includes some kind of identification in the form of a user name and password.

Lurking. Reading or "listening" to a mailing list discussion or USENET newsgroup without actively participating (i.e., without contributing to the discussion). Lurking is encouraged for beginners who wish to learn the history and habits of the group. In course-related discussion lists, lurking is discouraged because to be silent is to be invisible.

Mail Exploder. Part of an electronic mail delivery system that allows a single message to be delivered to a list of addresses. Mail exploders are used to implement mailing lists. Users send messages to a single address (e.g., mygroup-L~somehost.edu) and the mail exploder takes care of delivery to each of the individual subscribers to the list.

Modem (MOdulator/DEModulator). A device that converts the digital signals in your computer to analog signals, and vice-versa, to enable computer communication through analog telephone lines.

Moderator. The person who is "in charge" of a Listserv or Usenet newsgroup. On a moderated list, the moderator reads the messages prior to posting to the list, may edit them, and forwards them to the list for general distribution. On an unmoderated list, the moderator just steps in when discussion get out of control. On private lists the moderator may also subscribe and unsubscribe people.

MOO (MUD, Object Oriented). Offers a more complex, object-oriented virtual interaction among participants than a MUD. Usually participants take on a role and interact in character. The "objects" they create remain after a particular user has logged off.

Mosaic. The name of a popular Web browser from National Center for Supercomputing Applications (NCSA) for accessing the Web; the first BROWSER invented for the Web.

MUD. Multi-User Dungeons/Domains are text-based, virtual environments evolved from "Dungeons and Dragons" type games that allow multiple users to gather and interact together in real time. *see also* **MOO.**

MUSE (Multi-User Simulation Environment). A virtual reality interaction via the Internet that combines the elements of Internet Relay Chat (IRC) and a MOO. Participants may choose and create their own reality or participate in ongoing games.

National Education and Research Network (NREN). The National Research and Education Network is a proposed national computer network to be built on the foundation of the NSF backbone network, NSFnet, the current internet backbone. NREN would provide high-speed interconnection between various national and regional networks.

Netiquette. A contraction of "network" and "etiquette" referring to socially acceptable communication behaviors on a computer network, often in the form of a written document.

Netnews. *see* **Usenet.**

Netscape. A graphical Web browser that currently offers many cutting-edge HTML features.

Netweaving (netweaver). Netweaving occurs when connections between these networks are not automatic and messages must be individually moved by a human volunteer—who then becomes a netweaver.

Network. A group of computers connected together so they can transmit information to one another.

NIC (Network Information Center). An internet host computer designated to provide useful information services to network users.

Node. A computer that is attached to a network; also called a HOST.

NREN. *see* the **National Research and Education Network.**

NSFnet (National Science Foundation Network). TCP/IP-based network that is the backbone for data transmission in the United States.

OPAC. (Online Public Access Catalog). Most large academic and many public libraries have converted their card catalogs to electronic or "machine-readable" format. These online catalogs may be searched from remote locations via modem or remote login, and so truly have become public reference sources.

Peer-to-peer network. A LAN situation in which every computer on the network has equal status with every other computer. Users can share files or resources (e.g., printers) between any combination of computers, and typically no single computer acts as a host, or server. This type of network is often referred to as a workgroup.

Pirate. A software pirate; someone who steals computer programs. Usually pirates will sell or give away the programs they steal.

Postmaster. The person responsible for answering questions about users and electronic mail addresses at a site. Can sometimes be reached by sending mail to "postmaster@host.subdomain.domain" if you are having trouble reaching someone at that host machine or subdomain.

Protocol. A formalized set of rules governing the format, timing, and error control of transmissions on a network. The protocol that networks use to communicate with each other. TCP/IP is an example of a network protocol.

Remote Access. The ability to access one computer from another—from across the room or across the world. Remote access requires communications hardware, software, and actual physical links, although this can be as simple as common carrier (telephone) lines or as complex as a TELNET login to another computer across the Internet.

RFC (Request for Comments). The document series, begun in 1969, in which the Internet's standards, proposed standards, and generally agreed-upon ideas are documented and published.

Robot. An automated program that will go out and search or retrieve information for the user.

SEND. The interactive real-time messaging protocol for BITnet-connected VAXJVMS systems. (*see* **TELL** for the equivalent protocol for IMB mainframes)

Server. A dedicated computer that shares its resources, such as files and applications programs, with other computers on a network. *see* **CLIENT.**

Shareware. Microcomputer software, distributed through public domain channels such as ftp, for which the author expects to receive some compensation. Users are typically allowed a free 30-day evaluation, after which they can discard the software or are expected to pay for it. This free evaluation period and the ease of distribution by "everyday people" makes shareware a powerful means of distributing software and rewarding authors.

Signature (often .sig). The three or four lines at the bottom of an email message or a Usenet article that identify the sender. A .sig is a short file created in a mail program that often contains addresses, telephone numbers, e-mail addresses, and, sometimes, ingenious graphics built from keyboard characters. Large signatures (over five lines) are generally frowned on.

SLIP. Serial Line Internet Protocol. A communications protocol for internet connections over a serial line like phone lines with a modem.

SMTP. Simple Mail Transfer Protocol. The Internet standard protocol for transferring electronic mail messages from one computer to another.

Snail Mail. A pejorative term referring to the postal service.

Synchronous. Data communications in which transmissions are sent at a fixed rate, with the sending and receiving devices synchronized. Synchronous communication occurs in real time (e.g., with two or more users communicating online at the same time to one another.

Sysop, sysops. System operator, person in charge of maintaining a host, server, or network.

Talk. A protocol that allows two people on remote Unix computer systems to communicate in real time. When one issues the "talk user@machine.place.domain" command, and if the individual is logged and accepts the request, the screen display divides horizontally and one can type at each other in real time.

TELL. The interactive real-time messaging protocol for IBM mainframes running VM/CMS and with BITnet connections. (SEND is the equivalent protocol for BITnet-connected VAXNMS systems). At the system prompt one types

tell (or "send") user@machine a single line message

and the message will appear on user~machine's screen if they are logged in. It is unwise to send TELL or SEND messages to persons one does not know because, depending on the rank and mood of the recipient, it could result in revocation of one's access privileges.

TCP/IP (Transmission Control Protocol/Internet Protocol). The set of transmission standards on the Internet that provide the reliable communication service on which many applications depend for accurate data transfer. It allows the transfer of data between computers that use TCP/IP, and it supports other services (protocols) such as Telnet, FTP, and SMTP. TCP/IP is also often used for other networks, particularly local area networks that tie together numerous different kinds of computers or engineering workstations.

Telecommuting. The practice of employees working partially or primarily from home, using microcomputers and modems to access information systems and perform their daily duties without regard to their actual physical location.

Telnet. A basic function provided by the TCP/IP protocol on the Internet is Telnet, or remote login, or remote terminal connection service. This allows a user to interact with another computer as if she or he were directly connected to the remote computer.

Terminal Emulation Software. Communications software that permits one's personal computer or workstation to communicate with another computer or network as if one's machine were a specific type of terminal directly connected to that computer or network (e.g., VT100 or TN3270).

Terminal Server. A computer that connects terminals to a network by providing host TELNET service.

Thread. A series of postings to an electronic bulletin board, or other discussion group (e.g., Listserv), that have a common subject heading. A thread normally consists of responses to an original posting to a discussion topic, or an offshoot of another thread.

TN3270. A version of Telnet required by some IBM mainframes for remote logins.

UNIX. An operating system developed by Bell Laboratories that supports several users logged into a computer or workstation at the same time, and which supports multi-user and multitasking operations. That is, this operating system allows many people to share the processing capabilities of the computer on which it is running and to use several programs at once. Unix is case-sensitive so most commands to UNIX hosts must be typed in lower case.

Upload. Transfer electronic data from a local to a remote computer, or from a floppy disk to a hard drive on a personal computer. *see* **DOWNLOAD.**

URL (Uniform Resource Locator). A technical description of a resource's Internet address. A URL specifies what type of resource (a document at an FTP site, on a gopher, a WWW site, etc.) is being described and its location on a machine connected to the Internet using a standardized format. Most web browsers allow the user to enter a URL and gain access to the specified site. (Pronounced "earl."). *see* **HTTP**

Usenet (NETNEWS). A computer bulletin board system, originally distributed over computers running the Unix operation system to which many computer systems on and off the Internet now subscribe. Whereas Listserv software delivers discussion group messages as mail to individual mailboxes, messages from some or all of the over 2,000 Usenet newsgroups are typically stored on a site's mainframe computer. Readers can then log in to read the accumulation of messages which may amount to 15 to 20 megabytes of text a day. With the number of groups growing daily, there is truly something of interest to everyone on Usenet.

UUCP (Unix to Unix Copy). A protocol used for communication between Unix systems, on which mail and Usenet news services were built. Internet has largely taken over the transmission of such date exchange.

VAX (pl. VAXen). Mainframe and personal computers manufactured by the Digital Equipment Corporation and in wide use on the Internet. One of the prevalent terminal emulations used on the Internet is named for the VT100, an early DEC video terminal.

VAX Notes. VAX Notes is essentially a computer bulletin board set up with a series of topics numbered 1, 2, 3, and so on. Replies to each topic are attached to each topic note. Replies to topic 3 would be numbered 3.1, 3.2, and so on. This permits users to read, conduct, and respond to several different discussion topics simultaneously. It also saves and stores all topic notes and replies, permitting readers to connect at any time, even after a several day hiatus and catch up on the entire series of transactions.

Veronica (Very Easy Rodent-Oriented Net-wide Index to Computerized Archives). A search tool/utility used in gopher; performs a keyword search of the menus or documents of many gophers. Search results (these vary widely; sometimes many retrievals, sometimes none) are then displayed via newly created menus.

Virus. A program that infects other programs and computers, resulting in some sort of malfunction.

Virtual Reality. Systems that transform the computing environment by immersing the user in a simulated world, which also can include movement and tactile control. Virtual reality systems permit users to interact with computer systems in a manner that more closely mimics how humans naturally operate in the real world.

VMS. A Digital Equipment Corporation operating system for VAX machines.

VT100. A standard protocol for terminal emulation. This is the most common and often required protocol used when telnetting to a remote host. It is a bare-bones, lowest common denominator terminal emulation that does not usually allow for commands and features which are available with a workstation-based client

WAIS. (Wide-Area Information System). An information retrieval tool developed by Thinking Machines, Inc. WAIS provides a simple-to-use interface that allows a patron to search multiple sources for information with a single natural language question.

Web Crawler. A program that moves along the Web looking for URLs or other information; a type of intelligent agent. Used to build the search indexes available through Web browsers.

Web. *see* **World Wide Web.**

Web Server. Server software that allows an information provider to make documents (image, text, sound) available using a variety of platforms (DOS, Unix, Macintosh, etc.).

Wide-Area Network (WAN). A distributed network spanning hundreds or thousands of miles, connecting a number of Local Area Networks.

World-Wide Web (Web or WWW or W3). A global, hypermedia-based, distributed information system created by researchers at CERN in Switzerland. It allows users to create, edit, or browse hypertext documents containing text, images, and sound. The clients and servers are now easily accessible and available.

SOURCES USED IN THIS COMPILATION

Ask ERIC InfoGuide. (1993). *K-12 educators and the internet*. Available via anonymous FTP at ericir.syr.edu.

Cook, D., & Sellers, D. (1995). *Launching a business on the web*. Indianapolis, IN: Que Corporation.

Day, M. J. (1993). Private correspondence.

Jacobsen, O., & Lynch, D.. (1991). *A glossary of networking terms*. RFC 1208.

Kehoe, B. P. (1992). *Zen and the art of the internet*. Available for anonymous FTP on host FTP.CS.WIDENER.EDU, directory PUB/ZEN, filename ZEN-1.0.PS (Postscript file) and other formats.

Krol, E. (1991). *The whole internet user's guide & catalog*. Sebastapol, CA: O'Reilly and Associates, Inc.

Lamb, A., & Johnson, L. (1995). *Cruisin' the information highway: Internet in the K-12 classroom*. Evansville, IN: Vision To Action.

Longley, D. (1986). *Dictionary of information technology* (2nd ed.). NY: Oxford University Press.

Malkin, G., & Parker, T.L. (1993). *Internet users' glossary*. RFC 1392.

Mitchell, M., & Saunders, L. (1992). *Glossary*. Sent via private correspondence .

Mulliner, K. (1993). *Internet glossary*. Prepared for a workshop in Columbus, OH. Sent via private correspondence.

University of Wisconsin-Madison Libraries. (1995). *Basic internet glossary of terms and acronyms*. Madison, WI: Author.

Other miscellaneous glossaries and individual entries from unidentified sources that were sent to us as private correspondence.

AUTHOR INDEX

SUBJECT INDEX